Reasoned Freedom

By the same author

Descartes and the Enlightenment
The Imposition of Method: A Study of Descartes and Locke

REASONED FREEDOM

John Locke and Enlightenment

Peter A. Schouls

Cornell University Press

Ithaca and London

First published 1992 by Cornell University Press.

International Standard Book Number 0-8014-2758-4 (cloth)
International Standard Book Number 0-8014-8037-X (paper)
Library of Congress Catalog Card Number 92-52771

Printed in the United States of America

*Librarians: Library of Congress cataloging information appears on the
last page of the book.*

♾ The paper in this book meets the minimum requirements of the
American National Standard for Information Sciences–Permanence of
Paper for Printed Library Materials, ANSI Z39.48-1984.

To

Richard Bosley
Hendrik Hart
John King-Farlow

Contents

Preface

Human beings, for Locke, are born to be masters. They are born to be masters because it is their nature to be rational and free, and it is through deliberate exercise of their reason in all the exigencies of life that they achieve mastery. Human beings may be born to be masters, but, says Locke, it is obvious that most of them are in bondage. To mention three of Locke's favorite targets, they are in servitude to superstition, to human institutions, and to other human beings. This bondage has one chief cause, and that is wrong upbringing or education. One might then be tempted to say that there is also only one fully effective escape from this bondage, namely, right upbringing or, lacking that, proper re-education. Some influential commentators have in fact assumed this to be Locke's doctrine. However, neither right upbringing nor proper re-education guarantees a person his or her birthright. As we shall see, Locke's doctrine of human nature, particularly that of human autonomy, bars the way to such a facile conclusion. Right upbringing or proper re-education guarantees only that individuals find themselves in circumstances favorable for the achievement of mastery, for the salutary exercise of reason in all affairs of life. Whether this opportunity is going to be grasped is beyond the educator's control. If it is grasped, then right upbringing or proper re-education has placed individuals in a position favorable to full appropriation of their birthright. It has placed them advantageously for achieving a life of mastery, a life of which liberty and reason are the hallmarks.

For the academic year 1987–88 the University of Alberta appointed me to a McCalla Professorship, a position that enabled me to complete most

of this book in penultimate form. I deeply appreciate its generous support
of my work.

The major part of Chapter 3 was published as "Locke and the Dogma of
Infallible Reason" in *Revue Internationale de Philosophie* 42 (1988): 115–32. I
thank the editor of that journal for permission to use this material.

As always, I am indebted to many of my students, particularly to those
who took my graduate seminars and to graduate students Graham
McAleer for verifying quotations and Jeffrey McLaughlin for compiling
the index. I express my appreciation to Patricia Clements (Dean of the
Faculty of Arts) and to David Sharp (Chair of the Department of Philosophy) for their steadfast and wholehearted support of excellence in teaching
and research under conditions of financial stringency; to Pat Brunel for
making available typists Wendy Minns, Anita Theroux, Lenore Dafoe,
and Rosetta Bossio, who cheerfully helped me through various drafts; and
to Lois Larson for her patient guidance into computer literacy during the
last year of writing this project.

Pervasive in my life and work is the influence of my spouse, Jeanette.
Our support of each other's work enhances that of both in more ways than
can be easily identified.

Recognition is owing to the many colleagues who have influenced my
work through their own writings, through formal and informal discussions at various conferences, and through comments on various parts of
earlier drafts. Wherever possible, I have acknowledged indebtedness to
them on specific points in my footnotes. Special mention must be made of
the extremely conscientious readers for Cornell University Press: their
copious and penetrating comments substantially improved the quality of
the final product. My greatest debt is to Richard Bosley, Hendrik Hart,
and John King-Farlow. They have most generously given me of their time
for many years. This is the third of my book-length studies of which they
have read early drafts, on which they commented in most supportive,
critical and helpful ways. I acknowledge their collegiality and friendship
by dedicating this book to them.

PETER A. SCHOULS

Edmonton, Alberta

Reasoned Freedom

∼ I

Locke, Descartes,
and the Enlightenment

1. Locke as Intermediary

John Locke is often called the Enlightenment's great pro-
genitor.[1] There are, however, no sustained studies in which Locke's work
is discussed specifically in terms of the set of concepts which characterize
Enlightenment thought. In conjunction, the concepts of *freedom*, *progress*,
and *mastery* may be taken as expressing the core of Enlightenment thinking. These concepts, in turn, are closely related to *reason* and *education*.
This book examines the nature, function, and interrelations of these five
concepts as they are to be found in some of Locke's major writings. It will
not take long before we see that dealing with Locke through concepts
such as these allows for a discussion that touches the very heart of his
position.

Locke is not the greatest of the Enlightenment's forefathers. The place

---

1. There is an abundance of statements to this effect. See, for example: Richard I. Aaron,
John Locke, 3d ed. (Oxford, 1971), p. 334; Reinhard Brandt, ed., *John Locke: Symposium
Wolfenbüttel 1979* (Berlin, 1979), pp. 2–3; Crane Brinton, *Encyclopedia of Philosophy*, ed. Paul
Edwards (New York 1967) 2:519; S. C. Brown, ed., *Philosophers of the Enlightenment* (Hassocks, U.K., 1979), p. vii, and in the same volume John Rogers, "The Empiricism of Locke
and Newton," p. 1; Peter Gay, *The Enlightenment: An Interpretation, 2: The Science of Freedom*
(London, 1970), p. 625. Geraint Parry—in *John Locke* (London, 1978)—writes, "Freedom,
reason and self-reliance together constitute the 'Ariadne's thread' which permits one to trace
the connections of Locke's ideas" (p. 20); this promising theme he leaves practically undeveloped.

of pre-eminence belongs to Descartes.[2] Indeed, Locke might not have exerted much of an influence on the Enlightenment had it not been for the impact of Descartes' methodology on him.[3] In this book I therefore approach Locke as one whose work is linked intimately with both that of Descartes and that of the eighteenth-century Enlightenment.

Important though these links are, I will, even in this chapter, not give anything like the amount of space to Descartes and eighteenth-century thinkers as I reserve for Locke. It is he who is the focus of my attention. Others enter to indicate important dimensions of the historical context so that we may remain conscious of influences exerted on, and by, Locke's work. Awareness of the grip which, for example, Cartesian methodology had on Locke's thought will help keep us from misinterpretation at points where commentators still all too often misconstrue Locke's intentions. It will also help in drawing relationships among Lockean doctrines that critics have often left unrelated or, if not totally unrelated, whose precise relations have received insufficient notice. One of the most important— and, until recently, most neglected—of these relationships is that between the doctrines of the *Essay concerning Human Understanding* (particularly those about human nature, reason, and freedom) and Locke's views on education. There is as yet, even in the most recent and interesting treatments of Locke's thought, no sustained work in which the teachings of the *Essay* are used systematically to develop a satisfactory account of doctrines most central to the educational works.[4] One aim of my book is at least the partial filling of this gap.

My chief emphasis will be on certain of Locke's writings, particularly on the *Essay concerning Human Understanding, Of the Conduct of the Understanding*, and *Some Thoughts concerning Education*. (I shall often refer to these simply as the *Essay*, the *Conduct*, and the *Education*.) These three

2. This position I have argued in detail in my *Descartes and the Enlightenment* (Edinburgh, 1989). It is a position many would oppose. See, for example, *Philosophers of the Enlightenment*, p. xi, as well as Aaron, *John Locke*.

3. That Cartesian methodology plays a pervasive role in Locke's thought I have shown in *The Imposition of Method: A Study of Descartes and Locke* (Oxford, 1980), chaps. 6–8.

4. I have in mind Nathan Tarcov's *Locke's Education for Liberty* (Chicago, 1984) and James Tully's "Governing Conduct" in *Conscience and Casuistry in Early Modern Europe*, ed. Edmund Leites (Cambridge, 1988), pp. 12–71. Both Tarcov and Tully use the *Essay* to elucidate parts of Locke's writings on education. Tarcov, however, deliberately avoids the most pressing matter: how, if at all, Locke's doctrine makes it possible that habituation can lead to liberty ("A thorough examination . . . of pedagogical methods to be employed in the intellectual part of education . . . would require another study"—p. 198.) And Tully's conclusions abrogate the Lockean notion of autonomy. ("The aim is to inculcate . . . virtuous behaviour" so that one's "conduct" comes to "depend solely on one's tutor . . . or, as Locke calls him, one's 'governor' "— pp. 62, 65.)

works are linked because, in the parts on which I concentrate, they all deal with *mastery*. They deal primarily with self-mastery, but they also concern mastery of one's physical and cultural environment (where mastery of one's cultural environment excludes the legitimacy of certain ways in which others might be one's "masters" or ways in which one might be the "master" of others).

Three concepts, reason, freedom, and education, are my special concern. As we shall see in detail, each is, in turn, related to that of *mastery*. Hence, of the three major parts of this book, the first deals with reason and the nature of a master, the second with freedom and the nature of a master, and the third with the education of a potential master. The concept of *progress* will remain mostly in the background, but it is clearly not absent: for Locke, human beings are the kind of beings who can progress to ever greater self-mastery—a condition that places them in an advantageous position to achieve continual progress in procuring "the Conveniences of Life" through the development and application of "profitable Knowledge" (4.12.11, 12).[5]

The mention of mastery leads again to Descartes, as well as to the eighteenth-century Enlightenment. Descartes's statement that consistent use of the right method will enable us to "make ourselves, as it were, the lords and masters of nature"[6] is well enough known. For Descartes, the mastery in question was domination over physical nature through the science of mechanics; this was to obviate the drudgery and pain of labor expended in the provision of daily needs. It was, in addition, control over the body through the science of medicine; this was to banish illness with all its fear and suffering. Finally, it was command over the passions through the science of "morals"; this was to end all personal, interpersonal, and international strife because it would do away with envy and hatred and, consequently, with quarrels and wars. In short, through consistent use of the right method (I shall discuss the nature of that method in section 3 of this chapter) people were to become masters of their fate. By grasping the opportunities offered through proper education, each human being could come to possess such mastery.

5. "4.12.11, 12" signifies that the phrases in quotation marks are from the *Essay concerning Human Understanding*, Book 4, chapter 12, paragraphs 11 and 12. Throughout this book I shall identify passages from the *Essay* in this manner.
6. *Discourse on Method*, Part VI. The passage is on pp. 142–43, volume 1, of the two-volume *Philosophical Writings of Descartes*, trans. and ed. John Cottingham, Robert Stoothoff, and Dugald Murdoch (Cambridge, 1985). In *Oeuvres de Descartes*, ed. Charles Adam and Paul Tannery (Paris, 1965–75), it is on p. 62 of volume 6. In subsequent references to Cartesian texts, both sources will be indicated in abbreviated form, as follows, for example: CSM1, 142–43; AT6, 62.

These sentiments are not just Descartes's; they are equally those of many Enlightenment thinkers.[7] For them too, proper education primarily consisted in learning to use the right method as a matter of habit. That way of putting it is pertinent to what these thinkers took to be the right education of a child. But (they were convinced) adults also needed educating or, more accurately, re-educating. For adults, proper re-education demanded exercise of an aspect of this method not initially relevant to the education of children: adults were to use the method in the first instance to free themselves from prejudice, that is, to reject all beliefs and so-called knowledge hitherto acquired. Then, starting with a slate wiped clean, they were to construct a system of knowledge step by careful step through further use of the proper method.

For both adult and child, use of this method was to allow for what these thinkers took to be the employment of reason unhampered by prejudice. They believed that reason always leads to truth, and that submission to such truth always keeps one free. They therefore held that, for both adult and child, proper education was to consist basically in learning to use one's reason and learning to act on the dictates of one's reason. (How—if at all—such learning can take place, is discussed in the third part of this book.) In other words, these thinkers took the outcome of right education to be that of individual autonomy. For they believed persons to be autonomous when they could choose to act on nothing but the dictates of their own reason. Both Descartes and philosophes, including d'Alembert and Condorcet, subscribed to these statements about education, method, reason, and freedom. So did Locke.

7. There is a strain in Locke which distances him from Enlightenment thinkers and which might at first sight appear to conflict with that of "mastery." It is the theme of the human being as servant of God. As the *Second Treatise* has it, "Men" are "all the Workmanship of one Omnipotent, and infinitely wise Maker; All the Servants of one Sovereign Master, sent into the World by his order and about his business . . ."(§6). Of course, most Enlightenment thinkers had no truck with this notion of a divine master. The fact that they could, nevertheless, accept most of the rest of Locke's position (or better: the fact that the rest of Locke's position was a root of their own) is at least prima facie evidence that this "workmanship" hence "ownership" theme does not cancel that of mastery. To the contrary, to be God's "Property" guarantees the legitimacy of the autonomy expressed in the ideal of mastery in the sense that one ought not to be the property of a fellow human being. Hence the passage quoted from the *Second Treatise* continues as follows: "they are his Property, whose Workmanship they are, made to last during his, not one anothers pleasure. And being furnished with like Faculties . . . there cannot be supposed any such Subordination among us, that may authorize us to destroy one another, as if we were made for one anothers uses." John Dunn, in chap. 5 of *Wealth and Virtue*, ed. I. Hont and M. Ignatieff (Cambridge, 1983), imposes a "theocentric" view on Locke to the extent that it creates more of a difference between Locke and Enlightenment thinkers than is warranted. The "workmanship model" is developed in interesting ways by James Tully in chap. 1 of his *A Discourse on Property: John Locke and His Adversaries* (Cambridge, 1980); I have occasion to relate my argument to it later on.

It is important that from the outset there be some clarity about the relationship between Locke's thought and that of Descartes on the one hand and the Enlightenment on the other. The kind of confusion which exists on this point in the writings of otherwise insightful commentators is well illustrated by Richard Aaron when he ascribes greater influence to Locke's doctrines than to those of Descartes, where most of the doctrines in question are the ones which Locke adopted from Descartes. Aaron writes: "It is not at all strange that the *Essay*, the *Civil Government*, *The Reasonableness of Christianity*, and *Some Thoughts Concerning Education* should have led men to put their trust in reason. For they were written by a rationalist whose aim was to increase man's faith in reason."[8] One should not quarrel with a statement like this were it not for the fact that it is immediately preceded by the assertion that it is "Locke . . . and not Descartes" who "is the supreme formative influence on the France of the eighteenth century." Of course, Aaron is correct when he states that there are important links between Locke and the Enlightenment (in this case, particularly, between Locke and the philosophes). But when he juxtaposes Locke's influence to that of Descartes he reveals that he does not know the precise nature of these links—even though he is certainly right in holding that the relation of influence has to do with "putting trust" or "increasing faith" in "reason."

Many authors state as a fact that there exists an intimate relationship between Locke's thought and that of the Enlightenment. Exactly what this relationship might be their statements tend not to reveal. When, like Aaron (or to mention a more recent writer, like S. C. Brown),[9] they deny this relationship to Descartes at the same time as they ascribe it to Locke, it is clear that its particular character is really obscure to them. For this intimate connection exists between Locke and the Enlightenment precisely because it exists between Locke and Descartes.

It might be said that influence is attributed to Locke and denied to Descartes because the philosophes, for example, never tired of acknowledging Locke's influence and seldom resisted an opportunity of criticizing Descartes. It should be recognized, however, that the philosophes condemned only aspects of Cartesian *metaphysics*. They never censured Descartes's view of the workings of reason, that is, his doctrine of method. That doctrine they adopted as their own and believed that once it was put into practice, it would lead to revolution and liberation in all areas of life, freeing mankind from prejudice, superstition, drudgery, pain, guilt, and fear. That Cartesian doctrine they saw put into practice by Locke. They

8. Aaron, *John Locke,* p. 334.
9. Brown, *Philosophers of the Enlightenment,* p. vii.

considered Locke to be the first[10] who, through following the right method, had gained noteworthy victories especially in the battle against the entrenched powers of both church and state. They praised him, in addition, for what they took to be his practicable directives for the education of youth. They believed that, if implemented, his educational precepts would guarantee future generations the opportunity for freedom of the human spirit. It was typical of the philosophes to heap praises on Locke. It was just as characteristic for many of them to acknowledge Descartes's role.

D'Alembert's accolade in the *Discours préliminaire* of the *Encyclopédie* was widely acknowledged as well deserved. He praised Descartes as the first "to show good thinkers how to throw off the yoke of scholasticism, opinion, and authority" and of "prejudice and barbarism." He saw Descartes as the first of the revolutionaries. Of this archetypal revolutionary he said that his "revolt, the fruits of which we are gathering today . . . rendered philosophy a service, more difficult perhaps and more essential than all those which it owes to his illustrious successors." "Descartes," said d'Alembert, was to "be regarded as the leader of a conspiracy, the one who had the courage to rise up first against a despotic and arbitrary power."[11]

Aaron is correct when he characterizes Locke's writings as "written by a rationalist whose aim was to increase man's faith in reason." It was their common view of human ability and of the workings of human reason which accounts for the intimacy among Descartes, Locke, and key figures in the eighteenth-century Enlightenment. They all shared doctrines about human beings as rational beings, as free beings who can achieve mastery, beings whose destiny lies in their own hands, beings capable of progressing on the way to full realization of their destiny. Locke presents some of the elements of this complex view quite explicitly in the *Conduct of the Understanding*, where we read, for example:

10. As Condorcet put it: "Locke grasped the thread by which philosophy should be guided; he showed that an exact and precise analysis of ideas, which reduces them step by step to other ideas of more immediate origin or of simpler composition, is the only way to avoid being lost in that chaos of incomplete, incoherent and indeterminate notions which chance presents to us at hazard and we unthinkingly accept. . . . This method was soon adopted by all philosophers and, by applying it to moral science, to politics and to social economy, they were able to make almost as sure progress in these sciences as they had in the natural sciences." Condorcet, *Sketch for a Historical Picture of the Progress of the Human Mind*, trans. June Barraclough (London, 1955), pp. 132–33.
11. These are oft-quoted statements. See, for example, Gay, *Enlightenment*, p. 147; and Ronald Grimsley, *Jean D'Alembert* (Oxford, 1963), p. 269.

In these two things, viz. an equal indifferency for all truth; I mean the receiving of it, the love of it, as truth, but not loving it for any other reason, before we know it to be true; and in the examination of our principles, and not receiving any for such, nor building on them, till we are fully convinced, as rational creatures, of their solidity, truth, and certainty; consists that freedom of the understanding which is necessary to a rational creature, and without which it is not truly an understanding. It is conceit, fancy, extravagance, any thing rather than understanding, if it must be under the constraint of receiving and holding opinions by the authority of any thing but their own, not fancied, but perceived evidence. This was rightly called imposition, and is of all other the worst and most dangerous sort of it. For we impose upon ourselves, which is the strongest imposition of all others; and we impose upon ourselves in that part which ought with the greatest care to be kept free from all imposition.[12]

Most elements of this passage will not receive adequate attention until later chapters. What, precisely, is meant by "principles," how we distinguish right from wrong "principles," how we "receive" anything for true because "we know it to be true," and how we know something "to be true"—these are all matters whose precise details are for later concern. What needs detain us now is the prime importance Locke ascribes to "freedom of the understanding." He holds that without such freedom we cannot be rational creatures. The presence of this freedom is to keep us from "imposing upon ourselves"—an imposing that would occur once we accept as true anything which we ourselves do not perceive to be true. How we might come to such an imposition, and whether or not such imposition occurs frequently, Locke reveals in other passages of the same work. Of these, the following is representative:

Many men firmly embrace falsehood for truth, not only because they never thought otherwise, but also because, thus blinded as they have been from the beginning, they never could think otherwise, at least without a vigour of mind able to contest the empire of habit, and look into its own principles; a freedom which few men have a notion of in themselves, and fewer are allowed the practice of by others; it being the great art and business of the teachers and guides in most sects to suppress, as much as they can, this fundamental duty which every man owes himself, and is the first steady step towards right and truth in the whole train of his actions and opinions.[13]

12. This quotation is from para. 12 of the *Conduct*. It may be found on pp. 231–32, volume 3, of *Works of John Locke* (London, 1823; rpt. Aalen, 1963). All subsequent references to this text will be to this edition.
13. Para. 41, p. 276.

The doctrine of these two paragraphs is about human autonomy as this presents itself through human rationality. One might say that they state it as Locke's doctrine that *to be rational is to be critical*. To be critical consists in not accepting any thing as true or good merely on the grounds that many others accept it and may have done so for a long time, and in accepting as true or good only that which one has personally proved to be true or good. The "fundamental duty which every man owes himself" is to be critical of what custom or habit or tradition would make one accept on trust. Human beings can act on this duty because they are capable of "indifference." Because they can be "indifferent" they need not hold as true that which they have not examined and found to be true, and they can withdraw their commitment from any tenet once they recognize that they have accepted it on some authority other than that of their own reason. To be critical is to work at the realization of one's autonomy. It is each person's duty to be critical with respect to all principles, thoughts, and actions. One is human only when one is critical, for to be human is to be autonomous, and no autonomy is possible apart from this critical stance. To be critical, to be truly human, requires that one start de novo. It will be clear in a moment that this demands that one be a revolutionary.

These two passages present an attitude typical of the Enlightenment. Every major thinker of the movement, from Voltaire to Kant,[14] from Condorcet to Lessing,[15] adopted the position these passages express. This stance was also Descartes's. It was Descartes who gave it its first complete published articulation in his *Discourse on the Method of rightly conducting one's Reason*, a work whose thrust is aptly captured by the long title which Descartes had originally in mind for it: "The Plan of a Universal Science to raise our Nature to its Highest Degree of Perfection. . . ."[16] This work received a wide readership in a very short time.[17] Locke and many later

14. Recall Kant's definition of "enlightenment" in the opening sentences of "An Answer to the Question: What Is Enlightenment?": "Enlightenment is man's emergence from his self-imposed immaturity [*Unmündigkeit*]. Immaturity is the inability to use one's understanding without guidance from another. This immaturity is self-imposed when its cause lies not in lack of understanding, but in lack of resolve and courage to use it without guidance from another. *Sapere Aude!* 'Have courage to use your own understanding!'—that is the motto of enlightenment." The translation is from Ted Humphrey's *Immanuel Kant: Perpetual Peace and Other Essays* (Indianapolis, Ind., 1983), p. 41.

15. On Lessing's debt to Locke, see Brandt, *Symposium*, pp. 1–3.

16. See Descartes's letter to Mersenne, March 1636. The translation is that of Anthony Kenny. See Kenny, ed., *Descartes: Philosophical Letters* (Oxford, 1970), p. 28. This letter is now incorporated in *The Philosophical Writings of Descartes*, vol. 3, trans. and ed. Cottingham, Stoothoff, Murdoch, and Kenny (Cambridge, 1991), 50–52.

17. The original French edition was published in 1637. A Latin version appeared in 1644. And it was published in an English translation, with a preface by Henry More, the influential Cambridge Platonist, in 1649. Locke possessed both the Latin and English translations of the *Discours de la méthode*. Recent scholarship has established from Locke's notes and manuscripts

thinkers were revolutionary primarily insofar as they adopted and implemented the precepts of Descartes's method. Why Cartesian methodology
must be seen as demanding revolution and to what extent it influenced
eighteenth-century thought and action in France are matters I have discussed in detail elsewhere.[18] I shall say no more about this influence. But it
will, later on in this chapter, be useful to restate some of what I have said
about the revolutionary nature of Cartesian methodology. This will be
helpful in completing the tasks of providing justification for my characterization of Locke as a revolutionary and for my assertion that Locke was a
revolutionary because he accepted Descartes's method, the subjects of
sections 3 and 4 of this chapter.

First I must turn to the distinction, on which Locke insists in his use
of *reason*, between the reasoning which gives us "certainty" and that
which gives us "probability." I approach this distinction by way of another contrast Locke draws, that between "Master-Builder" and "Under-
Labourer."

I call attention to these well-known distinctions at this early stage of my
book to emphasize two points. The first is that in important respects
Locke was both less of a Cartesian and more of an Enlightenment thinker
than some of my comments in this section may have led one to expect.
The second and more important one is that I have placed a restriction on
myself; in this book I deal more with those aspects of the *Essay*, the
Conduct, and the *Education* in which Locke would have considered himself a "Master-Builder" than with those in which he saw himself as an
"Under-Labourer." This emphasis, in turn, entails that I focus on the
reasoning which affords "certainty" rather than on that which gives
"probability."

2. "Master-Builder" and "Under-Labourer"

In the *Essay*'s "Epistle to the Reader," Locke refers to the "Master-
Builders" ("a Boyle, or a Sydenham; . . . the Great—Huygenius, and the

---

that in the early and mid 1660s—the years of transition from "traditionalist" to "revolutionary"—he carefully studied the *Discourse*, *Meditations*, and *Principles of Philosophy*. I have
in mind J. R. Milton, "Before the Drafts: Locke's Intellectual Development 1658–1671," a
paper read to the British Society for the History of Philosophy Conference on John Locke,
Oxford, November 15, 1986.

18. For a fuller account of Descartes as a revolutionary than the one I will give in a
moment, see *Descartes and the Enlightenment*, passim, as well as the more extensive discussion
in "Descartes as Revolutionary," *Philosophia Reformata* 52 (1987): 4–23. For the fact that
Enlightenment thinkers saw Descartes as a revolutionary and were themselves revolutionaries in the sense in which I use that term, see chap. 3, part 5, of the first, and part 3 of the
second item.

incomparable Mr. Newton") and with respect to them pronounces himself to be an "Under-Labourer" whose task consists in "clearing Ground a little, and removing some of the Rubbish, that lies in the way to Knowledge." These "Master-Builders" deal with "nature," with "knowledge" of "substances" and their "qualities" and "relations," with the objects of which we are aware through the senses. They develop sciences like medicine and physics. In this context, Locke's role as "Under-Labourer" includes demonstrating that those who deal with "nature" cannot be armchair scientists because, for example, there is no innate knowledge. It also consists in discussions of ideas such as "substance," "quality," and "relation" in order to demonstrate the limitation of our knowledge in this area. And it involves providing directives[19] for achieving practical certainty or probability (as distinct from theoretical or absolute certainty) in these sciences.

Since there are many studies which deal with Locke's view of "substances," their "qualities" and "relations," and the appropriate way of reasoning about them, there is no urgency for another one.[20] This, however, is not my most important reason for refraining from extensive discussion of Locke on knowledge of "substances." From the relevant parts of the *Essay* as well as from these studies, it is quite clear that, unless we want to designate most of philosophy as "under-labour" to the sciences, Locke was far more than an "Under-Labourer." And when he was an "Under-Labourer" he often was so to himself as "Master-Builder." In addition to procedural directive for disciplines like medicine and physics, he advanced methodological principles for political theory and a hermeneutics for theology. In both these areas he was, no doubt, involved in clearing ground and removing rubbish, in the first by exposing "the well endowed Opinions in Fashion" (4.3.20),[21] and in the second by arguing that there is no place for "Enthusiasm" which "laying by Reason would

19. See, for example, 4.12.9–13. For grounds of such directives see passages such as 4.3.9–14 and 4.6.4–15.

20. The most impressive and exhaustive of these are Michael Ayers's *Locke, Volume I: Epistemology* and *Locke, Volume II: Ontology* (London, 1991). Some of the more interesting earlier studies are Peter Alexander's *Ideas, Qualities, and Corpuscles* (Cambridge, 1985); the first three chapters of J. L. Mackie's *Problems from Locke* (Oxford, 1976); H.A.S. Schankula's "Locke, Descartes, and the Science of Nature" in Reinhard Brandt, ed., *John Locke: Symposium Wolfenbüttel 1979* (Berlin, 1979); chap. 3 of R. S. Woolhouse's *Locke* (Brighton, 1983); as well as all of the latter's *Locke's Philosophy of Science and Knowledge* (Oxford, 1971); and chap. 6 of his *The Empiricists* (Oxford, 1988).

21. Locke's anti-Filmer *First Treatise of Government* consists almost entirely of demonstrations that the Royal and Tory view of kingship and the state is nothing but a web of constricting prejudice.

set up Revelation without it" (4.19.3).[22] But he then proceeded to erect edifices—not the least of which is the *Second Treatise of Government*—which in many ways have dominated the contours of the landscape to our own day.

Of course, the *Essay concerning Human Understanding* is itself an imposing and enduring structure. Two of my major subjects, those of human reason and human freedom, form main parts of it. Reason, or the understanding, is the chief subject throughout, but occupies center stage in Books 1 and 4. In the first of these Locke's interest lies in showing what reason is not (hence this part of the *Essay* might best be seen as the under-labor of removing rubbish) and in the second in what it is. To freedom Locke gave short shrift in the *Essay*'s first edition, but, once the inadequacy of that treatment was pointed out to him, the place in which he dealt with it (2.21) grew to be by far the longest chapter in the course of subsequent editions. Neither the doctrine of reason in Book 4 nor that of freedom in Book 2 has the character of under-labor, or, if they do, they are in the form of the foundations for structures that Locke himself erected on them in his political and theological writings and—as I intend this book to demonstrate—in his writings on education.

Before I deal with reason as one of these foundations I must first highlight and elaborate on both an important distinction which Locke draws and a restriction which I have placed on myself in terms of that distinction. The distinction is between reasoning and the nature of the results of reasoning concerning, on the one hand, "abstract ideas" (or "general ideas" or "universals") and, on the other hand, physical objects (or "substances"). The restriction is that, when dealing with reasoning, I limit myself almost entirely to the first of these. In preceding paragraphs I referred to medicine and physics as "sciences." Strictly speaking, Locke would not allow that name for such disciplines. In 4.12.10, for example, he writes:

> I deny not, but a Man accustomed to rational and regular Experiments shall be able to see farther into the Nature of Bodies, and guess righter at their yet unknown Properties, than one, that is a Stranger to them: But yet, as I have said, this is but Judgment and Opinion, not Knowledge and Certainty. This way of getting, and improving our Knowledge in Substances only by Expe-

---

22. In the *Letters concerning Toleration* following his first one, as well as in the *Vindications* which followed his *Reasonableness of Christianity*, Locke's main concern was the removal of the weeds that threatened to obscure the presence of these two original works, weeds sown by minds which were prejudiced hence predisposed against truth.

rience and History, which is all that the weakness of our Faculties in this State of Mediocrity, which we are in in this World, can attain to, makes me suspect, that natural Philosophy is not capable of being made a Science. We are able, I imagine, to reach very little general Knowledge concerning the Species of Bodies, and their several Properties.

For Locke, scientific knowledge is general knowledge. It is knowledge in which reason is concerned only with necessary connections between or among universals. Hence it is "Knowledge of universal Truths," is characterized by "Certainty" and is the result of "Demonstration" (e.g., 4.3.25–26). Usually Locke is more severe than he is in 4.12.10, where "Experiments" are said to afford "very little general Knowledge." A more typical statement is that of 4.3.26: with respect to the "Bodies, that fall under the Examination of our Senses . . . we are not capable of scientifical Knowledge; nor shall ever be able to discover general, instructive, unquestionable Truths concerning them. Certainty and Demonstration, are Things we must not, in these Matters, pretend to."[23] Thus the distinction Locke draws is that between "general" and "experimental" reasoning, between certainty and probability. It is these two functions and products of reason which we find juxtaposed in a single sentence in the *Essay*'s 4.17.2: "the Mind comes to see, either the certain Agreement or Disagreement of any two Ideas, as in Demonstration, in which it arrives at Knowledge; or their probable connexion, on which it gives or with-holds its Assent, as in Opinion."

Phrases like "we are not capable of" certainty and have "but Judgment and Opinion" in the fields of interest to scientists like Sydenham and Newton should not be read as disparaging comments which would downgrade the importance of either such Master-Builders or their achievements. In these areas, probability is not only all we can hope to attain, it is all we need. If we were to aim at the certainty of general knowledge here, we would be using the wrong method: "He that shall consider, how little general Maxims . . . helped to satisfy the Enquiries of rational Men after

---

23. The reason for the difference between the two realms is that universals, but not "substances," are made by the thinker; therefore we know the real essence of the first but not of the second. Once we know an entity's "real essence" we know "that Foundation from which all its Properties flow." Because we do not know these essences of physical objects, therefore we cannot know anything about them with certainty, for "general Certainty is never to be found but in our Ideas" and "Whenever we go to seek it elsewhere in Experiment, or Observations without us, our Knowledge goes not beyond particulars," for it is "the contemplation of our own abstract Ideas, that alone is able to afford us general Knowledge" (4.6.16; see also 4.12.9). I have dealt at some length with this making of universals and hence knowledge of essences in chap. 6 of *Imposition of Method*.

real Improvements; How little, I say, the setting out at that end, has for many Ages together advanced Men's Progress towards the Knowledge of natural Philosophy, will think, we have Reason to thank those, who in this latter Age have taken another Course, and have trod out to us . . . a surer way to profitable Knowledge" (4.12.12).

If starting with "general Maxims" does not lead to "real Improvements," does this then imply Locke's disparagement of "general knowledge"? Answering that question affirmatively would be as wrong as it would have been earlier to take Locke as deprecating "probable knowledge." There are two domains in which reason is active: that of universals and that of physical objects. Reason's mode of procedure in the first of these is quite different from that in the second. Whereas in the first it makes abstractions and looks for necessary connections between and among the universals it obtains through this process of abstraction (e.g., 4.12.7), in the second it uses the senses to make observations and conduct experiments. Successful labor in the first of these domains gives us the general knowledge that, once we act on it, engages us in the pursuit of the *"Summum Bonum"* and so holds out the promise of freedom from the fear and bondage entailed by passion and prejudice. Success in the second domain progressively frees us from the drudgery and pain of daily life as the "mechanical sciences" allow us to procure "the Conveniences of Life" and medicine allows us their greater enjoyment through better health and longer life (e.g., 4.12.11–12),

Now that this distinction is in clear focus there remains the matter of why I stress the first and largely disregard the second of these uses of reason. It is not because I take the distinction to be unimportant—quite the contrary, if only because it marks a clear difference between Locke and Descartes. For Descartes, all knowledge is characterized by certainty, one and the same method is to be applied to all areas of knowledge, *and physical nature (including the human body) is one of these areas.* Because it all rests on clear and distinct foundations and is characterized by clarity and distinctness as it is developed on these foundations, all knowledge for Descartes possesses the same attribute of certainty irrespective of what it is about, so that the phrase "probable knowledge" is a contradiction in terms. As we have seen, Locke agrees with Descartes on this characteristic only as long as we limit our discussion to the realm of general knowledge, but he fundamentally disagrees in the realm of knowledge of physical objects.

In his insistence that in the realm of knowledge of nature probability is all we can attain, and all we need for the achievement of mastery, Locke makes himself an object of admiration for eighteenth-century Enlighten-

ment thinkers at precisely the point where Descartes aroused their antagonism. Descartes's insistence that he knew the real essence of matter was,
for these thinkers, an instance of the metaphysics which, "vain and am-
bitious," "wants to search into every mystery" and does not "wisely keep
within the bounds prescribed by nature."[24] It was, for them, an example
of philosophic "bad taste" when Descartes refused to place "strict limits
on the mania for explaining everything" and so disrespected "the wise
timidity of modern physics."[25] There was, to them, no vanity in Locke's
removing such "rubbish," nothing but good taste in his clearing the
ground for the Master-Builders by insisting on the use as well as the
limitations of the senses—especially when these limitations in no way
stood in the way of the utility that Descartes had foreseen as fruit of the
diligent pursuit of the sciences of nature.

Why, then, not focus on the function of reason for which Locke insisted
on "wise timidity"? To reiterate: it is not primarily because others have
done much work on Locke on substances and our knowledge of substances. It is, rather, that in significant respects the function of reason that
deals with universals and gives us the "certainty" of general knowledge
has the more crucial place in Locke's works.

There are two main grounds for this claim. First, it is this function of
reason which tells us what real essences are, how to obtain knowledge of
them,[26] that we are barred from such essences in the realm of "substances"
and that consequently we are there dependent on "Experiments" and
"Histories." It is this reasoning which juxtaposes the two realms in the
words from the headings of the *Essay*'s 4.12.7 and 4.12.9—"The true
method of advancing Knowledge, is by considering our abstract Ideas,"
"But Knowledge of Bodies is to be improved only by Experience"—and
which, in the latter paragraph, then insists:

> In our search after the knowledge of Substances, our want of Ideas, that are
> suitable to such a way of proceeding, obliges us to a quite different method
> [from that characteristic of this function of reason]. We advance not here, as
> in the other (where our abstract Ideas are real . . . Essences) by contemplating
> our Ideas, and considering their Relations and Correspondencies. . . . Here
> we are to take a quite contrary Course, the want of Ideas of their real Essences
> sends us from our own Thoughts, to the Things themselves, as they exist.
> Experience here must teach me, what Reason cannot.

24. These phrases are from Etienne Bonnot de Condillac, *An Essay on the Origin of Human Knowledge*, trans. Thomas Nugent (New York, 1974), p. 2.
25. Quoted from d'Alembert's *Encyclopedia* entry "Taste" in Nelly S. Hoyt and Thomas Cassirer, *Encyclopedia Selections* (Indianapolis, Ind., 1965), pp. 362–63.
26. See, again, chap. 6 of *Imposition of Method*.

Second, in subsequent parts of the book I demonstrate that it is this reasoning (rather than that about "substances") whose very process is of prime importance in the destruction of prejudice, thus in the liberation of the reasoner's mind, and in placing the reasoner in the only position from which legitimate mastery may be achieved—whether this be the mastery over self, over nature, or over one's cultural context. Since it is mastery over self that is the first and foremost aim of what Locke takes to be right education, it is this reasoning in which youth (or, for that matter, wrongly educated adults) have to acquire facility to the extent that its exercise becomes habitual for them.

Fundamentally, it is this reasoning on which, for Locke, both human freedom and progress depend. As we can now see, this holds even for progress in the sciences of nature. For without this function of reason directing us here "to take a quite contrary Course . . . from our own Thoughts, to the Things themselves," reason's necessary mode of operation in the realm of universals would, in the realm of physical objects, have become "the source of innumerable errors, as it fills the mind with vague and indeterminate notions, and with words that have no meaning."[27] It is, in short, this function of reason which makes Locke's philosophy revolutionary and which allows for the characterization of Locke as philosopher of mastery.

3. Locke as a Revolutionary

Especially in view of recent remarks that "the concept of revolution" has "cognitive opacity,"[28] it is necessary first to state the meaning that I attach to "revolution." One way to come to such a statement is by distinguishing "revolutionary" from "reformer."

I take a reformer to be a person who accepts the most important part of an existing set of principles or beliefs and the practices built upon them, but who recognizes that some (perhaps many) of the beliefs of this set may be false and some (perhaps many) of these practices less than good. While accepting much of a particular set of beliefs as true and praising many of the actions based on it, reformers aim to purify both thought and action

27. In this sentence, the first quotation repeats phrases from the passage I have just quoted from the *Essay*'s 4.12.9. The second quotation sounds very Lockean and evokes all sorts of passages from the *Essay* (for example, the last six paragraphs from its "Epistle to the Reader"). It is, however, an immediate continuation of the statement quoted a few paragraphs earlier from Condillac's *An Essay on the Origin of Human Knowledge*.

28. The phrase is from John Dunn's "Revolution," in *Political Innovation and Conceptual Change*, ed. Terence Ball, James Farr, and Russell Hanson (New York, 1989).

through identifying some of the beliefs of this set as false and some of its related actions as harmful, and through replacing such beliefs with true beliefs and substituting for such actions those they consider to be salubrious. In their attempts to achieve this aim, reformers are radical because they want to set things straight by returning to the root of the matter: they judge their contemporaries' beliefs and practices by principles that were once accepted but are no longer heeded. In contrast, revolutionaries are more than radical: they mean to uproot all beliefs and practices, and consider themselves free from all of society's present and past principles and from all actions based on them.

Revolutionaries always attempt to start de novo.[29] Their intent is to be, or become, free from all beliefs and practices that their context would impose, free as far as possible from this context itself. They recognize that they must begin their activity somewhere, must start out from some "given." But this given is always kept as minimal as possible and as close to an aspect of (presumed) first–person experience as possible. If Luther is a good example of a reformer, Descartes is a prime example of a revolutionary. All Descartes initially accepts as true is that there is thinking going on. He does not even at first accept this as *his* thinking, that is, as the thinking carried out by the person René Descartes. For this would introduce many other givens, not the least of which are the doctrines of soul and body, the realms of mind and matter. Even the use of "accept" in the statement "he accepts that there is thinking going on" is saying too much if it implies that there is a given. To Descartes, initially nothing is "given" if "to be given" implies a distinction of giver and receiver. Initially, he "gets rid of" all his opinions (and hence all the objects of his opinions) "all at one go" (CSM1, 117; AT6, 13)—as others[30] translate this statement, "he sweeps them completely away"—and then, free from anything his physical or cultural context would impose on him, he starts only with consciousness aware of its own activity.

---

29. It is unlikely that the term "revolutionary" can be used univocally, so that, for example, the eighteenth-century French and the twentieth-century Russian "revolutions" are essentially similar in all aspects. There may be enough similarities to continue a cautious application of this term to both events. But in the way I develop the term here, it applies better to events and persons in the seventeenth and eighteenth than to those in the nineteenth and twentieth centuries. (The difference is, no doubt, to be accounted for in terms of the advent of Hegel and of historicism.) If there is no strictly univocal use of "revolutionary," then we cannot take any person or event as paradigmatically revolutionary. This holds for Descartes and for any other thinker to whom we might want to apply the term. Again, see Dunn's nuanced treatment of the topic in his "Revolution."

30. E. S. Haldane and G. R. T. Ross, *The Philosophical Works of Descartes*, 2 vols. (Cambridge, 1911), 1:89.

Elsewhere, I have tried to capture a broad spectrum of statements on the meaning of "revolution" in the definition: "revolution is the introduction of discontinuity, that is, of a radically new situation, order, or condition; the discontinuity is for the sake of obtaining freedom."[31] Given Descartes's position that, at the foundation of one's knowledge, there must be items which are contextless, that is, items which are self-evident or known per se, Descartes is a thinker whom we may call "revolutionary" in this sense of that word. And because of Descartes's influence on him, we may say the same of Locke. But before we go to Locke, it will be helpful to say just a bit more about the revolutionary nature of the Cartesian position. Let me do this by introducing Descartes's criteria of knowledge, "clarity" and "distinctness" (criteria Locke employed much in the way Descartes did). Descartes stipulates that the criteria of clarity and distinctness must jointly apply to an item if it is legitimately to be called an item of knowledge. He calls "clear" that which "is present and accessible to the attentive mind," and "distinct" that which "is so sharply separated from all other perceptions that it contains within itself only what is clear" (*Principles* I 45: CSM1, 207–8; AT8-1, 21–22). In order therefore for us to be capable of judging anything properly it is not sufficient that we are just fully aware of all of that "thing." That much is compliance only with the first criterion, with "clarity." And such compliance may leave the "thing" intricately enmeshed with many other "things" none of which need themselves be fully understood. "Distinctness" demands that we have before the mind nothing but what pertains to having that item fully before the mind. "Distinctness" therefore requires that, through reductive analysis, we separate that item from all other items that accompany it in our everyday sensuous or intellectual experience.

Thus these criteria dictate that we cannot initially accept as knowledge that which is not epistemically completely simple. Even if we are confronted with a complex item which is clear and distinct to others, it cannot be so immediately to us. For, as complex, it is a compound of other items, all of which we must ourselves grasp as clear and distinct. Only then can the relations that hold between and among such items be understood; only then can a complex item be clear and distinct. These criteria therefore demand that at the foundation of knowledge there be utterly simple items, that is, items known apart from any other items, items known per

---

31. Critical notice of Richard Ashcraft's *Revolutionary Politics and Locke's Two Treatises of Government*, in *Canadian Journal of Philosophy* 19, no. 1 (1989): 101–16. The definition is on p. 107.

se rather than per aliud. They demand that the materials foundational to knowledge be context-independent in the strongest possible sense: their self-evidence determines them to be context*less*.[32]

That which the senses give us is concrete, enmeshed in its context, and therefore cannot be known immediately. If we call "nature" that which the senses give us, then "nature" cannot be known immediately. It can be understood only once it has been fitted into the rational schemes of a "mechanics," "medicine," or "morals." These "rational schemes" themselves cannot be developed prior to the advancement of the "rational schemes" called "metaphysics" and "physics." These in turn rest on the prior knowledge of certain concepts and principles known per se.

The same holds for what our education or general cultural environment places before us. For neither Euclid's *Elements* nor Aristotle's *Ethics*, neither Aquinas's *Summa Theologica* nor Galileo's *Two New Sciences* show that it derives its conclusions from indubitable principles known per se. None of them even went so far as to attempt to state these principles. Even had they stated them, and even had they derived their conclusions from them by uninterrupted chains of argument, I myself cannot begin at the end, with conclusions. If I am to understand, I must begin where they began to understand, at the level of items known per se. But such items are not "given."

Descartes's epistemology therefore dictates that, whether it is my physical or my cultural context that I am attempting to understand, if I am to understand I must understand for myself, radically so. In the words of the opening paragraph of the *Meditations*, "anything at all in the sciences that" for someone else "was stable and likely to last" is initially of little use to me as a person aspiring to know. For I will not be able to understand it unless I myself "start again right from the foundations." And no foundation is ever given. The foundation is always to be established. Whoever wants to understand will first have to establish his or her own foundation. Moreover, no foundation can be established apart from obeying the reductionistic precepts of the method which Descartes proposes. Thus when in the *Discourse* Descartes writes that "my plan has never gone beyond trying to reform my own thoughts and construct them upon a foundation which is all my own" (CSM1, 118; AT6, 15), he speaks for himself and, he believes, for whoever seeks to understand. The need for

32. It is reductive analysis that is to lead to clarity and distinctness. This analysis of the Cartesian methodology is therefore quite different from the "analysis" of many of the ancient and medieval philosophers for whom "analysis" did not result in "contextlessness." For them, "contextless items" (if that notion was at all intelligible) would be taken to be unknowable; knowledge of an item involved relating that item to some "universal," to, say, the Good, or God.

revolution is dictated by a methodology that goes hand-in-hand with the criteria of clarity and distinctness, as well as with a doctrine of radical epistemic individualism.[33] Locke, too, is a revolutionary rather than a reformer. He is a revolutionary because he follows Descartes (a statement which must appear contradictory given that I have just said that "revolutionary" involves both contextlessness and individualism; I shall deal with this apparent contradiction in the next section). It is not that Locke follows Descartes in accepting what we would call Cartesian metaphysical doctrines about soul and body, mind and matter; these are among the Cartesian doctrines which he rejects. And out of the rejection of Descartes's doctrine concerning matter there flows the important difference between the two on the kind of *knowledge* of matter or of "nature" that is possible. In spite of all their differences, what accounts for their strong kinship is Locke's adoption of Descartes's method for "general knowledge." When Locke adopts Descartes's methodology, he becomes a revolutionary in the areas covered by "general knowledge." I shall first discuss the phrase "Locke's revolutionary methodology." Discussion of the sentence "Locke accepts the Cartesian revolutionary methodology" will be left for the next section.

It has of course been noted by others that, in the sense in which I use the term, Locke is a revolutionary. The most recent extensive treatment of Locke as revolutionary is Richard Ashcraft's *Revolutionary Politics and Locke's Two Treatises of Government*.[34] Ashcraft, however, divorces Locke's revolutionary stance in politics from his methodological and epistemological doctrines; in this respect, his treatment is retrogressive.[35] For earlier writers did recognize that the revolutionary thrust of Locke's thought is not to be restricted to his political writings. Peter Laslett, for example, has said that "the implications of Locke's theory of knowledge for politics and political thinking were considerable and acted quite independently of the influence of *Two Treatises*." Laslett added that it was the implications of Locke's epistemology which "made men begin to feel that the whole world is new for everyone and we are all absolutely free of what has gone before."[36] As an example of an epistemological tenet with such an influence Laslett points to the doctrine of the tabula rasa. As we shall see at

33. With emendations, the five preceding paragraphs are from the article mentioned in note 18 above.

34. Richard Ashcraft, *Revolutionary Politics and Locke's Two Treatises of Government* (Princeton, 1986).

35. For my critique of Ashcraft, see the article mentioned in n. 31 above.

36. Peter Laslett, "Introduction" to *John Locke: Two Treatises of Government* (Cambridge, 1960; rev. 1963; first Mentor printing, 1965). All quotations from the *Second Treatise* are from the Mentor edition. The above quotations are from p. 97.

the end of this section, that particular doctrine is not really as fundamentally important as he assumes it to be. More important are the principles of Locke's methodology for development of "general knowledge." They are more important because, in contrast to the doctrine of the tabula rasa, they are unequivocally revolutionary. The aspects of Locke's epistemology which in fact dictate a revolutionary postion are themselves determined by the methodological principles. In these principles Locke transcends the boundaries of what is peculiar to his own position. At bottom, it is these principles that bind him, for example, to his later French *confrères* such as d'Alembert and Condorcet as well as to Descartes. It is these principles that lead to the social and political atomism which Laslett correctly identifies as a direct implication of Locke's theory of knowledge.[37] The application of the principles (about whose nature I will say more in a moment) led to atomism not just in social and political thought. For when others (like Boyle or Hooke or Newton) applied them to "nature" they led to a mechanistic picture of the universe and to theories of an atomistic kind in chemistry and physics. It is Locke's principles that helped bring about the atomism which many have pronounced typical of Enlightenment thought.

This idea of the relation between methodology and atomism, rooted in the seventeenth century and prevalent in the eighteenth, has not infrequently been a topic for comment. Consider Isaiah Berlin, who writes that "the great popularizers of the age . . . headed by Voltaire, Diderot, Holbach, Condorcet, and their followers, whatever their differences," shared the "dominant trend" of "analyzing everything into ultimate, irreducible atomic constituents, whether physical or psychological."[38] It has been widely recognized that such "ultimate components" were not held to be restricted to the realms of the physical or psychological; there were also believed to be epistemic and social or political irreducible constituents. Of the latter, the person of Locke's *Second Treatise of Government* is acknowledged as a prime illustration. The former are the foundational ideas of both Descartes and Locke. Whether, with Descartes, we call these "simple natures" or, with Locke, "simple ideas" or uncompounded

37. Laslett does not recognize that, in the end, this atomism is a consequence of Locke's methodology. Hence he (mistakenly) denies the existence of important "connecting links" between the *Second Treatise* and the *Essay*. Cf. *Two Treatises*, pp. 97–105. With respect to this aspect of Laslett's position, Ashcraft's is not as retrogressive as it may at first appear (although he, too, denies the importance of Locke's methodology to his political thought). For an antidote to both Laslett and Ashcraft, see Ruth W. Grant, *John Locke's Liberalism* (Chicago, 1987).

38. Isaiah Berlin, *The Age of Enlightenment: The Eighteenth Century Philosophers* (Oxford, 1956), p. 20.

"universals," in either case they are characterized by both Descartes and Locke as "clear and distinct" or (to use a word Locke introduces in later editions of the *Essay*) as "determinate." For both Locke and Descartes, a clear and distinct idea is the end product of reason's activity of analysis, or, speaking in terms of methodology, it is the final product of the process of reduction or decomposition. For Locke as for Descartes, it is only from the foundation of these fully known contextless items that theorizing can start, that systematic ("general") knowledge can be achieved. Whether in theory or in practice, to aim for a starting point which is to be character- ized as "contextless" is to intend to start de novo. As we have seen, such an intent is typical of the seventeenth- and eighteenth-century revolutionary.

Some of those who connect atomistic doctrines with methodology label these doctrines as revolutionary in import and explicitly attribute them to (among others) Locke. So Charles Taylor writes of "atomist doctrines" which "underly the seventeenth-century revolution in the terms of normative discourse," doctrines "which we associate with the names of Hobbes and Locke," doctrines whose "central . . . tradition" in the domain of political thought "is an affirmation of what we could call the primacy of rights."[39] There is thus nothing new in speaking about Locke's ideas as "revolutionary." That is how his ideas appeared to many of his contemporaries—for example, to William Molyneux—as well as to his immediate successors. In spite of the fact that we today find Locke's philosophy "frequently obvious and almost commonplace" (which is "the measure of its influence on us")[40] many recent critics remain struck by its revolutionary character.

Some, like Berlin, without elaboration, summarily refer to Locke's ideas as "genuinely revolutionary."[41] Others attach this label to specific works or to specific themes in them. Among these, John Passmore speaks of the "revolutionary implications" of *Some Thoughts concerning Educa- tion,"[42] John Yolton refers to Locke's "religious views" as "foremost in the ranks of those considered radical and revolutionary,"[43] and Ashcraft calls Locke a "hard-line radical" who published the *Second Treatise* as a "public and solemn statement on . . . the rightness of . . . revolution."[44] What

39. Charles Taylor, "Atomism," in *Powers, Possessions and Freedom: Essays in Honour of C. B. Macpherson,* ed. Alkis Kontos (Toronto, 1979), p. 39.
40. These phrases are Aaron's; *John Locke,* p. 44.
41. Berlin, *Age of Enlightenment,* p. 31.
42. John Passmore, "The Malleability of Man," in *Aspects of the Eighteenth Century,* ed. Earl R. Wasserman (Baltimore, 1965), pp. 37–38.
43. John Yolton, *John Locke and the Way of Ideas* (Oxford, 1956), p. 203.
44. Ashcraft, *Revolutionary Politics,* p. 600.

basically accounts for the revolutionary character of Locke's thought is a point on which many of these writers remain imprecise. Most of them, in fact, pass it by altogether. Taylor provides a valuable hint when he relates "revolutionary" and "atomistic." So does Yolton when he writes, "It would be a gross overstatement to claim that Locke was unaware of the implications for religion of many of his epistemological doctrines, for a man so well versed in the controversies of his day could not fail to grasp the revolutionary character of many of these doctrines for religion."[45] Both Taylor and Yolton point in the right direction: the revolutionary power of Locke's thought is related to the atomism demanded by his epistemology. But neither of them quite reveals the heart of the matter. For the characteristic nature of Locke's epistemology comes about through the adoption of a particular methodological stance and it is, therefore, the revolutionary character of Locke's reductionistic methodology which lends revolutionary force to his epistemology. His methodology and epistemology together, in turn, account for the "revolutionary implications" of his works on politics, on religion, and on education.

Locke himself was quite conscious of the fact that it was from his methodology that revolutionary power emanated into the rest of his writings. This, as we shall see in a moment, is clear enough from his *Essay*. But the point may also be established from other works. Take, as an example, the opening pages of the *Conduct of the Understanding*. Here Locke writes about "the logic, now in use . . . these two or three thousand years" as "not sufficient to guide the understanding." He impugns that "logic" for having "served to confirm and establish errors, rather than to open a way to truth." What is therefore called for, he continues, is "that a better and perfecter use and employment of the mind and understanding should be introduced."[46] "Logic" is here spoken of as "a way," "a use." In other words, logic is to be taken as method. Implied is the revolutionary nature of the new method. The old method debarred us from attaining truth. Its well-entrenched products obstruct our intellectual progress and will have to be expunged. Employment of the new method will lead us totally to abandon the old method and to sweep its products completely away. When we have reached that point we must begin anew in the attempt to develop knowledge. For once we are rid of the old we are still only at the stage where we can "open a way to truth." Truth still has to be won.

A move just made requires, for a moment, interrupting the discussion

---

45. Yolton, *Locke and the Way of Ideas*, p. 116.
46. Para. 1, p. 206–7. Some of these phrases Locke quotes from Bacon's *Novum Organum*.

of Locke as "revolutionary." It is my characterization of Locke's writings on logic as works on method. This identification is plausible if only because of Descartes's influence on Locke, for Descartes writes about his *Discourse on Method* as a work "where I summarized the principal rules of logic."[47] But especially for my discussion of education in later chapters, it is important to establish the legitimacy of this identification more firmly and to demonstrate that Locke himself made it.

The new "logic" is one which Locke took himself to have propounded and used in the *Essay*. That this logic is in fact what (with Descartes and many others) we would call "method" can perhaps be established more easily from that part of the correspondence which passed between Locke and William Molyneux when Locke was preparing his *Some Thoughts concerning Education* for publication.

In a letter of July 16, 1692, Locke thanks Molyneux for "the extraordinary compliment you were pleased to make me in the Epistle Dedicatory" of *Dioptrica Nova. A Treatise of Dioptrics*. This compliment reads as follows:

> But to none do we owe for a greater Advancement in this Part of Philosophy, than to the incomparable Mr. Locke, Who, in his *Essay of Humane Understanding*, has rectified more received Mistakes, and delivered more profound Truths, established on Experience and Observations, for the Direction of Man's Mind in the Prosecution of knowledge, (which I think may be properly term'd *Logick*) than are to be met with in all the Volumes of the Antients.[48]

Throughout the seventeenth and eighteenth centuries works on method were announced as writings on "Truths . . . for the Direction of Man's mind in the Prosecution of knowledge." Molyneux's phrase evokes the titles of Descartes's works on method, the *Discourse on the Method of rightly conducting one's Reason and seeking the Truth in the Sciences*, and the earlier *Rules for the Direction of the Mind* (known to many in manuscript form and first published in Dutch in 1684).[49] His phrase also calls to mind titles and

---

47. CSM1, 186; AT9–2, 15.
48. For both Locke's statement and that of Molyneux, see *The Correspondence of John Locke*, ed. E. S. de Beer, 8 vols. (Oxford, 1976–88), 4:479. No doubt Locke was sincere in calling the compliment "extraordinary." In it, Molyneux spoke of Locke the way Locke had spoken of Newton, so that Locke and Newton now shared the attribute of incomparability. For Locke's compliment to Newton, see the *Essay*'s "Epistle to the Reader," pp. 9–10 of the Nidditch edition. Locke would have been less pleased had he known that, in addition to Newton, he shared this attribute with one of the main targets of his scorn: "that incomparable politician, Sir Robert Filmer." (See Ashcraft, *Revolutionary Politics*, p. 225.)
49. This Dutch edition was followed by the publication of the original Latin text in 1701.

sentences from later works. There is Arnauld's *La logique, ou l'art de penser* (published in 1662, with an explicit acknowledgment that parts of it were taken directly from the manuscript of Descartes's *Rules*),[50] in which the opening sentence of the Introduction begins with the words "Logic is the art of directing reason to a knowledge of things . . . ." And to mention just one of the works written in the eighteenth century, there is Isaac Watts's *Logick: or, the Right Use of Reason in the Enquiry after Truth, with a Variety of Rules to Guard against Error, in the Affairs of Religion and Human Life, as Well as in the Sciences*; the opening chapter begins with the statement "Logick is the Art of using Reason well in our Enquiries after Truth."[51] From the correspondence it is evident that Molyneux sees the basic importance of Locke's *Essay* as lying in the area of "logic" or methodology, and that Locke's great service still to be performed is to republish just these "truths . . . for the direction of man's mind" in a form suitable to be a guide for the education of the young.

Locke takes no exception to Molyneux's identification of logic and method: "as to the method of learning," he wrote, "perhaps I may entertain you more at large hereafter."[52] Molyneux then informs Locke that, through a third party, he was told that while exiled in Holland Locke was busy preparing just "such a Work as this I desire" on "the Method of Learning."[53] Locke confirms the correctness of this information, hence explicitly identifying the thrust of the *Essay*'s method with that of the precepts of his major work on education: "The main of what I now publish"—i.e., *Some Thoughts concerning Education*—"is but what was contain'd in several letters to a friend of mine, the greatest part whereof were writ out of Holland."[54] In reply, Molyneux writes that "I can give no better proof of my liking your Book in all these Precepts, than by a strict Observance of them in the Education of My Own. . . . I know no Logick that Deserves to be Named, but the Essay of Humane Understanding."[55]

Locke continues to use "logic" with the sense of "method." And, like Molyneux, he continues to see logic or method as the *Essay*'s epitome:

50. See the translation of James Dickoff and Patricia James, *The Art of Thinking* (Indianapolis, Ind., 1964), p. 302.

51. This work, widely read throughout the middle decades of the eighteenth century, both in England and abroad, presents a Lockean epistemology and methodology. Its dedication speaks of "Logick" as "not that noisy Thing that deals in all Dispute and Wrangling, to which former Ages had debased and confined it." Quoted from "The Second Edition, Corrected" (London, 1726); republished (New York 1984), ed. Peter A. Schouls.

52. 20 January 1693; *Correspondence* 4: 627.

53. 2 March 1693; *Correspondence* 4: 649.

54. 28 March 1693; *Correspondence* 4: 665.

55. 12 August 1693; *Correspondence* 4: 715.

two years after this period of correspondence he tells Molyneux that the third edition of the *Essay* is about to appear and that "what perhaps will seem stranger, and possibly please you better, an abridgment is now making . . . by one of the university of Oxford, for the use of young scholars, in the place of an ordinary system of logick."[56]

These items of correspondence state that the logic of the *Essay* is to be taken as a method for the direction of the mind. They explicitly link the *Essay* and the *Education*. They do not, however, say anything specifically about the main topic of this section, to which I now return: the revolutionary nature of this method. But if we consider some of the *Essay*'s passages in which Locke writes of what he believes the employment of the method will accomplish, then it becomes quite legitimate to say that the designation "revolutionary" is appropriate. Introduction of just a few passages from the first book of the *Essay* will suffice to substantiate this point.

In the third chapter of that first book Locke attempts to explain how it comes about that people "even of good understanding in other matters," in morality and religion "embraced as first and unquestionable" principles and doctrines which, because of "their absurdity, as well as opposition one to another, it is impossible should be true" (1.3.21). He asks, first, what are "the ways, and steps by which it is brought about" that "Doctrines, that have been derived from no better original, than the Superstition of a Nurse, or the Authority of an old Woman" come to "grow up to the dignity of Principles in Religion or Morality"? (1.3.22). Once we have correctly answered this question, we know which wrong ways or methods of thinking and of education we ought to break free from. Second, he asks: how is it possible that in spite of their very wrongness, such methods can be so effective in blinding us to truth? Part of the answer to the first question is that any method is wrong if it does not teach people to be critical of whatever is placed before them. Part of the answer to the second is that a child is very impressionable and has little or no defense against the power of those who dominate its surroundings; it is anything but difficult for adults to impose their principles on the vulnerable child. Parents in particular and educators in general therefore have the task of preventing even the principles dearest to themselves from being impressed on the child's consciousness. The only principle that ought to guide parents is not "to principle" children but to encourage them to develop their power of questioning, of not accepting what may enjoy popular acceptance unless it can withstand criticism, that is, unless the issue in

56. 26 April 1695; *Correspondence* 5: 351.

question can be seen by the maturing child to be clear and distinct. Children acquire prejudices whenever they accept as true or good an item which they have not criticized, that is, have not submitted to the criteria of clarity and distinctness. Whether or not the belief accepted is in fact true is not the issue. The point is whether the child adopting it may legitimately adopt it as true. Only when children have themselves recognized, clearly and distinctly, the truth of a belief is their acceptance of that belief legitimate.

Although the question of precisely how the child is to become "critical" must be left for the third part of this book, it is clear that for Locke, the only principle which ought to guide parents is to keep the child from becoming prejudiced. Alas, says Locke, parents and educators generally act quite contrary to this principle.

> For such, who are careful (as they call it) to principle Children well, (and few there be who have not a set of those Principles for them, which they believe in) instil into the unwary, and, as yet, unprejudiced Understanding, (for white Paper receives any Characters) those Doctrines they would have them retain and profess. These being taught them as soon as they have any apprehension; and still as they grow up, confirmed to them, either by the open Profession, or tacit Consent, of all they have to do with; or at least by those, of whose Wisdom, Knowledge, and Piety, they have an Opinion, who never suffer those Propositions to be otherwise mentioned, but as the Basis and Foundation, on which they build their Religion or Manners, come, by these means, to have the reputation of unquestionable, self-evident, and innate Truths. (1.3.22)

In this way what is really artificial and relative comes to be accepted without question as natural and absolute. That which we should have critically examined we "take . . . upon trust."[57]

Upbringing or education is the greatest culprit but not the only one, for "some, wanting skill and leisure, and others the inclination, and some being taught, that they ought not, to examine; there are few to be found, who are not exposed by their Ignorance, Laziness, Education, or Precipitancy, to take . . . Principles . . . upon trust" (1.3.24). What follows is one of the most revolutionary passages of the *Essay*:

---

57. In his "Governing Conduct" Tully writes: "Principles or ideas and dispositions that are said to be innate are, in fact, the *product* of custom and education. By being called 'innate' or 'divine' and 'first principles' they are insulated from examination and taken on 'trust'. . . . This concept of 'trust' is of course the central target of the *Essay*" (pp. 21–22). Locke's anti-trust stance will surface as crucially important throughout my study. It is a stance dictated by Locke's revolutionary "logic."

This is evidently the case of all Children and young Folk; and Custom, a greater power than Nature, seldom failing to make them worship for Divine, what she has inured them to bow their Minds, and submit their Understandings to, it is no wonder, that grown Men, either perplexed in the necessary affairs of Life, or hot in the pursuit of Pleasures, should not seriously sit down to examine their own Tenets; especially when one of their Principles is, That principles ought not to be questioned. And had Men leisure, parts, and will, Who is there almost, that dare *shake the foundations of all his past Thoughts and Actions*, and endure to bring upon himself, the shame of having been a long time wholly in mistake and error? . . . he will be . . . afraid to *question* those Principles, when he shall think them, as most Men do, *the Standards set up by God in his Mind*, to be *the Rule and Touchstone of all other Opinions*. And what can hinder him from thinking them sacred, when he finds them the earliest of all his own Thoughts, and the most reverenced by others? (1.3.25, my italics)

For the adult not educated in accordance with the right method one of the "truths . . . for the direction of man's mind in the prosecution of knowledge" is that he must be thoroughly critical of absolutely every belief he happens to hold. For that, he must "shake the foundations of all his past Thoughts and Actions" even if such foundations commonly function as standards and touchstone, even if he himself and those around him believe they have been established by God. Discussion of how this shaking of the foundations is to be accomplished must also be postponed to a later chapter. Suffice it to say here that the principle behind the procedure involved in shaking the foundations is no different from what is present in the upbringing of a young person who is being educated according to the right method. In either case the principle is that of (epistemic) autonomy; in either case it demands the revolutionary's attitude. Nothing believed to be sacred or ultimate by yourself or by society is to be accepted as absolute. All that parents and teachers are allowed to pass on to children is that they must be thoroughly critical of whatever comes before their minds. Thus educators are duty bound to impress upon the pupil not to accept anything as true unless it has withstood criteria imposed by the pupil's own understanding. The criteria in question are those of clarity and distinctness. This manner of educating, according to Locke, is the only way for a new generation to have the best chance of maturing free from prejudice. To be free from prejudice or bias, free from principles whose acceptance one's own reason has not authorized, is the only state in which a person can successfully direct his or her "mind in the prosecution of knowledge." The results then obtained will themselves be free from bias because they carry reason's authoritative stamp.

In the *Essay* Locke does not just advocate this method; he actually uses it. To the extent that he employs it successfully, the *Essay* itself is then a revolutionary document not merely in the method it advocates but also in the manner it deals with its subject matter and in the results it achieves. Book 1 illustrates this well. It introduces a doctrine, that of innatism, which is dear, even sacred, to many of Locke's contemporaries; Locke reduces this doctrine to the obscure ideas and contradictory principles upon which it rests, and then rejects it; and he puts in its place a new doctrine, that of the tabula rasa. The closing paragraphs of Book 1 attest to the fact that Locke was well aware of the revolutionary character of his program. There we read: "What censure, doubting thus of innate Principles, may deserve from Men, who will be apt to call it, pulling up the old foundations of Knowledge and Certainty, I cannot tell." And, it is clear, he does not really care. He continues, "This I am certain, I have not made it my business, either to quit, or follow any Authority in the ensuing Discourse" (1.4.23). What he has made his business is to employ nothing but his own reason on the materials derived from his own experience. As he states in the final sentence of this first book, his business was to present "an unbias'd enquiry after Truth." As we now know, for Locke "unbias'd enquiry" is possible upon disregarding what one's culture would have one accept in the first place. It is necessary to be "indifferent"; hence "I have not made it my business, either to quit, or follow any Authority." It is in the contextlessness created through rejecting the relevance of his culture's authorities that Locke obtains a foundation that he is convinced can stand the test of rational scrutiny: "All that I shall say for the Principles I proceed on, is, that I can only appeal to Mens own unprejudiced Experience, and Observation, whether they be true, or no."

Earlier in this section, I said that when we discuss the revolutionary nature of Locke's position, it will become clear that the doctrine of the tabula rasa does not occupy as fundamental a place as considerations about methodology. We can now see why this is so. The doctrine of the tabula rasa need not have revolutionary implications. For it is not inconceivable for such a doctrine to coexist with one that portrays human beings as social beings, as the kind of beings which are, however, only potentially social. They could then be the kind of beings which cannot come to the realization of their potentiality except through their cultural context, that is, through becoming imbued with the beliefs and attitudes prevalent at the time during which they are in the process of growth and maturation. Such a holistic doctrine is far removed from the atomistic one Locke presents. The one would hold that no beings become fully human unless they come to be imbued with the web of beliefs prevalent in their culture; the other, that they do not become fully human unless they initially reject all prevalent doctrines and opinions and accept only such doctrines as can pass a certain test imposed by each individual's own intellect. Either view might incorporate the doctrine of the tabula rasa. Whether the position is holistic or atomistic, conservatist or revolutionary in implication, the doctrine of the tabula rasa may be used to express the view that we are not born with some (ineradicable) beliefs. In the one case, a being is to become human through uninhibited exposure to its culture's beliefs and principles, in the other through initial shielding from them. In the one the slate is to be inscribed with the prevalent cultural attitudes at the earliest opportunity, in the other it is to be kept as clean as possible. In the former it might be held that precisely because society can write on the "white paper," new generations of social (hence human) beings can come on the scene. In the latter it might be believed that because minds are like "white paper" people can become ruined for life and never really attain humanhood because of their early upbringing; or that they can be brought up well by being taught to let only their own reason write on the slate; or that they can redeem themselves from the disaster of the wrong kind of upbringing by forcing themselves to erase all marks found on the paper and to let only their reason write on it henceforth.[58] The last two statements are sketches of how Locke sees the emergence of a new truly human being. In both of them the revolutionary implications of the doctrine of the tabula rasa are borrowed from the broader methodological picture in which this doctrine is given its place.

It might be said that only one of these doctrines is consistent, namely, the one which holds that children must be influenced as soon as possible by their cultural context. It might be said that the other really reduces to that position when it submits children to a set of beliefs precisely in its attempt at shielding them from their culture. To this one might object that the injunction "Do not accept any belief until . . ." is itself advice and not belief. But why would one offer, or follow, the advice unless one believed that offering or following it would lead to good results? Thus some beliefs of goodness or utility would seem to be presupposed.

4. Locke and Cartesian Methodology

Two questions remain for this chapter. First, may Locke's method, characterized as revolutionary, be called new? If by "new" we mean

---

58. In view of the traditional and still influential distinction between empiricism and rationalism, I should stress that my use of reason in these statements is not meant to play down the role of the senses.

original with Locke, the question must be answered negatively. The method Locke advocates for the pursuit of general knowledge[59] is that which Descartes first articulates in a complete and systematic way. This of course immediately raises the second question: given my description of what it means to be revolutionary, how can I call Locke a revolutionary? If Locke accepts the method propounded by Descartes, can he then be said to have swept all away and started anew, from fresh foundations? Can Locke be a revolutionary if he is a *follower* of a revolutionary?

It is, I think, undeniable that in the *Essay* Locke does espouse a method for the pursuit of general knowledge which is essentially Descartes's. Since I have argued this point in detail elsewhere, I need not provide support for it here.[60] This method is equally present in Locke's writings on education. (In both places it is of course not the only method present, for in both there is knowledge of substances as well as general knowledge. But for reasons stated earlier, I shall continue to focus on the method for attaining general knowledge to which, for brevity's sake, I shall refer as "the" method.) Little else can be expected since (as eighteenth-century Enlightenment thinkers were quick to notice) Locke's educational writings show the philosophy of the *Essay* at work. Although the method in these works is Cartesian, Locke's position in them is nevertheless revolutionary. Because Locke's views on education are considered in detail in later chapters, I shall at this point introduce only such passages from the *Conduct of the Understanding* as are sufficient to provide support for the claim that, in this work also, Locke's method is Cartesian. Furthermore, these passages will help make it possible to determine the sense in which this sharing of methodology does not conflict with the assertion of revolutionary originality.

In the opening paragraph of the *Conduct* we find the statement to which I already directed our thoughts, that about "The logic, now in use . . . these two or three thousand years" being "not sufficient to guide the understanding" because it has "served to confirm and establish errors, rather than to open a way to truth." In the second paragraph Locke adds that the absence of proper methodic procedure has made people "guilty of a great many faults in the exercise and improvement" of the understanding, faults that "hinder them in their progress, and keep them in ignorance

---

59. The restriction that, according to Locke, this is the method to be used in *general* knowledge need, I take it, not be emphasized beyond what I have said on it in the second section. To remind ourselves of the restriction once more: this method holds for mathematics, morals (which includes ethics and political theory) and theology; according to Locke it does not hold for the sciences that preoccupied Boyle and Newton, those that we call the "sciences of nature."

60. For the relevant details, see chap. 6 of *Imposition of Method*.

and error all their lives." In the third paragraph these faults are enumerated in language reminiscent of several Cartesian texts (for example, of the ninth and tenth rules of the *Rules for the Direction of the Mind*). These "faults" are "the want of determined ideas, and of sagacity, and exercise in finding out, and laying in order, intermediate ideas." How do we obtain determined ideas, and how do we become sagacious in their use? Like Descartes in the *Rules* and in the *Discourse*, Locke, in the fourth paragraph, advises practice rather than memorization of maxims: "it is practice alone that brings the powers of the mind to their perfection," for "Nobody is made any thing by hearing of rules, or laying them up in his memory." It is practice that "must settle the habit of doing, without reflecting on the rule." No one can be made "a strict reasoner, by a set of rules, showing him wherein right reasoning consists." This stress on practice reveals the required logic or method to be internal to the understanding. Rules and maxims that one has not experienced at work are meaningless. There is nothing to be said against an articulated methodology, as long as one recognizes that its rules are of use only if they are, and through individual experience are known to be, an articulation of the way the understanding works in its successful pursuit of truth. An account of the complete set of correct methodic procedures is nothing but reason's self-portrait. But it cannot be recognized as such except through its use in actual reasoning. Hence what is called for is practice, exercise in realms in which reason has been successful in achieving incontrovertible truth. This doctrine is purely Cartesian.[61]

In the *Conduct* Locke follows Descartes also concerning the area in which such practice can best be obtained. As we read in the sixth paragraph: "Would you have a man reason well, you must use him to it betimes, exercise his mind in observing the connexion of ideas, and following them in train. Nothing does this better than mathematics, which, therefore, I think should be taught all those who have the time and opportunity; not so much to make them mathematicians, as to make them reasonable creatures."[62]

---

61. That for Descartes method is intrinsic rather than extrinsic to the understanding is, of course, a well-established point which has been made in the standard commentaries. See, for example, L. J. Beck, *The Method of Descartes* (Oxford, 1952), p. 205; Alexandre Koyré, "Introduction" to G. E. M. Anscombe and Peter Geach, eds., *Descartes: Philosophical Writings* (London, 1954), p. xxv; and Norman Kemp Smith, *Studies in the Cartesian Philosophy* (1902; New York, 1962), p. 23.

62. The doctrines that you cannot become a reasoner through memorizing a set of rules, and that practice in mathematics makes us reasonable creatures, become commonplaces in eighteenth century writings. Sometimes they are stated with an explicit reference to Locke, as by Isaac Watts, *Logick*, pp. 326–27.

The passages cited so far are, in the main, about synthesis or composition. But Locke also writes quite Cartesianly of how we obtain the foundations from which we must reason. That is, he adopts the Cartesian doctrine of analysis or reduction. The following passage from paragraph 39, explicitly about *the* method to be used with respect to *any* subject matter if we are to obtain general knowledge of it, is little more than a paraphrase of the second and third methodic precepts of Descartes' *Discourse*: "Things . . . must be approached by gentle and regular steps; and what is most visible, easy, and obvious in them first considered. Reduce them into their distinct parts; and then in their due order bring all that should be known concerning every one of those parts into plain and simple questions." This procedure of reduction Locke calls "methodic application" to the problem. Since it is the prerequisite for composition, for the "distinct gradual growth in knowledge" which is "firm and sure" and "carries its own light with it in every step of its progression in an easy and orderly train," there is, Locke adds, "nothing of more use to the understanding" than this "methodic application." Indeed, without this application the understanding cannot function properly; apart from it no reasoning can take place. In its absence fancy will usurp the place of reason, ignorance and superstition that of knowledge and liberty. These too are sentiments shared with Descartes. Both believe that reduction of whatever intelligible complexity confronts the human mind leads to the simple self-evident foundations of knowledge which we must apprehend in order to be able to develop systematic knowledge.

After both reduction and composition have been discussed, the *Conduct* (in paragraph 41) reverts to the language of Book 1 of the *Essay*, with all of its revolutionary implications:

> There is, I know, a great fault among all sorts of people of principling their children and scholars, which at last, when looked into, amounts to no more but making them imbibe their teacher's notions and tenets by an implicit faith, and firmly adhere to them whether true or false. . . . I can see no other right way of principling them, but to take heed, as much as may be, that in their tender years ideas that have no natural cohesion come not to be united in their heads; and that this rule be often inculcated to them to be their guide in the whole course of their lives and studies, viz. that they never suffer any ideas to be joined in their understandings in any other or stronger combination than what their own nature and correspondence give them, and that they often examine those that they find linked together in their minds, whether this association of ideas be from the visible agreement that is in the ideas themselves, or from the habitual and prevailing custom of the mind joining them thus together in thinking.

As we saw earlier in discussing the *Essay*, so we now see in reflecting on the *Conduct*, that even if what the teacher reports or proclaims is true, it is the teacher's duty to impress on the student not to accept it "by an implicit faith." The teacher's main task is to encourage the pupil to adopt the habit of striving for epistemic autonomy. The critical examination this requires of whatever comes before the mind is one whose criteria are explicitly bound up with Cartesian reductionistic methodology. Students always have the duty to attempt to reduce whatever confronts the mind to clear and distinct self-evident concepts and principles and to reconstitute it into the kind of complexity which is determinate, the kind of complexity which embodies no obscurity for the mind that carried out the reduction and recomposition. In short, the fundamental duty all human beings owe themselves—that of epistemic autonomy—can be carried out only through the application of this Cartesian methodology. And the only test that can indicate whether a person has in fact performed this duty also necessarily implicates this methodology. Because of the indispensable role it plays in it, Cartesian methodology is crucial for what some call Locke's "Enlightenment position." This, as we have seen, is clear from the *Conduct*. But it could have been illustrated as well from Locke's other writings on education.[63]

Thus the negative answer given to the first of this chapter's final questions has been confirmed as correct. Even though Locke's method is revolutionary, it cannot be called new. These two works, the *Essay concerning Human Understanding* and the *Conduct of the Understanding*, clearly show the method to be one he shared with others, notably with Descartes.

That leaves the second question. If he accepts a method propounded by Descartes, can Locke then be called a revolutionary? Suppose that Locke accepts as correct my description of revolutionary activity, so that he would agree with the statement that a revolutionary thinker can take nothing for granted and must start de novo. Suppose further that Locke would also agree with me that the method he adopts is that propounded by Descartes. If we then ask him whether he would consider his own stance to be revolutionary, the answer consistent with his position would still have to be in the affirmative. It is not difficult to support this point.

Consider Locke's response to one of Stillingfleet's attacks on the *Essay*:

> My book . . . hath had this misfortune to displease your lordship, with many things in it, for their novelty; as 'new way of reasoning; new hypothesis

---

63. See, for example, *Some Thoughts concerning Reading and Study for a Gentleman, Works*, 1823, 3:294; as well as the *Discourse*-like statements about "good method" and the statements against bad logic, reminiscent of the *Rules for the Direction of the Mind*, in *Some Thoughts concerning Education*, paragraphs 195 and 188 respectively.

about reason; new sort of certainty; . . . new method of certainty,' . . . .
But as to the way your lordship thinks I should have taken to prevent the
having it thought my invention, when it was common to me with others; it
unluckily so fell out, in the subject of my Essay of Human Understanding,
that I could not look into the thoughts of other men to inform myself. For
my design being, as well as I could, to copy nature, and to give an account of
the operations of the mind in thinking, I could look into nobody's understanding but my own, to see how it wrought; nor have a prospect into other
men's minds to . . . observe what steps and notions they took . . . in their
acquainting themselves with truth, and their advance to knowledge. . . .
    All therefore I can say of my book is, that it is a copy of my own mind, in
its several ways of operation. And all that I can say for the publishing of it is,
that I think the intellectual faculties are made, and operate alike in most men;
and that some, that I showed it to before I published it, liked it so well that I
was confirmed in that opinion.[64]

If we take this passage in conjunction with some of the material I quoted
from the *Conduct* (particularly the statements about the use of mathematics and the nature of deduction), then we can support the point that the
method, though not "new" because shared with a predecessor, is nevertheless revolutionary and causes the practitioner of it to be a revolutionary. Locke's doctrine is as follows. When my understanding leads me to
results that I experience as clear and distinct and thus pronounce to be
incontrovertible, I can observe the workings of my mind in its process of
attaining these results. I may then extrapolate and say that a statement of
this process is a statement of the universal method, that is, of the procedure that must be followed in any area where human beings can gain
general knowledge if such knowledge is to become a reality. Locke would
stress the following as grounds for this extrapolation.
    In areas where I feel most assured of having attained truth, say in an area
like arithmetic, others report they too feel quite assured, and the results I
and these others attain are identical. When I explain to these others how I
have obtained these results, they profess to have traveled an identical path.
The path I went is the path they went; the results obtained by each are the
same as for the others; and all hold these results to be incontrovertible.
They are taken to be incontrovertible because they are held to be founded
on indubitable, self-evident, clear and distinct foundations, foundations

64. *Works*, 1823, 4:137–39. Locke's insistence that a statement of method, of "the operations of the mind in thinking," is in the first instance based on observation of his *own* mind
"in its several ways of operating" is, of course, not an afterthought to the *Essay*. The point is
made emphatically in the *Essay*'s 2.11.16. I return to this issue in the third chapter.

that clearly and distinctly allowed the establishment of the relationships between them which produced these results.

However, the way to obtain these self-evident, clear and distinct foundations, necessitates being critical of whatever confronts the mind; it requires that I never accept anything presented ready-made by my surroundings. In other words, it demands of me an ahistorical, revolutionary activity of rejecting whatever is not (yet) clear and distinct to my mind. For the way to truth begins with reduction or decomposition of beliefs into their constituents until no further division is possible. And such reduction is the disintegration and hence rejection of these beliefs. That is the way my understanding works. The description of that manner of procedure is, in effect, a partial definition of reasoning (partial, because it deals only with reduction and not with composition). But evidence suggests that this is the way others' understandings work as well. The methodological writings of Descartes indicate that his understanding also worked that way. When, therefore, he wrote about the way to attain truth, his doctrine and that of anyone else writing with care and without bias on that subject would necessarily tend to show strong agreement. But what each is saying is that reason itself is revolutionary. And since the locus of reason is in each individual, each individual cannot but act in a revolutionary manner when exercising reason.

This, I think, would be Locke's answer. Like Descartes', its methodological and epistemological individualism is not taken to lead to subjective relativism but instead is meant to overcome the relativism of belief conditioned by specific cultural epochs. For methodic procedure, reason's way of working, is the way of "natural reason," of the natural ability to attain truth—an ability that belongs to all human beings by virtue of their nature. As we read in the *Conduct* (§3): "Every man carries about him a touchstone, if he will make use of it, to distinguish substantial gold from superficial glitterings, truth from appearances. And, indeed, the use and benefit of this touchstone, which is natural reason, is spoiled and lost only by assumed prejudices, overweening presumption, and narrowing our minds."

For Locke, as for Descartes and Enlightenment thinkers such as the philosophes, the articulation of the method of reduction and composition gives us a functional definition of reason. Because reduction is one of the two chief parts of this definition, it is reason itself which dictates revolution. All these thinkers hold that it is reason which "must be our last Judge and Guide in every Thing" (*Essay*, 4.19.14). For them, reason judges all things but is itself beyond the pale of evaluation. There is, therefore, for them no question about the authority that would sanction the implementation of the method. This authority is reason itself. And reason not only sanctions but, in fact, demands a revolutionary stance. For to recapitulate: Reason demands that, to begin with, one may not accept, trust, or conform to anything. Acceptance, trust, or conformation is legitimate for people only once their reason has authorized such acts. No such authorization is possible until all beliefs have been completely swept away and hence all objects of these beliefs have lost whatever authority or compulsion they may have seemed to possess. Reason demands revolution because it requires of each person, at the beginnings of each attempt to make sense of one's context, that one reject as valid all one's beliefs about that particular context. To begin with it demands contextlessness. Hence the importance at the foundation, not of one's culture's "principles" but of self-evident items, not of items known per aliud but of items known per se.[65]

Locke holds reason to be beyond the pale of evaluation because he holds it to be infallible. It is, therefore, the infallibility of reason which places the legitimacy of the imposition of the method beyond question. It is reason's infallible voice that commands the revolutionary posture. How does Locke know that what he takes to be human reason is really infallible? That question is of prime importance. If it were the case that he did not know but merely assumed that reason was infallible, then Locke's revolutionary stance—in epistemology as well as in his educational theory— would rest upon dogmatic belief. The call for the kind of revolution that forbids all dogmatism would then itself be dogmatic. The question about knowledge of the infallibility of reason will therefore have to be considered with care if we are to be able to place ourselves in a position from which we can properly evaluate these aspects of Locke's thought. I discuss the relation of reason to human nature in the next chapter. I then devote the following chapter entirely to this question about knowledge of reason's infallibility.

Before we turn to these discussions it will be well to remind ourselves of the supremely important role that reason plays in Locke's thought. In the fourth paragraph of the *Conduct* Locke writes: "We are born with faculties and powers capable almost of anything, such at least as would carry us farther than can easily be imagined." He adds: "but it is only the exercise of those powers which gives us ability and skill in any thing, and

---

65. It is clear that when critics accused Locke of relativism or skepticism because they saw him as "pulling up the old foundations of Knowledge and Certainty" (*Essay* 1.4.23) they missed Locke's point. These old foundations must be pulled up so that knowledge and certainty can be established. For Locke, one is a revolutionary in order to overcome epistemic skepticism and cultural relativism.

leads us towards perfection."[66] Reason and freedom are these faculties and powers (with freedom taken as the power to suspend action with respect to whatever reason has not examined). Education (or re-education) is the chief tool that is to place us in a position advantageous to the exercise of these powers, so that we may come to use them to attain ability and skill in any thing. In this sense education is instrumental in making possible our progress toward the "perfection" which is true mastery. At bottom, however, no such progress can occur unless we employ the faculty of reason and the power of freedom. No human perfection is possible except through the deliberate exercise of revolutionary reason.

66. Implicit in this statement is the Enlightenment doctrine that genius is a matter of freedom from prejudice combined with assiduous practice in method. That such practice is better than genius is stated as early as 1724 by Isaac Watts, *Logick*, p. 327: "This Habit of conceiving clearly, of judging justly, and of reasoning well, is not to be attained merely by the Happiness of Constitution, the Brightness of Genius, the best natural Parts, or the best Collection of logical Precepts. It is Custom and Practice that must form and establish this Habit."

A

⌒

Reason and the
Nature of a Master

Locke teaches that a human being is born to be master. This is a statement which few commentators would find controversial. Disagreement exists about the answer to the question: According to Locke, what makes it possible for a human being to achieve mastery? Some answer by drawing upon what they take to be Locke's view of human nature; some answer without reference to human nature because they believe that, for Locke, human beings have no nature at all. Whereas the first stress nature and limit the role of nurture, the second allow room only for nurture. The first hold that sentences like "individuals can make themselves masters" and "one's fate is in one's own hands" properly express Locke's view; the second make that claim for a sentence like "environmental forces ultimately mold a person." Neither camp denies the importance of education. And, within either camp, there are few who deny Locke's basic optimism about the future of both the individual and the human race: people can and likely will attain mastery. (Notable exceptions in this respect are Peter Laslett and John Dunn, both of whom ascribe a pessimistic stance to Locke.)

I believe the second type of answer to be mistaken. It fails to do justice to much of what Locke specifically says on the issues of nature and nurture throughout his various writings (nearly all of which deal with these issues in one way or another). More generally, it would seem to militate against the position that Locke is a revolutionary: if it is the influence of *others* which is crucial in determining whether one will achieve mastery, there would seem to be no room for radical newness or thoroughgoing autonomy. (I here use the phrase "would seem to be" in order to indicate that this assertion is hardly unproblematic. Can one be *molded* into a revolutionary in the Cartesian-Lockean sense? Can one be *molded* into an autonomous being? Both questions would seem to contain a contradiction. Such questions are central to my chapters on education.) Possibly the best known formulation of the second answer—an answer given in the eighteenth century by writers including David Hartley and Etienne de Condillac—is J. A. Passmore's in his "The Malleability of Man in Eighteenth-Century Thought." I discuss it in the third section of the following chapter. In its first two sections I expound the view which I take to be Locke's, namely, that a human being has a nature and that it is this nature which enables a person to achieve mastery; that nurture may help or hinder a person in this pursuit, but that it is never the final explanation of either triumph or failure.

Locke believes human beings to possess a rational nature. He adds that human beings are not just rational; they are also creatures of passion. It is because passion is also a part of their nature that human beings are susceptible to prejudice. Unless prejudice is overcome, mastery cannot be achieved. This sort of blanket statement cannot, however, be made about the passions; for Locke holds that no mastery can be achieved except through giving free rein to one certain passion. I shall call this the "master passion." It is the desire for mastery. Human beings achieve mastery through properly relating the other passions and reason to the master passion. Indeed, as we shall see, all other passions, and reason itself, are to be servants of this master passion. The relationships involved here are discussed in this part's final chapter (Chapter 4). Before I turn to that relationship, I address the important issue of the infallibility of reason in the middle chapter of this part (Chapter 3).

To deal with human nature in terms of rationality, prejudice, and passion is to deal with it only in part; it is at least as important to consider human freedom. Freedom will be my prime concern in Part B of this study. The upshot of my argument in Parts A and B is that, for Locke, without reason and freedom a person cannot attain mastery. Both are necessary (but, as will become clear, not sufficient) conditions for the attainment of mastery. The reason and freedom in question Locke holds to be essential to human nature.

ᗄ2

Human Nature and Reason

1. Natural Rationality

Locke begins his *Essay concerning Human Understanding* with the sentence "Since it is the Understanding that sets Man above the rest of sensible Beings, and gives him all the Advantage and Dominion, which he has over them; it is certainly a Subject, even for its Nobleness, worth our Labour to enquire into." A few lines later he adds that the enquiry into our understanding or reasoning is an investigation of our selves. Reasoning or understanding is the activity Locke explicates in terms of "abstraction" (which he also calls "reduction" and "decomposition") and "composition" in the second and fourth books of the *Essay*. It is an activity which distinguishes us from all other corporeal beings. It fixes our place and determines our task: it elevates us above all other earthly creatures and enables us to exercise mastery over them as well as over ourselves.

When, in the *Essay*'s second book, Locke turns to this distinction between human and other corporeal beings, he does so explicitly in the terminology of abstracting and compounding. In 2.11.9 he explains that through abstraction a person obtains abstract ideas or universals. General knowledge is not possible without these foundational ideas.[1] The next paragraph, 2.11.10, draws a sharp line of demarcation between people and animals, for in it "the power of Abstracting" is said to be "not at all in"

---

1. As the heading of 4.12.7 later on puts this: "The true Method of advancing Knowledge, is by considering our abstract Ideas."

animals and so this power "puts a perfect distinction betwixt Man and Brutes."

In the fourth book Locke discusses in detail the understanding's operations in its production of general knowledge. He does so under the heading "Of Reason," where "Reason" "stands for a Faculty in Man, That Faculty, whereby Man is supposed to be distinguished from Beasts, and wherein it is evident he much surpasses them" (4.17.1). The phrase "is supposed to be distinguished from Beasts" may seem to relativize what was said in the previous quotation where reason is "not at all in animals" and "puts a perfect distinction betwixt Man and Brutes." As we will see more clearly in the next part of this chapter, there is more to being rational than being able to form universals. There is a *normative* dimension to rationality. So even if this phrase from 4.17.1 were to relativize those from 2.11.10, the normative dimension—which is found in the willingness to submit to the dictates of reason—retains the idea of "perfect distinction." In the next part it will become apparent that the "is supposed to" of 4.17.1 may well be a hint of that aspect of Locke's doctrine.

Statements such as those from 2.11.10 and 4.17.1 give grounds for the way many commentators have read Locke as one who holds that we are rational by nature. Passages such as these justify, for example, John Dunn's comment that "the central truths and duties of human experience are accessible to all through their intellects" and that this "confers an irreducible autonomy on every human individual."[2] To speak of the autonomy of each human being is one way of pointing at the difference between humankind and beasts, an irreducible difference which derives from their respective natures, from the presence in the one and the absence in the other of intellect or reason. Such passages warrant a contention such as Hans Aarsleff's that "Locke never believed that basic man was a product of society," that instead "Locke's civil society was made according to the nature of man in order to preserve that nature to the highest possible degree." The nature to be preserved is rational human nature. It is, says Aarsleff, "Locke's fundamental belief . . . that man is 'by nature rational'."[3]

Locke never abandoned this belief in our natural rationality. He knows that without it, neither his central political nor his most important theological doctrines can survive scrutiny. Thus his works on politics and

2. John Dunn, "The Politics of Locke in England and America in the Eighteenth Century," in *John Locke, Problems and Perspectives*, ed. J. W. Yolton (Cambridge 1969), p. 56.

3. Hans Aarsleff, "The State of Nature and the Nature of Man in Locke," in *John Locke, Problems and Perspectives*, ed. Yolton, p. 100.

religion regularly presuppose or restate or augment but never abandon the *Essay*'s teaching on this point. In the *Second Treatise* one meets doctrines which presuppose it. So we read that in the pre-political state of nature "the Law of Nature" or "the Law of Reason" is "plain and intelligible to all rational Creatures" (§124); and that whether we speak of people as being in a political or in a pre-political condition, in either case this "law" is "no where to be found but in the minds of Men," that is to say, in the understanding of individual human beings (§136). In the *Reasonableness of Christianity* we often find explicit restatements of this belief in natural human rationality. This work contains many sentences such as "God is an holy, just, and righteous God, and man a rational creature" (112). It also contains passages which go beyond the *Essay*'s doctrine when rational human nature is described as containing a "spark of the divine nature": "God had, by the light of reason, revealed to all mankind, who would make use of that light, that he was good and merciful. The same spark of the divine nature and knowledge in man, which, making him a man, showed him the law he was under, as a man; showed him also the way of atoning . . . when he had transgressed that law. He that made use of this candle of the Lord, so far as to find what was his duty, could not miss to find also the way to reconciliation" (133). The last two sentences state specifically with respect to our religious duties what the opening paragraphs of the *Essay* set forth for human life in general. In these paragraphs we read that God has given us "Whatsoever is necessary for the Conveniences of Life, and Information of Vertue" and so "we can find out those Measures, whereby a rational Creature put in that State, which Man is in, in this World, may, and ought to govern his Opinions," because "the Candle, that is set up in us, shines bright enough for all our Purposes" (1.1.5, 6).

These quotations from Locke's writings all contain a compound doctrine which may be called "the universal uniformity of rational human nature." It is Locke's position that each human being is rational by nature, and that the meaning of "rational" remains constant: "rational" always designates the human power of reasoning and the human willingness to act in accordance with the dictates of one's reason. As we shall see, this compound doctrine is fundamental to Locke's views on education, and it is the cornerstone on which rests his optimism concerning progress. To deny Locke this doctrine (as some, including Passmore, have done) results in a misinterpretation of Locke's educational writings and creates conflicts where none exist. That, however, is the story of the third section of this chapter. First it is important to say something more about this compound doctrine itself and to stress that it is not peripheral to, but instead permeates, Locke's thought. Second, I must state a significant corollary to this doctrine. It concerns knowledge and truth.

Locke's doctrine of the uniformity of rational human nature incorporates the notion that human nature is not a product of the particular political society in which a human being happens to mature. But there is more to it. If we were to concede that historically people have not always lived in political society but were nevertheless always social beings because they lived in some sort of enduring interpersonal non- or pre-political relationships, then (Locke would say) human nature is not the product of that social relationship either. Suppose there is a meeting of two beings from quite different political or pre-political social backgrounds. It could plausibly be supposed that the nature of the social or political contexts in which each matured might well make a meaningful relationship between them impossible: there might, for example, be nothing but suspicion, distrust, fear and hatred between the two. Locke, however, would reject the use of the word "impossible" here. For he holds that in spite of the distrust and hatred which the two societies might harbor for each other, a meaningful relationship is possible between these two beings because each of them is human, that is, rational. They can therefore judge the situation for themselves, free from whatever attitude their societies would have wanted to inculcate. Hence they can act as human beings—as beings more fully human to the extent that they reject as automatically binding the principles which their cultural contexts would impose. Each is then capable, for example, of an act which evinces trust, of the act of making and keeping promises. The rationality which the act bespeaks—an act that may well negate all the attitudes of the societies from which each came—then expresses the essence of these beings. Hence this essence is independent of particular social or political contexts. This independence allows for the notion of uniformity of rational human nature.

Introduction of even a few passages from Locke's works will be sufficient to illustrate the pervasiveness of the doctrine that people are naturally rational. Taken together, these passages show the presence of the main elements of this compound doctrine: that rationality is original in the sense that it cannot be explained through either social or political forces, and that this rationality is uniform.

The doctrine of the uniformity of rational human nature is present in the part of the debate with Stillingfleet described in the first chapter. The implication there is that the doctrine is assumed throughout the *Essay*, for only on its assumption can a single person's understanding, making itself "its own Object" come to conclusions about "the Original, Certainty, and Extent of humane Knowledge" (1.1.1, 2). It is assumed in the move from the particular case—it is Locke's understanding which examines itself—to the general one of "humane Knowledge."[4]

That is not the only way in which this doctrine is present in the *Essay*. It also comes to the fore when Locke considers the effect on human beings of the different social and political conditions to which they may be subject. Does human nature vary with variations in these conditions? Locke's answer (as in 4.20.2–4—an important passage to which I refer often in this book) is a clear negative. Some people, as "poor and wretched Labourers," are "enslaved to the Necessities of their mean Condition." Others, with "largeness of Fortune," are "cooped in close, by the Laws of their Countries, and the strict guards of those, whose Interest it is to keep them ignorant, lest, knowing more, they should believe the less in them." Like the "wretched Labourers" these, too, are "confined to narrowness of Thought, and enslaved in that which should be the freest part of Man, their Understandings." Both are far "from the Liberty and Opportunities of a fair Enquiry." Nevertheless, individuals from neither social group necessarily live subhuman lives. They are not bound by "Accident, and blind Chance, to conduct them to their Happiness, or Misery." They have the ability and at least some opportunity to gain knowledge "in Matters of Religion," that is, in a person's "greatest Concernments," in "his everlasting Happiness, or Misery." No one need here follow "current Opinions"; each remains epistemically and morally autonomous. They all remain responsible for their own beliefs and actions because all human beings by nature possess the power of reason which, whatever their social or political condition, they retain sufficiently to make them personally accountable for their most important concerns.[5]

The doctrine is not confined to the *Essay*. In the *Second Treatise* it underlies, for example, the statement that "The Promises . . . between . . . a Swiss and an Indian, in the Woods of America, are binding to them, though they are perfectly in a State of Nature, in reference to one another." Part of the explanation given for this state of affairs between two

---

4. Locke does, of course, offer some argument for the assumption. When others read his *Essay* he found they agreed with his description of reason's procedure. Nevertheless, no amount of inductive generalization allows for certainty of statements of a universal nature. He recognized that as to its universal import, the statement remains an assumption. Cf. *Works*, 1823, 4:138–39. I say more about the nature of this assumption in the next part, when I deal with the problem of essence. And I deal with an important implication of this assumption in Chap. 3.

5. The question whether Locke is too optimistic in this ascription of epistemic and moral autonomy will receive some discussion in the next section.

beings who share neither a political nor a social context is that "Truth and keeping of Faith" (which, according to Locke, come about only through free submission to one's reason) "belong to Men, as Men, and not as Members of Society" (§14).[6]

Neither the absence of political structures nor other differences in cultural contexts create variations in rational human nature. Locke implied as much already in his first *Letter concerning Toleration*, before the publication of the *Essay* and of the *Second Treatise*. There he speaks of "American Indians" as "innocent pagans, strict observers of the rules of equity and the law of nature" (36). And in the *Second Letter* he writes about "pagans" who are "all agreed in the duties of natural religion," who have "a pure heart, not polluted with the breaches of the law of nature," to whom "Reason discovered . . . that a good life was the most acceptable thing to the Deity" (156).

Locke never abandoned this doctrine of universal uniform rationality. When, in the closing years of his life, he writes his *Paraphrase and Notes on St. Paul's Epistle to the Romans*, he renders the phrase "reasonable service" of Romans 12:1 as "such a way of worship as becomes a rational creature." Since (in spite of St. Paul's limited aim) Locke takes this epistle to be relevant to all human beings in all ages A.D., wherever they may happen to reside and whatever their state of social or political development, he therefore takes each human being to be a rational creature. And since the reasonable service dictated by the rationality of all of these creatures is of the same kind, the assumption of a uniform rationality is, again, presupposed.

The important corollary to this doctrine concerns claims to knowledge and assertions of truth. Given the constancy of rational human nature, it follows for Locke that controversies about what is taken as known or as true are to be explained in terms of factors which hinder the use of reason.[7]

---

6. On the reasoning powers of those living in other cultures, see also the *Essay* 4.4.4. Locke's assumption of the universality of human nature is, in fact, broader than that based on the communality of reason. There is a communality of needs and wants, and of what counts as the fulfillment of these needs and wants. As Alan Ryan has pointed out, "When Locke defends the inequality of a more advanced economy by appealing to the pay-offs to the worst off, he does so by arguing that the Devonshire day labourer has a higher standard of living than does the Indian chief in the wastes of middle America." Ryan adds that "Locke plainly assumes that we can . . . hold human nature constant. . . ." See his *Property and Political Theory* (Oxford, 1984), pp. 41, 42.

7. There is of course an additional assumption at work here. Not only is human reason universally the same, but so is reason's object when that object is, for example, the laws that hold in mathematical theory or the laws that ought to be obeyed by persons living together in a political state.

Throughout his writings Locke's stance is, therefore, anti-relativistic. Let me illustrate this from *The Conduct of the Understanding*, the *Paraphrase and Notes on St. Paul's Epistle to the Romans*, and the *Essay concerning Human Understanding*.

In the *Conduct* Locke blames "Fashion, discipline, and education," for having "put eminent differences in the ages of several countries, and made one generation much differ from another in arts and sciences." Cultural relativism is to be condemned because "truth is always the same; time alters it not" (246–47). It is this anti-relativistic stance that leads Locke to say that it is possible to consult authors of various cultures and different ages and, in spite of the variety of doctrine to be met on this intellectual journey, to return from it with greater knowledge and more truth than one possessed before.

> He that will inquire out the best books in every science, and inform himself of the most material authors of the several sects of philosophy and religion, will not find it an infinite work to acquaint himself with the sentiments of mankind, concerning the most weighty and comprehensive subjects. Let him exercise the freedom of his reason and understanding in such a latitude as this . . . and the light, which the remote and scattered parts of truth will give to one another, will so assist his judgment, that he will seldom be widely out, or miss giving proof of a clear head and comprehensive knowledge. (Ibid., 213)

Because of the uniformity of human nature, truth is not relative to time or place or cultural condition. Each of us can discern whatever truth there may be in the products of different cultures because, as rational creatures, we carry with us the touchstone necessary for such discernment. Fashion and education may have hindered the exercise of reason in various cultures, but they have never altogether frustrated reason's power and in the "best books" of all times truth shines through.[8] On these "remote and scattered parts of truth" a person can lay hold if he "settle in his head determined ideas of all that he employs his thoughts about" (ibid.). Because it is a statement of reason's procedure, the methodology of the *Essay* (see Chapter 1) is the path to follow in this attempt to obtain such determined ideas. Hence this doctrine of the universal uniformity of reason and its corollary about knowledge and truth do not detract from

---

8. It is therefore quite in character when Locke recommends to Richard King (who wanted to know what to read to gain insight into the nature of government) his own *Two Treatises of Government*, Hooker's *Ecclesiastical Polity*, and Aristotle's *Politics*. See Peter Laslett's Introduction to *Two Treatises of Government*, p. 15.

what I said before about Locke as revolutionary, and do not conflict with the idea that each person is epistemically autonomous. Nothing one reads in texts, not even in the most venerated, may be simply accepted as truth. All purported knowledge must first be reduced to its simplest constituents, and that is a process which is tantamount to its initial rejection. Hence the stress on "the *freedom* of his reason," and the continuation of this passage from the *Conduct* with the admonition that if there is any truth in these "sentiments of mankind," it can be winnowed, but only if a person "never fail to judge himself, and judge unbiassedly, of all that he receives from others" so that "Reverence or prejudice" do not "give beauty or deformity" to what he encounters in his reading. Coherence of the truths thus winnowed from the chaff plentiful even in the best books—"the light, which the remote and scattered parts of truth will give to one another"—then confirms the legitimacy of using reason as the touchstone. In this passage Locke shows his commitment to the universal uniformity of rational human nature, to the objectivity of knowledge, and to the coherence of truth.[9]

This anti-relativism presents itself in the *Paraphrase* when we read that "the moral rule to all mankind" is "laid within the discovery of their reason" (note to Romans 2:26), and that "Mankind, without the positive law of God, knew, by the light of nature, that they transgressed the rule of their nature, reason, which dictated to them what they ought to do" (note to Romans 5:13). Statements such as these are basic to Locke's position of objectivity in "morals," a position which makes possible mutual encouragement when all tend to act rightly and admonition or censure when some turn to wrong paths. In this work Locke's doctrines of individual epistemic and moral autonomy allow for each of us to know when we act or fail to act in accordance with what is right; and the non-relativity of truth allows for others to judge our behavior, which they can discern as either in keeping with or in violation of what is right.

This anti-relativism also plays a crucial role in the *Essay*, not least in the important chapter "Of Power." In it, the intellectual power of foresight—another power characteristically belonging to all human beings—makes it possible for us to recognize that the present moment is not our eternity. Reason and foresight, together with the power of suspension, can lead us to awareness of an absolute standard for human action; it is conformity to this standard which enables us to transcend the subjective relativism of a

---

9. The latter notion explicitly comes to play a very important role in Locke's theological works. See my account of what I called Locke's "coherence principle" in chap. 8 of *Imposition of Method*.

simplistic hedonism. Since that part of the *Essay* has much to say about freedom and has great relevance to Locke's views on education, it demands careful and detailed attention. I shall devote most of the second part of this book to it. All that needs to be noted now is that without the doctrine of the universal uniformity of a rational human nature, and its corollary about knowledge and truth, some of the most important theses developed in "Of Power" have no foundation.[10]

2. Potentiality and Essence

Two issues should be settled at this point. The first may be identified by means of the following questions. Is it not Locke's doctrine that everyone is born with only the *potential* to become rational, that no one is born possessing reason? Moreover, does not Locke hold that everyone acts irrationally some of the time, perhaps even that many if not all act irrationally most of the time? And according to Locke, are not there some whose behavior is so irrational that they have become degenerate and have sunk to the level of animals? If all or even a single one of these questions is to be answered affirmatively, would not this imply that it is incorrect to ascribe to Locke the view that we are essentially rational by nature? The second issue, that of *essence*, may also be presented through questions. Does not Locke draw a distinction between a human being's real and nominal essence and does not he state in the *Essay* that we cannot know anything about this real essence and that therefore we cannot know whether it is our real essence to be rational, potentially or actually? So even if (contrary to what some critics hold) Locke teaches that we have a nature, do we speak of our real essence when we characterize human nature as rational?

Behind each set of questions there hides a single query. It concerns the importance of rationality in Locke's thought. The first set of questions amounts to asking: Is rationality as centrally important to Locke's position as I have made it out to be? If the answer is affirmative, the second asks: In

---

10. About Locke's objectivity Yolton writes: "The revelations of this natural faculty [of reason] are of the utmost importance for morality and religion. Locke was seeking to justify a system of morality by grounding the moral law in something objective. The law of nature is a decree of God, not of man's reason. It is part of God's will." *Locke: An Introduction* (Oxford, 1985), p. 48. In his juxtaposition of man's reason and God's will Yolton seems to imply that subjectivism would result if the "moral law" were only a "decree . . . of man's reason." Given the doctrine of the universality and uniformity of reason, this does not follow. In fact, given this doctrine, reference to God's will is not necessary in order to escape subjectivism (which of course is not to say that Locke made no such reference).

view of certain other Lockean doctrines, specifically, in view of Locke's distinction between real and nominal essences, can the notion of rationality play so crucial a role? I shall deal with the two sets of questions in the order in which I raised them.

First. Locke of course holds that we are not born in possession of that which reason helps to make accessible to us.[11] If therefore by "rational" we mean "possessing certain concepts or principles," then no human being is born a rational being. This Locke stresses so conspicuously throughout his writings (most especially in Book 1 of the *Essay*) that no more need be said about it. Even to say that human beings are born with the capacity to reason and to submit to the dictates of their reason would be saying too much. Since no newborn infant, no very young child even, is able to reason and to submit itself to reason, the best that may be said is that human beings are born as potentially rational beings. Whether they will become actually rational depends on behavior in later life. If this behavior is of a certain kind, it justifies saying that the very young are potentially rational. This last statement requires explication.

People are born *to be* masters; no human being is a master at birth. As we shall see in detail in later chapters, a human being becomes a master through rational action. Only human offspring can achieve mastery because only human offspring are potentially rational. But since not all human offspring come to act rationally therefore not all attain mastery. Later chapters explain that human offspring who do not achieve at least some degree of mastery come to be incorporated into the causal mechanism of nature. This interpretation helps to indicate that, for Locke, it is not the case that by nature we are either potentially rational or potentially non-rational. For non-rational behavior leads to incorporation into nature, that is, into the system governed by natural causality; but Locke holds a human being to be *essentially* different from nature. Hence Locke characterizes those who fail to achieve any degree of mastery as non-human: they have destroyed their own humanity by refusing to develop the rational potential which naturally characterizes the newborn child.

I continue the discussion of the potential rationality of the child in my next section. In the meantime, we have some understanding of why Locke holds that rational behavior of the maturing human being justifies saying that the very young are potentially rational. Does it also justify

---

11. I say "reason helps to make accessible" rather than "reason makes accessible" because of the restrictions which Locke consistently places on reason. Reason alone cannot give us knowledge; it is impotent unless provided with materials on which to work. These materials come only from experience, that is, from sensation and reflection. Cf. *Essay* 2.1.2.

calling them "human"? And if it does, can we then in view of the mere potentiality of their rationality say that mankind is universally rational? I take the answer to both these questions to be affirmative. The potential rationality of the young should present no obstacles to this move. To be rational by nature does not entail any signs of rationality from the beginning. The fact that there are rational acts in subsequent years implies that, before the beings in question actually proved themselves to be rational, they were the kind of beings who could develop into those guided by their own reason. There is a promise attached to human offspring that distinguishes them from the offspring of any other corporeal beings. The promise of rational action allows for their classification as "human," without jeopardizing the truth of the statement that human beings are universally rational. The child is the easier case, the adult the more difficult one. And before I say more about the rationality of the very young I must develop some of the hints dropped in the preceding paragraphs about the adult.

To say that, for Locke, all or even most adults live completely rational lives would be saying far too much. Locke stresses that most adults fall short of a fully rational life. Many of the major doctrines of his various works revolve around this point. Take the *Second Treatise*. Here the reason given why a person is willing to help form, or to join, a political state, why willing to "part with his Freedom," is that all are "his Equal, and for the greater part no strict Observers of Equity and Justice" (§123). Since, in this treatise, reason is identified with the law of nature, and since the law of nature dictates a life of "Equity and Justice," therefore not being "strict Observers of Equity and Justice" is the same as not always living by the dictates of reason. And "the greater part" of mankind leads such a life. Does this then imply that mankind is anything but rational? Does it imply that the greater part of mankind is degenerate and hence really undeserving to be called part of mankind? Neither conclusion is the correct one.

In his *Second Treatise* Locke frequently speaks of degeneracy. The action of a degenerate human being is characterized as anti-rational, illegal, animalistic. Such beings have "quit the Principles of Human Nature" because they departed "from the right Rule of Reason"; and so each of them has become "a noxious Creature" (§10); each is "a Criminal" who, because having "renounced Reason," "may be destroyed as a Lyon or a Tyger, one of those wild Savage Beasts, with whom Men can have no Society nor Security" (§11); they may be killed like an animal because they are "not under the ties of the Common Law of Reason" and have "no other Rule, but that of Force and Violence, and so may be treated as Beasts of Prey, those dangerous and noxious Creatures" (§16).

The greater part of mankind, those who are "no strict Observers of Equity and Justice," are not to be identified with these degenerates. In the words of paragraph 10, theirs is not "the crime which consists in violating the law and varying from the right rule of reason, whereby a man so far becomes degenerate and declares himself to quit the principles of human nature." The degenerates did know the law of nature but expressly rejected it as binding on their action; they chose to live by force rather than by reason. Living by force, they "quit the principles of human nature"; they stopped acting rationally. Because they knowingly act against the dictates of reason their action should be called anti-rational.

The degenerate have not reverted to the status of the very young. Young children have not quitted "the Principles of Human Nature" simply because they cannot yet know enough or do enough to declare themselves in their behavior for or against these principles. They do not yet act, whether rationally or anti-rationally.

Neither do the degenerate belong to what Locke takes to be the majority of mankind. In the *Second Treatise* he speaks of this majority as "the greater part," in the *Reasonableness of Christianity* as "the greatest part." The "greater part" of the *Second Treatise* is more comprehensive than the "greatest part" of the *Reasonableness*; the former includes the latter.

In the closing paragraph of the *Reasonableness*[12] Locke writes about "the greatest part" of mankind as comprising the laborers, that is, all whose preoccupation with acquiring daily necessities allows them no leisure for thinking critically: "The greatest part of mankind have not leisure for learning and logic." It is lack of opportunity, not lack of talent, which keeps these people from acquainting themselves with matters like the ones "that the books and disputes of religion are filled with." Nevertheless, theirs too is the task to live by reason. And Locke believes them to be capable of the task. In religion, for example, they are able to grasp and rationally commit themselves to the fundamentals of the faith and thus secure their eternal bliss: it is "plain and intelligible" to them that they should accept Christ "to be the Saviour promised, and take him now raised from the dead, and constituted the Lord and Judge of all men, to be their King and Ruler."

The lack of critical thinking therefore need not entail anti-rational action. As we saw in the first chapter, Locke holds that all human adults have sufficient talent and opportunity to get to know the basic rules of right and wrong. This knowledge, he believes, enables them to discern

---

12. Unless otherwise indicated, all quotations in the six following paragraphs are from this closing paragraph of the *Reasonableness*.

well enough to apply these basic rules in all vicissitudes of their lives so that the sum of each day's actions adds up to a rational life. They are capable of this but, Locke admits, only barely so: "It is well if men of that rank (to say nothing of the other sex) can comprehend plain propositions, and a short reasoning about things familiar to their minds, and nearly allied to their daily experience. Go beyond this, and you amaze the greatest part of mankind; and may as well talk Arabic."

This greatest part of mankind is not degenerate. Those belonging to it are not the thieves and murderers of the *Second Treatise*, and they have no excuse for becoming thieves and murderers, for if they were to go those paths they would go against what their own reason tells them. In that case they would consciously "quit the Principles of Human Nature" and become degenerate. But no adults are degenerate by virtue of their social or cultural condition. The greatest part is human not just because it is capable of exercising its reason: it is human because it exercises its reason and submits to reason's dictates.

Clearly, there are problems here for Locke. Is it really so plain and intelligible what are, and what are not, the fundamentals of the Christian faith? If it were so plain and intelligible, why the need to write an entire book proving the point (as Locke did in the *Reasonableness*)? And even if it is plain and intelligible (even if, for instance, all that needs to be done in a work like the *Reasonableness* is to remove obscuring prejudices), it is one thing to know the fundamentals but quite another to know what, specifically, they require of one in one's daily practice. In public worship, for example, ought one to join the dissenters or the conformists? Or is that a matter of indifference? If the latter, that was manifestly not plain and intelligible to most of Locke's contemporaries, for they fought a bloody war over it. And if the question of what constitutes the life of reason in daily activity is not so easy to answer with respect to formal religious practice, neither is it in the other realm which so exercised Locke and his contemporaries, that of politics. Ought one to follow Charles II or the Earl of Shaftesbury, James Stuart or William and Mary? Should one heed Robert Filmer or John Locke? (both of whom were preached about, pro and con, from more than one pulpit even in laborers' parishes). In this realm too, wrote Locke, there is a fundamental principle at stake, that of the primacy of the individual characterized by inalienable rights to life, liberty, and property. But how plain and intelligible is it that this is the right principle? For, again, it took Locke an entire book (the *First Treatise of Government*) to expose certain fundamentals as spurious, and, once the right principle was articulated, it required another book (the *Second Treatise*) to make clear what the principle entailed for the daily lives of both commoners and kings. In his assurance that "the bulk of mankind" (to pick another phrase from the final paragraph of the *Reasonableness*) is capable of "reasoning about things familiar to their minds, and nearly allied to their daily experience" Locke is at best naively optimistic. For standing out as things familiar in daily experience are issues such as: to conform or dissent, to join the cause of the Duke of Monmouth or that of King Charles II. So familiar were these matters to the daily experience of two generations of the bulk of British mankind that for many of them they were an issue of life or death.

Locke's optimism at this point is unwarranted. As additional grounds for this charge consider the following. Suppose one said it would have been more realistic for Locke to hold that the greatest part is capable of living a rational life because (*a*) it can know the basic rules of right and wrong, and (*b*) this knowledge, though not adequate to guide it in all the many problems of life, is sufficient to allow it to model its action on the example of others who do have the "leisure for learning and logic." Through knowing the fundamentals (granting for the moment that these are accessible in spite of lack of "leisure for learning") those belonging to the greatest part could then remain epistemically and morally responsible for following the example on which they had fastened. They would then live the life of reason: their own reason to begin with, to which—through following the right examples—one could add what might be called "borrowed reason." Though this might appear more realistic it would, in fact, be inconsistent for Locke to hold anything like this position.

For, first of all, Locke's individualistic epistemology precludes the meaningfulness of a concept like that of borrowed reason: "we may as rationally hope to see with other Mens Eyes, as to know by other Mens Understandings" and "The floating of other Mens Opinions in our brains makes us not one jot the more knowing, though they happen to be true" (*Essay* 1.4.23). And, second, if the notion of borrowed reason were admissible, how would those who follow examples recognize an example to be rational? The two possible answers either make the recognition impossible, or the example superfluous. On the one hand, such recognition would seem to demand the protracted exercise of reason—precisely that for which the greatest part is said to lack the necessary leisure. And, on the other hand, if no considerable time-consuming use of reason were needed in the analysis of the example, the greatest part would end up where it would not need to follow examples but could follow nothing but its own reason. Assuming that in this situation examples would not from the outset be redundant, then, given the revolutionary character of analysis (as explicated in my first chapter), critical reflection on an example would make it—and hence borrowed reason—obsolete.

I shall not be further detained by the complications of what, in the *Reasonableness* and elsewhere, Locke presents as straightforward doctrine: that the greatest part of humankind is rational; that although it has not developed its rationality as far as others more fortunate in circumstances may have done, it is not on that account degenerate. What should be added is that Locke holds that there is always the chance that any one belonging to the bulk of mankind may become degenerate. But that chance, he adds, exists equally for members of the leisured class, even if they have been fortunate enough to have received the right kind of education. For as we shall see in a later chapter, reason by itself has no compelling force: Locke holds that knowing truth or goodness does not necessarily lead to action in accordance with such knowledge, that we can consciously and persistently disobey the dictates of our reason. Such disobedience results in degeneracy. It is Locke's view that most do not act in this way.

It is also his view that most of us do not always obey the dictates of our reason. That is because we are not only rational beings but also creatures of passion. The discussion of reason and passion will have to wait till the fourth chapter. Suffice it to say here that it is the co-presence of reason and passion that makes human beings "for the greater part no strict Observers of Equity and Justice."

The "greater part" of the *Second Treatise* includes "the greatest part" of the *Reasonableness*; it comprises the uneducated as well as the educated, the working as well as the leisured class. This greatest part is human because, by and large, it can be counted upon to act rationally.[13] They have enough rational sense to recognize that passion makes most of them "no *strict* Observers of Equity and Justice," and they are willing to limit their opportunity for disregarding reason's dictates by parting with some of their freedom and creating a political state.

Those whom Locke calls "degenerate" he believes to be relatively few in number. They are literally the exception, in a double sense of the word. They are the odd case. And these odd cases have excepted themselves

---

13. The last part of this sentence portrays Locke as an optimist. The question of whether or not Locke is an optimist is distinct from that of whether Locke can consistently be an optimist. It is the latter question which I addressed in the preceding paragraphs. It will demand our attention on a number of occasions. The question whether Locke is in fact an optimist I have addressed in a paper ("John Locke: Optimist or Pessimist?") given at the John Locke Conference held at Christ Church, Oxford, 5–7 September 1990. In it, I consider what some take to be "pessimistic" statements about either human reason or human freedom (statements especially from the *Reasonableness* and from Locke's correspondence) and conclude (contra Laslett and Dunn) that Locke remains an "optimistic" thinker. That, in terms of both human reason and freedom, he has no right to such an optimistic position, is one conclusion I will reach in this book.

from the human race. They are no longer autonomous beings. They are the kind of beings which, when they are too much of a nuisance or threat, may be locked away or destroyed like any other non-autonomous being. Because the degenerate have excluded themselves from the human race, no account must be taken of them when we ask whether human beings are universally rational.[14]

Second, there is the question about *essence*. All things or substances may be spoken of in terms of their real and their nominal essences. When we know the real essence of a thing we can know why a thing functions as it does. We can develop general knowledge only when we know real essences; where no real essences are accessible we must be satisfied with belief and probability. In Locke's words, we know a thing's real essence when we know its "true internal Constitution" from which its "Qualities flow"; we do not know the real essence of things when we are ignorant of "the internal Constitution, whereon their Properties depend" (3.6.9).

The individual things which we handle in our daily living are all substances. Of these substances Locke writes that "the real Essences, on which depend their Properties and Operations, are unknown to us" (4.6.12). We have seen (in Chapter 1, section 2) that careful observation of the behavior of such substances often gives us very useful ideas about them. Such observation allows for their classification and for a certain amount of prediction. It allows for sciences like physics and chemistry. This classification, however, always retains a degree of arbitrariness— although both the appearances of things and the demands of communication rule out unrestrained arbitrariness (cf. 3.6.28). In the case of these substances we may speak of human acquaintance with essences, but those with which one is acquainted are the *nominal* essences. The nominal essence refers to nothing but that group of "obvious appearances," the qualities and patterns of the behavior of things, which we have picked out and have grouped together; these qualities and patterns of behavior are then reflected in a complex idea, and designated by a certain name (cf. 3.6.25). These groups of "Qualities we observe in them, and of which our complex Ideas of them are made up . . . will be able to furnish us but very sparingly with any general Knowledge, or universal Propositions capable of real Certainty" (4.6.12).

Although all substances have real essences, only God (and perhaps angels) know what they are (3.3.10; 3.6.3). We have no God's-eye-view and Locke says we do not need it. The isolated beliefs together with the

---

14. Cf. Yolton, *Locke: An Introduction*: "anyone who . . . intentionally acted against this law [of nature] . . . for Locke ceases to be a person, at least ceases to be a moral agent" (38). See also Schouls, *Imposition of Method*, pp. 205, 210–11.

system of beliefs that we acquire about substances through careful observations, and reasoning about these observations are of sufficient utility to allow us a safe and comfortable life. We have seen that probable reasoning about nominal essences is of immense importance to Locke. It accounts for progress already achieved, and on it depends the possibility of further progress, in health and in "the Conveniences of Life" through developments in medicine and in "natural Philosophy."

Human beings are also substances. Of them, too, Locke holds that only God knows their real essences. The definitions of "man" proffered over the ages are all nominal definitions. The very fact that they differ from age to age—some saying that the name "man" designates a being "of Sense and spontaneous Motion, join'd to a Body of such a shape," others that it stands for "*Animal rationale,*" others again that it denotes "*Animal implume bipes latis unguibus*" (3.6.26)—is by itself enough to prove the point, for a thing's real essence is one and unchangeable, and knowledge of a thing's real essence necessarily reflects this unity and unchangeability. Therefore, of human beings, it also holds that we do not know why they function as they do. This doctrine Locke states quite explicitly. It occurs in several passages in addition to the one just introduced. "And had we such a Knowledge of that Constitution of Man, from which his Faculties of Moving, Sensation, and Reasoning, and other Powers flow; and on which his so regular shape depends, as 'tis possible Angels have, and 'tis certain his Maker has, we should have a quite other Idea of his Essence, than what now is contained in our Definition of that Species, be it what it will" (3.6.3; see also 3.6.22; 3.6.27; 4.4.16).

It is crucial to notice that all of these passages have one thing in common: they all are about *natural man.* They are about the kind of beings of which we have knowledge limited by what our senses reveal about them. We can only examine them on the outside and judge "by what our Faculties can discover in them as they exist" (4.4.16). All of these passages are about the kind of being which is as natural a phenomenon as is a dog or a nugget of gold. None of them are about *moral man,* the being whom one expects to keep promises, the being who can live as a member of a political state fully accountable for keeping its laws, the being who is personally responsible for its eternal weal or woe. Of *moral* man we *can* know the real essence. In this case we are able to attain "general Knowledge, or universal Propositions capable of real Certainty." In the case of moral beings we know exactly why they function as they ought. Or, if they do not function as they ought, we can discern the causes which keep them from proper functioning (whether these are internal like overweening passion or external like political oppression).

Locke also speaks of moral man in the *Essay* and, when he does so, it is

clear both that he distinguishes moral man from natural man and that he
believes we can know the former's real essence:

> For as to Substances, when concerned in moral Discourses, their divers
> Natures are not so much enquir'd into, as supposed; *v.g.* when we say that
> Man is subject to Law: We mean nothing by Man, but a corporeal rational
> Creature: What the real Essence or other Qualities of that Creature are in this
> Case, is no way considered. And therefore, whether a Child or Changeling
> be a Man in a physical Sense, may amongst the Naturalists be as disputable as
> it will, it concerns not at all the moral Man, as I may call him, which is this
> immoveable unchangeable Idea, a corporeal rational Being. (3.11.16)

At first sight it may look as if Locke is here speaking of the nominal
essence of moral man. Two sets of phrases may give rise to this impression. (*a*) "What the real Essence or other Qualities of that Creature are in
this Case, is no way considered." However, "real Essence" in this case
refers to the real essence of that creature as a merely natural being, as
"Man in a physical Sense." We do not worry about whether moral man is a
child or changeling or (as he says in the continuation of this passage)
whether it is "a Monkey, or any other Creature." What we worry about is
whether he has "the use of Reason, to such a degree, as to be able to
understand general Signs, and to deduce Consequences about general
Ideas"; for if he were to possess these properties then he would be "subject
to Law, and, in that Sense, be a Man, how much soever he differ'd in
Shape from others of that Name" (ibid.). (*b*) In "moral Discourses, their
divers Natures are not so much enquir'd into, as supposed." If it is mere
supposition, there would seem at least a measure of arbitrariness, and the
essence in question would be nominal rather than real. But that would
make the essence variable depending on who does the supposing—which
conflicts with what Locke here says about this essence, namely, that it is
captured in an "immoveable, unchangeable Idea." The "name," "a corporeal rational Being," denotes the real essence. Nominal and real essence
coincide in this instance of moral man (as they do also in names of
mathematical entities). The supposing, in this case, is a matter of legisla-
tion which really does justice to the nature of the thing.[15]

About this supposing I shall say more in a moment. Locke holds that no
supposing which really does justice to the nature of the thing can occur
about gold or about natural man, for in these cases we are ignorant of the
properties from which the overt qualities and behavior in question flow.

---

15. This supposing is a form of invention (cf. *Essay* 2.22.9). I have discussed this particular
invention in *Imposition of Method*, chap. 7, part 2.

In the case of moral man the behavior is that of a being subject to law. The law in question is fully knowable. And the behavior which consists in action subject to that law flows from, that is, is fully explicable in terms of, moral man's essential properties of being corporeal and rational.

Of course, none of this is to say that there are no mysteries about "rational" (or, for that matter, "corporeal"). Locke believes that we are immediately aware of ourselves as thinking beings, and that we know how reason functions in its pursuit of truth (whether he can legitimately make this knowledge claim will be examined in the next chapter). But this does not entail for him that we know that from which this faculty of reasoning flows. Again, we have no God's-eye-view; we can make no ontological knowledge claim in this case. " 'Tis past controversy, that we have in us something that thinks, our very Doubts about what it is, confirm the certainty of its being, though we must content our selves in the Ignorance of what kind of Being it is" (4.3.6). That is (as the context of the sentence makes explicit) we do not know whether thought or reason flows from extended material or unextended immaterial being. This, however, is an issue of interest to—though not answerable by—the naturalist and the metaphysician. It does not concern moral philosophy, that is, ethical and political theory. Neither does it concern educational theory. Also in education the distinction between natural man and moral man will be found to be crucial. It is moral man, the corporeal rational being, who is educable; and this makes education quite different from the training which we would call conditioning. That, however, is a story for much later.

We possess (or can come to possess) general knowledge, real certainty, in the realms of mathematics, ethics, and politics precisely because of the coincidence of real and nominal essence in our ideas of mathematical entities and of human beings. As Locke says in 4.12.11, again juxtaposing natural and moral realms, nominal and real essences:

> It is obvious to conclude, that since our Faculties are not fitted to penetrate into the internal Fabrick and real Essences of Bodies; but yet plainly discover to us the Being of a GOD, and the Knowledge of our selves, enough to lead us into a full and clear discovery of our Duty, and great Concernment, it will become us, as rational Creatures, to imploy those Faculties we have about what they are most adapted to. . . . For 'tis rational to conclude, that our proper Imployment lies in those Enquiries, and in that sort of Knowledge, which is most suited to our natural Capacities, and carries in it our greatest interest, i.e. the Condition of our eternal Estate. Hence I think I may conclude, that Morality is the proper Science, and Business of Mankind in general; (who are both concerned, and fitted to search out their *Summum Bonum*).

Wherever real and nominal essences coincide, knowledge is possible because we can know the nature of the origin of the behavior we study. This
is Locke's doctrine from the early *Essays on the Law of Nature* onwards. In
its tenth question we read that

> [The law of nature is] a fixed and eternal rule of conduct, dictated by reason
> itself, and for this reason something fixed and inherent in human nature. And
> it would be necessary for human nature to change before this law could either
> change or be abrogated. For there exists a harmony between the two of these,
> and what now conforms to a rational nature, insofar as it is rational, must
> necessarily conform eternally. And this same reason will dictate the same
> rules of conduct everywhere. Inasmuch, therefore, as all men are rational by
> nature and there exists a harmony between this law and a rational nature—a
> harmony knowable by the light of nature—it is necessary that all men
> endowed with a rational nature—that is, all men everywhere—are bound by
> this law, so that if the law of nature should be binding on at least some men,
> by this same title it must clearly be binding on all as well. The basis of this
> obligation is equal among all men, the mode of their coming to know it the
> same, their nature the same, for this law depends not on a will which is fluid
> and changeable, but on the eternal order of things. In my opinion, some
> states of things seem to be immutable, and some duties, which cannot be
> otherwise, seem to have arisen out of necessity; not that nature (or, to speak
> more correctly) god could not have created man other than he is, but, since
> he has been created as he is, provided with reason and his other faculties,
> there follow from the constitution of man at birth some definite duties he
> must perform, which cannot be other than what they are. For it seems to me
> to follow as necessarily from the nature of man, if he be a man, that he is
> bound to . . . perform . . . duties which are in conformity with a rational
> nature—that is to observe the law of nature—as it follows from the nature of
> a triangle, if it be a triangle, that its three angles are equal to two right
> angles.[16]

Moral man is the being whose behavior is subject to the law of nature,
which is the law of reason and, as such, the law of moral man's nature.
The behavior which consists in action subject to the law of nature flows
from or is fully explicable in terms of the essential properties of corporeality and rationality.[17] It is not just moral beings themselves, but also

---

16. *John Locke: Questions concerning the Law of Nature*, ed. and trans. Robert Horwitz, Jenny
Strauss Clay, and Diskin Clay (Ithaca, N.Y., 1990), pp. 227–29.

17. The view that our reason dictates to us how we ought to govern our actions—
conversely, that correct human action flows from our rational nature—is certainly not an
early view that Locke subsequently abandoned. In the *Paraphrase and Notes on the Epistles of
St. Paul*, the last of Locke's works, we already noted the statement that "Mankind, without

the institution in which they live most usefully and securely, namely, the political state, which flows from or is explained in terms of these properties. In the field of political theory the concept *corporeal rational being* is the fundamental abstract idea whose consideration advances general knowledge. For example, if it is asked how the nature and extent of the power of the state is delimited, or what the duties of the citizens are, or whether anyone (whether citizen or sovereign) can lay claim to inalienable rights and what these rights might be, the answer in each case is "deduced"[18] from the concept *corporeal rational being*. This concept plays as fundamental a role in political theory as, for example, the concept *unity* performs in arithmetic. When any of the numbers or simple modes of arithmetic is explained through definition or resolution into its constituent parts, resolution stops at the concept of *unity*. Alternatively, the mind can make the simple modes of arithmetic only through generating them out of the concept of unity. The concept of unity is fundamental in arithmetic because all of this science's simple modes are to be explained in terms of it, all of them are ultimately composed out of it, and it itself neither is reducible to nor can be composed out of other concepts. The science of arithmetic flows from this concept (cf. the *Essay*'s Book 2, chapter 16). In political thought the concept *corporeal rational being* plays the role which unity plays in arithmetic. It is not reducible to simpler concepts within the framework of political thought. Neither a purely rational being (e.g., God) nor a merely corporeal being (e.g., a piece of gold) can serve as foundational concept in political theory. And the various important doctrines of political theory flow from this concept of corporeal rational being. It is consideration of this concept that leads the theorist to set specific limits to governmental power or to determine the citizens' duties and rights.[19]

Moral man has a nature, a real essence, an essence we can know as the complex idea or mixed mode *corporeal rational being*. As we saw from 3.11.16, human beings are supposed to have this nature. That "supposed" here does not mean something like "arbitrarily assumed" but has universal legislative power can now be illustrated. The illustration will connect this part of the discussion with that of degeneracy of preceding pages.

---

the positive law of God, knew, by the light of nature, that they transgressed the rule of their nature, reason, which dictated to them what they ought to do" (note to Romans 5:13).

18. By "deduced" I do not, of course, refer to Aristotelean deduction in this instance. Instead I refer to the "deductive" part of the (Cartesian) "analytic" method.

19. For my attempt at an exposition of how Locke "deduces" his political thought from the concept *corporeal rational being* see *The Imposition of Method*, chap. 7. For a more recent and much fuller exposition along not dissimilar lines, see Grant, *John Locke's Liberalism*.

Moral man "is this immoveable unchangeable Idea, a corporeal rational Being." It is from this essence that our duties flow. In other words, our own nature dictates certain duties, certain patterns of behavior, just as much as the real essence of gold is the cause of the behavior of gold, of its melting in fire and dissolving in aqua regia. Gold cannot behave except in ways dictated by its real essence; whatever does not behave like gold (e.g. whatever does not dissolve in aqua regia) is not gold. Unlike gold, human beings can act against the dictates of their real essence, that is, against their reason. But if this behavior is more than an occasional relatively minor aberration then, as in the case of gold, the behavior is not that of a human being. Thus, human beings can, on occasion, act against the dictates of reason. But we suppose that beings which we take to be human will as a rule act rationally. If such beings persistently act anti-rationally, then we suppose or legislate them to be non-human.[20] The legislating or supposing is not taken to be arbitrary: that which persistently acts anti-rationally cannot be a human being, for no consistently anti-rational behavior can flow from a corporeal rational creature. By persistently going against what was and ought to have remained their own nature, by constantly willfully acting as they are not supposed to act, these beings alienate themselves from their moral nature and remove themselves from the human race. When they are imprisoned because of theft or executed because of murder, no selves are being violated, no autonomy infringed upon. The degenerate, to the extent that they are degenerate, cannot claim autonomous status because they no longer act according to the law which their own understanding pronounces. Their action now flows from calculating brute force. They have ceased to be corporeal rational beings because they refuse to conform their behavior to what they know to be the dictates of reason.[21]

20. In this context, Polin speaks of "moral man" as a "model": "L'idée complexe de l'homme est donc susceptible de trouver une signification, non pas au niveau de la nature physique et de la référence à des substances, mais au niveau de 'l'homme moral' . . . l'idée de l'homme apparaisse, non pas comme un fait, mais comme un modèle [Thus the complex idea 'man' can have signification, not at the level of physical nature and with reference to substances, but at the level of 'moral man'. . . . The idea 'man' is to be understood not as a fact, but as a model]." This notion of model does not detract from the content I have given to that of supposing. Polin holds that in order to be truly human, we must strive for the realization of this model in our actions. To be human is rationally to determine what is one's true happiness, and to act in accordance with this judgment. See Raymond Polin, *La politique morale de John Locke* (Paris, 1960), pp. 15, 22–23, 24–26. (This work has been republished by Garland Publishing, New York, in 1984, in the series The Philosophy of John Locke, ed. Peter A. Schouls).
21. Working from different premises, James Tully (in chap. 1 of *A Discourse on Property*) reaches conclusions similar to those I reached in these last pages. "Locke does not enquire

3. "Man Has No Nature at All"

There is more to moral man, to the corporeal rational creature, than I have so far made explicit. Our real essence, according to Locke, is that of autonomous beings, of beings whose reason is the source of laws which, if they accept them as normative for their actions, make it possible for them to obtain true and lasting happiness. Hence implicit in this notion is that of freedom; and related to it is that of desire for true and lasting happiness. It is this desire which is to rule all of a person's actions; and it is to manifestations of this desire that I attach the name "master passion." In addition to reason, both freedom and desire for mastery are dimensions of moral man. Of these two, freedom belongs as much to the essence of the corporeal rational being as does reason; for as I have stressed all along, rational action involves both knowing what is true or good and freely acting on this knowledge. Whether also the desire for mastery belongs to the essence of moral man is not so clear; my earlier statement that "human beings are born to be masters" does not decide that issue one way or the other. And it need not be resolved for my present purposes.[22] For enough has been said so far to make it at least plausible to hold that, for Locke, human beings have a nature, that we can know what this nature is, and that this is knowledge of moral man's real essence. These statements will continue to gain plausibility when, in subsequent chapters, I present arguments about passion (including the master passion), prejudice, and freedom. But before I discuss items such as these we should first examine whether any credibility might attach as well to an opposing claim, namely, that for Locke man has no nature at all. This is the claim advanced by John Passmore.

Passmore is not the only one who interprets Locke as saying that human beings have no nature and that therefore nurture is all-important. Neither is this interpretation limited to philosophers.[23] But among philosophers Passmore's stand is extreme. Some take a position somewhere between Passmore and me: they do not reject the tenet that all education is habituation or training but they do reject (or are at least tentative about) what for Passmore is its antecedent, the doctrine that human beings have no nature.

---

into the cause of rationality or corporeality, which would be the case if this were an ontological claim. The theory applies only to men who make themselves, through education, conformable to this idea" (p. 28). See also pp. 16, 21–23, 27.

22. Desire for happiness is part of a human being's essence (cf. 1.3.3). But it will become clear in the fourth chapter that the desire for mastery is an acquired passion.

23. See, for example, Frank E. Manuel, *The New World of Henri Saint-Simon* (Cambridge, Mass., 1956), chap. 25.

Those who take this position become disposed to ascribe confusion or tension to Locke. In his *Locke: An Introduction*, Yolton adopts such an in-between stance. On the one hand he holds that, for Locke, there is a human nature ("To guide one's self by the law of nature and reason is not merely to live an orderly and virtuous life: it is to have the very essence of humanity," p. 37). On the other he also writes as if he believes that, for Locke, education consists in nothing but habituation or training (see pp. 22–25). Does this very essence of humanity come about through training? That is what parts of Yolton's text would lead one to believe, as when he writes that it is training that gives rise to autonomous individuals, to persons who act virtuously because they submit themselves to the dictates of their own reason (23). Yolton then finds it difficult to reconcile the doctrines of habituation and autonomy. He asks whether Locke's "emphasis on habituating the child to virtue and good manners, the emphasis on conforming to accepted modes of behaviour, allow[s] room for individual initiative and decision?" and he replies that "Locke clearly believed that the answer to my question was 'no' "(52). This is not Yolton's last word on the matter, for he then speaks of the "tensions between individual freedom and social pressures" which "are found in a number of places in Locke's writings" (53). With respect to education Yolton does not attempt to look for a resolution of these tensions, and so we are left with the impression that in his works on education Locke may well have been less than clear about human nature and confused about education.[24] The first step away from this impression of confusion about education is to be quite precise on what Locke says about human nature. Examination of Passmore's stand will confirm the correctness of the position I have adopted and will enable me later on to deal more effectively with what Yolton calls the "tensions between individual freedom and social pressures."

Passmore's discussion of Locke draws primarily on *Some Thoughts concerning Education*, a work which will be central to my discussion in the third section of this book. But since I take it as Locke's teaching that human beings have a nature, it is important to come to grips with Passmore's claim at this early stage. Doing so now will not lead to repetition later, for when I come to deal with Locke's educational theory I won't need to say much more about Passmore. Moreover, doing so now does not call for extensive discussion of items which are better left for a later stage; although a few such items will need to be introduced, they need not

---

24. Yolton reiterates this position in the Clarendon edition of *John Locke: Some Thoughts concerning Education* (Oxford, 1989). I refer to it in Part C of this book. In his "Governing Conduct" James Tully's position seems to be close to Yolton's; see pp. 54–55.

be treated in detail. More important is that I have already presented much of the material upon which I need to draw in order to counter Passmore's claim. It is material from the *Essay concerning Human Understanding*. The weakness of Passmore's discussion arises primarily from the fact that he pays little attention to what the *Essay* has to say about human nature, and none to the implications for Locke's educational thought of the *Essay*'s epistemology and methodology. It is these facts especially that make Passmore's discussion of Locke on human nature uncharacteristically superficial and that lead him to misread the *Education*.

Passmore's phrase "man has no nature at all," purportedly descriptive of Locke's position, occurs in his article "The Malleability of Man in Eighteenth-Century Thought."[25] This article, though mainly about eighteenth-century Enlightenment thinkers, explicitly deals on nearly every page with Locke's teachings as background to these thinkers.

In this description of Locke, Passmore denies what I affirm, namely, that for Locke human beings do have an essence or nature to begin with, that is, prior to the process of socialization, particularly, of education. I affirm it to be Locke's position that a human being is a rational being. With respect to the young child this is an affirmation to the effect that it is born with the (undeveloped) capacity to discern truth from error and good from evil as well as with the (undeveloped) capacity which allows for action in accordance with truth and goodness. (Since, even when developed, they only *allow for* action in accordance with truth and goodness, I am not asserting it to be Lockean doctrine that human beings are born with a natural inclination which would automatically lead them toward truth and goodness; as I said before, these capacities, though necessary, are not sufficient for virtuous action.)

Because Passmore conflates human essence, natural (emotional) tendencies, and moral character, it is not always evident that he in fact denies what I assert. Before I continue, it should be established that, in spite of some confusion in Passmore's article—confusion which sometimes makes me agree with one part of a statement or argument and reject another part of that same statement or argument—we are in the end speaking about the same thing.

I agree with Passmore when he writes that, for Locke, a human being "has no natural tendency to goodness, none to depravity" so that "he has in this respect no nature at all," but I disagree with the rest of this sentence,

---

25. The phrase occurs on pp. 36–37 of this article, published in *Aspects of the Eighteenth Century*, ed. Earl R. Wasserman (Baltimore, 1965). From here on all page references to this article will be given directly in the text.

which is that a human being has "no inherent free will" (24). In addition, if I were to agree with Passmore's statement that "Locke . . . denied that there were any innate passions at all" (33), I would still disagree when he opposes Locke to Hume—Locke who, in his *Some Thoughts concerning Education* advances "the doctrine that man has *no nature at all*," Hume who, in his *Enquiries Concerning the Human Understanding* and *Concerning the Principles of Morals* "does not so much as discuss" this doctrine because it is obvious to him that "passions" such as "self-love, or resentment of injuries" are "innate" (36–37). To assert that human beings have no innate passions is not necessarily to hold that they have no original nature. So (granting that Passmore is partially correct in his juxtaposition of Hume and Locke) the conflict between them need not be about whether human beings have any "nature at all." In fact, the conflict is about what this "nature" consists of. For Hume, nature includes passion. By this stage of his argument Passmore concludes that because, for Locke, human beings are not naturally good, not naturally depraved, and have no innate passions, therefore they have no nature at all.

This conclusion operates throughout Passmore's discussion of Locke's theory of education. Take the following passage from an early page of his article: "what Pascal fears—that what men call 'natural' in fact derives from custom—is, from the point of view of Locke . . . greatly to be welcomed. If men have a fixed, determinate nature, education is so far limited; if they have *no* nature, then its possibilities are boundless" (25). What should immediately caution us against ascribing this position to Locke is his repeated assertion that whether a person's education is good or bad, he can go against it; hence, for Locke, the possibilities of education are not at all boundless. Educators do not have the power of infinitely molding their pupils. A plausible inference is, then, that Passmore is wrong in ascribing to Locke the view that a human being has no determinate nature; that, instead, Locke holds there to be something beyond the educator's control: the pupil's freedom. Because of the individual's natural freedom, wisdom and virtue (or foolishness and vice) are ultimately to be explained in terms of the individual, not in terms of the individual's education.

Of both reason and freedom, Passmore denies that the individual possesses them originally. This is evident, for example, from what he writes about La Mettrie. He quotes La Mettrie's words: "Whence comes skill, science and virtue if not from a disposition which makes us suitable to become skillful, wise and virtuous? And whence comes this disposition, if not by Nature?" (40). La Mettrie, Passmore writes, recognized "the importance of the innate characteristics of the human being"; in this respect, he adds, La Mettrie opposed himself to Locke, for whom man has no such nature and who therefore expounded the "conception of man as infinitely malleable" (ibid.).

By discussing the supporting passages he introduces from Locke's text, I can now firmly establish that Passmore is wrong about Locke's doctrine concerning human nature. Although I discuss only the thesis about human nature, this will nevertheless directly allow me to make certain judgments about Passmore's assertions concerning both the degree of malleability and the role of education.

When in his opening sentence Passmore quotes the well-known statements from the opening paragraph of Locke's *Education*—"nine parts of ten are what they are, good or bad, useful or not, by their education. It is that which makes the great difference in mankind"—he does draw attention to what he calls Locke's cautious limitations in the phrases "nine parts out of ten" and "the *great* difference in mankind." This is his only reference to these cautious limitations. But if we take them seriously then Locke is here saying that some people—one out of ten—are what they are not because of their education but, perhaps, even in spite of it. What makes persons capable of becoming good or bad, useful or not apart from or even in spite of the pressures of their environment? I shall return to this question in a moment.

Passmore did well to quote the famous words from the opening paragraph of Locke's *Education* in his own opening sentence. But these words, whether about the explicit nine out of ten or the implicit one out of ten do not imply that either group has no nature. Consider the following example. Assume that creatures other than humans are born with no nature at all so that, for example, dogs are neither friendly nor vicious by birth. A dog may become friendly or vicious, but it does not then become morally good or bad. It is the person who trained the dog to be vicious whom we declare in this respect to be morally bad. If we consider the case of a maturing child rather than a dog, the situation differs in an important respect. Locke holds that as it grows up the child may become good or bad. He also holds that education may be extremely important to this process. But if, as it matures, the child becomes evil, we cannot put all the blame on the educator. The responsibility involved is that of both educator and maturing child. And as we shall see in later chapters, it is the responsibility of the maturing child which Locke holds to be of the greater importance. This alone would make it credible to posit as Locke's thesis that human beings are the kind of beings who, as they grow up, can and

ought to discern good from evil, and are obliged to act in accordance with
what they discern to be good because they are rational beings.[26] If they use
their powers of reason and freedom well they will become morally good
and live happily; if they neglect the first and misuse the second they will
become morally evil and live in misery. Because he holds that these
powers are inborn rather than inculcated Locke (in another statement
from the *Education*'s opening paragraph, this time one unheeded by Passmore) says "Men's Happiness or Misery is most part of their own making." Because of their nature human beings are responsible for the moral
character which they acquire.

Passmore absorbs nature into character. Once that move is made,
education becomes training and human beings become infinitely malleable. Concepts such as individual responsibility, freedom, autonomy—
concepts that loom so large in the *Essay*, the *Second Treatise*, the *Reasonableness*—would then play no role in the *Education*. They certainly play no
role in Passmore's article. His absorption of nature into character leads
him to present Locke as a thinker for whom nurture is all-important and
nature not important at all.

If Passmore's account were correct, there would be a rift in Locke's
thought between important doctrines of the *Education* and doctrines
characteristic of all of Locke's other major works. His account would
also create antagonism between Locke and a host of eighteenth-century
thinkers precisely on points where in reality there is agreement; and it
would create affinity between Locke and a minority movement in eighteenth-century thought precisely on points where no affinity exists. It
would make Mandeville and Helvétius followers of Locke, the former
when he holds that man's "capacity for being civilized" derives from
education (31), the latter when he holds that education "is the sole source
of virtue" (43). Locke held neither of these beliefs. In contrast, it would
create conflict between Locke on the one hand and Hume and Rousseau
on the other. It would result in conflict with Hume when the latter "thinks
of education mainly as a means of acquiring belief" (35) and with Rousseau when he teaches that "the function of education, at least in its early
years, is entirely negative: 'it consists, not in teaching virtue or truth, but
in preserving the heart from vice and the spirit from error'" (42). Locke
held both these beliefs.[27]

In the *Essay* Locke stresses repeatedly that knowledge cannot be imme-

26. The grounds, if any, for this ascription of obligation will be discussed in Chapter 6. In
the meantime, see here Yolton's discussion of "moral man" and "person": *Locke: An Introduction*, pp. 28–32.

27. That Locke agrees with Rousseau's remark is evident from what he says about the
"principling" of children, as I discussed in Chap. 1, section 3. That he agrees with Hume's

diately communicated, that one must think for oneself if one is to attain knowledge. Just note again the statement "we may as rationally hope to see with other Mens Eyes, as to know by other Mens Understandings. So much as we our selves consider and comprehend of Truth and Reason, so much we possess of real and true Knowledge. The floating of other Mens Opinions in our brains makes us not one jot the more knowing, though they happen to be true" (1.4.23).[28] To this doctrine of epistemic autonomy there corresponds that of moral autonomy. Passmore, however, speaks as if knowledge and virtue can be immediately communicated, as if neither epistemic nor moral autonomy is a part of Locke's position: "in his *Some Thoughts Concerning Education* he [Locke] is only marginally interested in the communication of knowledge. 'It is virtue', he [Locke] writes, 'direct virtue, which is the hard and valuable part to be aimed at in education'" (21–22). But, for Locke, to aim at virtue is not to communicate virtue. As we shall see in detailed discussion later on, in the *Education* Locke presents it as his doctrine that, strictly speaking, neither knowledge nor virtue can be communicated. Each of us gains knowledge only through the processes of our own reason and virtue only through voluntary submission to the dictates of our own reason. Neither habituation nor custom can be the real source of knowledge or of vice and virtue. Passmore can offer no defense for his statement that "Locke's *Concerning Education*" makes "habituation by 'government and education' the source of our virtues as well as our vices" (24). The passages he adduces as support do not warrant his conclusion.

For example, he introduces a passage from the *Education* that he takes to be in contrast to what Leibniz wrote in the Preface to his *Theodicy*. In that Preface we read that "The practices of virtue, as well as those of vice, may be the effect of a mere habit, one may acquire a taste for them; but when virtue is reasonable . . . it is founded on knowledge" (25). In paragraph 42 of the *Education* Locke writes (according to Passmore in contrast to Leibniz):

> Every man must sometime or other be trusted to himself and his own conduct; and he that is a good, a virtuous, and able man, must be made so within. And therefore what he is to receive from education, what is to sway

---

comment, and disagrees with those of Mandeville and Helvétius, will become firmly established in Part C of this study.

28. This statement already shows at least prima facie affinity with Hume. If "other Mens Opinions" can "float" "in our brains" without making us "one jot the more knowing," these "opinions" can at best be "belief." If Passmore has accurately described Locke's educator as one who merely instills habits, then it would seem that for Locke education cannot be the direct way to knowledge.

and influence his life, must be something put into him betimes; habits woven into the very principles of his nature; not a counterfeit carriage, and dissembled outside, put on by fear, only to avoid the present anger of a father, who perhaps may disinherit him. (25)

Even in the context of the *Education* alone (and certainly in that of Locke's other writings) this passage does not allow Passmore's conclusion that education or habituation is all-important. As we shall see later, the *Education* makes it very clear that, for Locke as for Leibniz, truly virtuous action is rational action, and the reason in question is our own reason, so that it is only our own action which can make us "virtuous . . . within." The role of habit consists merely in accustoming a person to stop and think rather than act precipitously or to accept on faith. But even that habit must be made one's own through, first, an examination of it and, second, repeated conscious activity to establish it. The legitimate weaving of that habit "into the very principles of his nature" presupposes acts of both an individual's reason and will. It assumes the antecedence of what Passmore denies to exist: an original human nature characterized by reason and freedom. It is, Locke believes, only the individual who can weave into the very principles of his nature the habits which make possible a life of virtue. Unless we are rational by nature we can come to possess neither knowledge nor virtue.

There is only one passage (p. 23) in which Passmore gives what may look like Lockean grounds for his thesis:

"It seems plain to me," Locke writes in *Concerning Education*, "that the principle of all virtue and excellency lies in a power of denying ourselves the satisfaction of our own desires, where reason does not authorize them. This power is to be got and improved by custom, made easy and familiar by an early practice" (§38). Notice the phrase "*got* and improved": we become free, capable of resisting our desires, by habituation, we are not born free by nature.

This is too weak a ground on which to support so weighty a thesis. There is no objection, for example, to read the "got and improved" as referring to the actualization of a natural potentiality. But even if we don't take it that way there is a difficulty with Passmore's reading. For, Locke holds, education often leads us to being controlled by desires, none of which have been authorized by our reason. The desires whose satisfaction we are to deny ourselves are often those which become ours through education or habituation. (We must not lose from sight that for Locke, as for most eighteenth-century thinkers, existing education is the wrong kind of education.) From such bondage we ought to escape. And we can, because even while so bound we possess an original freedom which enables us to deny ourselves the satisfaction of these desires. This freedom must be called "original" because in these circumstances it cannot be through education or habituation that we become free; instead, we use this freedom to reject our education, to overcome our habits. Passmore does not consider this crucial aspect of Locke's doctrine. But it is of central importance and plays a major role in the *Essay*'s chapter "Of Power" as well as in Locke's various works on education and religion. I will deal with it in Part B of this book.

The passage Passmore quotes presents a further problem for his thesis. Even if we grant Passmore his reading concerning freedom, Locke clearly stipulates that "the principle of all virtue" has a dual root: there is (i) "a power to deny ourselves the satisfaction of our own desires," of desires which have not been (ii) "authorized" by "reason." The question then is: whence this authorizing reason? In view of Locke's epistemology it can only be each individual's reason. It is not Locke's doctrine that habituation ultimately accounts for our rationality. For that aspect of his thesis Passmore has been unable to introduce a single text that even looks as if it might provide its support.

Passmore's reading of Locke is a misreading. For Locke, human beings have a nature, and they are not infinitely malleable. They are malleable to a large extent (Locke does not neglect the importance of nurture) but not infinitely malleable. Their rational nature sets limits to their malleability, and even then they remain personally responsible for their character though circumstances helped in its formation. It is Locke's belief that we are perfectible; but there is for him no necessary link between malleability and perfectibility. Human beings are perfectible, but in the end their own autonomous action accounts for the degree of perfection they achieve or fail to achieve. Locke's consistent emphasis on epistemic autonomy, which derives from his conception of the nature of reasoning itself, makes a necessary link between perfectibility and malleability impossible. It is Locke's doctrine that people cannot be perfected unless they act according to the dictates of their own reason. As we saw in the first chapter, a person's own reason requires initial rejection of all the beliefs, customs and habits that one's cultural context would have one accept. Perfectibility, according to Locke, is possible only if, and to the extent that, the power which cultural circumstances have over a person can by that person

∼ 3

The Dogma of
Infallible Reason

Descartes draws a distinction between fallible belief and infallible knowledge. He bases it on the difference between potentially deceptive sensation, "deceitful memory," and "illusory imagination" on the one hand, and what he takes to be actually infallible reason on the other. Much has been written about Descartes' claim that reason is infallible; the grounds for this claim—presented most eloquently in the *Meditations*—have proved to be of abiding interest to scholars and continue to be the subject of several publications each year.

Unlike Descartes in the *Meditations*, Locke does not attempt to argue extensively the thesis of reason's infallibility in the *Essay* or elsewhere. But like Descartes, Locke draws the distinction between belief and knowledge, in part on similar grounds: reason is infallible in that what it gives us is unfailingly true; reason gives us knowledge, therefore knowledge is infallible; and one can know that one reasons and hence that one knows. And in a few places Locke asserts grounds for his confidence in reason and its revelations.

Commentators are well aware of this aspect of Locke's thought. Take one recent example. In contrasting what Locke says about fallible belief and infallible knowledge, John Dunn presents Locke's doctrine in the words: "God . . . may know vastly more" but "any human being whose wits are sufficiently in order to consider the question may be perfectly confident, may *know*, that he or she *can* know."[1] Like most commenta-

---

1. John Dunn, *Locke* (Oxford, 1984), p. 71.

tors, Dunn remains silent on what it would involve to consider the question. Typically, commentators do not discuss how, according to Locke, one can infallibly know that one knows; they do not examine whether this perfect confidence is well grounded.

If, on examination, it were to be found that Locke's position does not legitimately allow the conclusion that one can infallibly know that one knows, then there is no room for perfect confidence in this instance. And not just in this instance. For if I can never infallibly know that I know when I know, then I can never legitimately pronounce any knowledge claim to be infallibly correct.

In this chapter, I shall first briefly indicate both the pervasiveness of, and some of the restrictions placed upon, this doctrine of infallibility in Locke's writings. In sections two and three, I then ask whether Locke can infallibly know that he knows and hence can have grounds for the doctrine of the infallibility of reason. My answer will be that, strictly on his own terms, he cannot. Hence, the conclusion has to be drawn that Locke's insistence on the infallibility of reason amounts to no more than a dogmatic assertion.

1. The Infallibility of Reason

Throughout Locke's writings we find the doctrine that reason is infallible, that in the field of general knowledge, the products of reasoning always possess the properties of certainty and truth. In the *Essay concerning Human Understanding* reason's infallibility derives from the nature of intuition and from the role intuition plays in demonstration. Intuition always reveals "the Truth, as the Eye doth light" (4.2.1). And "in every step Reason makes in demonstrative Knowledge, there is an intuitive Knowledge of that Agreement or Disagreement, it seeks, with the next intermediate Idea, which it uses as Proof"; hence "it is plain, that every step in Reasoning, that produces Knowledge, has intuitive Certainty" (4.2.7). In the *Reasonableness of Christianity* we meet this doctrine of infallibility in the words "reason and her oracles, which contain nothing but truth" (144). In the first *Letter concerning Toleration* it presents itself in the phrase "when he knows, i.e. is infallibly certain (for so is a man in what he knows)" (180).

The sources of these last two quotations reveal that the products of reason thus characterized as true and certain are not restricted to abstract sciences like arithmetic and geometry. The infallibility of reason extends to "morals," to knowledge of how we ought to act in the concrete ethical and political situations of daily life. Locke holds that we can, indeed must, entrust ourselves to reason for the realization of our highest aspirations. If we follow its dictates, we can be assured not only of temporal happiness, but also of eternal bliss—even without recourse to special revelation. To return to a passage from the *Paraphrase and Notes on the Epistle to the Romans*, "Mankind, without the positive law of God, knew, by the light of nature, that they transgressed the rule of their nature, reason, which dictated to them what they ought to do" (note to Romans 5:13). In the *Essay*, we find a statement in part parallel to, in part more radical than that just quoted. It is more radical because it affirms that if we heed what our reason tells us, we can have greater assurance of eternal bliss than if we trust what are taken as the divine pronouncements of special relevation. For "though every thing said in the Text" of the Old and New Testament "be infallibly true, yet the Reader may be, nay cannot chuse but be very fallible in the understanding of it." Therefore

> we ought to magnify his Goodness, that he hath spread before all the World, such legible Characters of his Works and Providence, and given all Mankind so sufficient a light of Reason, that they to whom this written Word never came, could not (when-ever they set themselves to search) either doubt of the Being of a GOD, or of the Obedience due to Him. Since then the Precepts of Natural Religion are plain . . . and other revealed Truths, which are conveyed to us by Books and Languages, are liable to the common and natural obscurities and difficulties incident to Words, methinks it would become us to be more careful and diligent in observing the former, and less magisterial, positive, and imperious, in imposing our own sense and interpretation of the latter. (3.9.23)[2]

There is nothing tentative about these declarations. In these pronouncements (which are but a small sample of those one finds on this issue throughout Locke's major writings) the infallibility of reason and the perfect trustworthiness of knowledge are announced without hesitation or doubt. The finality of his statements witnesses to Locke's assurance that he knows—that he is infallibly certain—of reasons's infallibility.

---

2. In this passage from the *Essay* Locke's position is not far from that common among eighteenth-century deists. Thomas Paine, for example, took only a small step beyond Locke when, in *The Age of Reason*, he argued from "The continually progressive change to which the meaning of words is subject" to the conclusion that "human language, whether in speech or print, cannot be the vehicle of the Word of God," that "the Word of God exists in something else." The small step taken is really only one of explication: as the guide for life Paine openly dethrones the Scriptures and in its place installs human reason. See *The Age of Reason* (1794). In the Prometheus Books edition (New York, 1984), this passage occurs on p. 24. See also pp. 32 and 69.

Two questions now arise. (i) How does Locke know that reason is infallible? (ii) Given the doctrine of the infallibility of reason, how does Locke account for the existence of controversy and error in matters where reason is supposedly able to give us certainty and truth? In this chapter, I limit myself to the first of these questions. In the next chapter I consider the second question by focusing on the relations among reason, prejudice, and passion. Before I deal with the first question however, I must make clear what it is that infallibility is said to pertain to.

The reasoning Locke holds to be infallible is that which results in "general knowledge"; it is discursive reasoning about universals. The qualification "about universals" is crucial. It is not as if, say, physicists, whose interests are in a science of "substances," of physical objects, do not use discursive reasoning. But as we saw in chapter 1, because their reasoning involves ideas that are not really abstract or universal in the requisite sense, their ideas concern only the nominal—but do not capture the real—essence of whatever they reason about. The real and nominal essences of these ideas differ because their "archetypes" or "formal constitutions" are not made by these physicists and hence not perspicuous to their intellect (cf. 3.11.22). I then noted an important difference between Descartes and Locke. For the latter, since the physicist's reasoning is about nominal essences only, the products of such reasoning are characterized by probability rather than certainty. The truth in this case is probable truth and, by definition, there attaches no infallibility to reason's activity in the fields of the natural sciences. Thus, for Locke, the products of reason can be either certain or probable, depending on whether we deal with true universals or with ideas of physical objects.

The reasoning in question is, then, deductive or discursive reasoning about abstract ideas or universals. But there is more to it, for the possibility of deduction requires the presence of intuition. In the development of general knowledge, intuition plays a dual role. (*a*) As with all reasoning, this deductive reasoning must be given materials with which to work. Thinkers are said to obtain these materials, the universals, through reduction or decomposition of the contents of a variety of their sentient states. The end products of such a reductive process are the simplest abstract ideas, the foundational universals. One is said to know them through reason functioning intuitively. (*b*) Intuition also enters into deduction itself rather than just into the process of providng its materials. We saw this when I quoted from 4.2.7 in this section's opening paragraph.

Speaking in terms of Locke's methodology, we may say that the two processes involved in this discursive reasoning are reduction and composition. Reduction of the complex contents of our sentient states to the simplicity which characterizes simple abstract ideas allows for intuitive knowledge of universals. Locke holds such intuitive knowledge to be infallible. Composition results in general knowledge. It is the process of connecting universals through discovering necessary relations which hold between or among them.[3] Locke does not say that composition without fail gives us products characterized by infallible certainty. However, the lesser degree of certainty of deduction as compared with that of intuition is put to the charge of the limitations of memory rather than to reason. In composition, too, reasoning is held to be infallible.

This notion of reason and of rational procedure has surfaced before. It did so in the third section of the first chapter, where we clearly saw that the reductive aspect of reasoning accounts for the genuinely revolutionary nature of Locke's program. It did so as well in the opening part of the second chapter when we noted that, according to Locke, it is in the possession of the powers of reduction and composition that human beings are essentially distinct from beasts. Reason will be in the foreground again especially in its reductive function when, in later chapters, I focus on Locke's educational theory.

It is not relevant to introduce many more particulars about the processes of reduction and composition.[4] For the present, we have nearly all the details we need to answer the question: How does Locke know that reasoning, that is, intuiting combined with deducing, always gives the person performing these operations certainty and truth? Or in terms of methodology: how does Locke know that proceeding by means of composition always leads to general knowledge? There is just one aspect that still needs to be made explicit.

As we have seen, in his debate with Stillingfleet[5] Locke stressed the point that what the *Essay* says about "the new way of reasoning" is nothing but "a copy of my own mind, in its several ways of operation." Thus, if by "know" in "how does Locke know that intuiting and deducing always give truth," we mean to refer to an item of general knowledge, then it is Locke's position that he does not know that reasoning always gives truth. In terms of methodology, we may say that he does not claim

3. Locke discusses deduction primarily in Book 2 of the *Essay* (see especially chaps. 11, 12, 13). He deals with intuition in Book 4 (especially chaps. 2, 12, 17). For the process of reduction which is to result in knowledge of the simple abstract ideas which are the foundational universals—concepts such as *unity* and *existence*—see the following passages: 2.11.9, 2.12.1, 2.13.27, and 3.11.9.

4. I have given a detailed account of the development of "general knowledge" in chap. 6 of *Imposition of Method*.

5. For the relevant part of this debate, see Locke's *Works*, 1823, 5: 137–39.

to know that there is a universal method which, when applied to a certain kind of subject matter (namely, that in which we deal with universals) always allows us to attain certain knowledge. In other words, Locke does not pretend to be able to offer an infallibly correct abstract theory of method. What he says about the workings of our minds in pursuit of general knowledge is characterized as probable rather than as certain, as opinion rather than as truth. Locke emphasizes this point in the *Essay* when, in the middle of his account of reduction, he writes, "These are my Guesses concerning the means whereby the Understanding comes to have, and retain simple Ideas, and the modes of them, with some other operations about them" (2.11.17).

Locke's knowledge of method, of reason's procedure in its successful pursuit of general knowledge, is gained in the first place from observation of his own mind. As we read in 2.12.8, "If we will trace the progress of our Minds, and with attention observe how it repeats, adds together, and unites its simple Ideas received from Sensation or Reflection. . . ." He stresses more than once that this observation is strictly confined to what takes place in the mind of the observer. "I can speak but of what I find in my self" (2.11.16); and, what thinking is "every one will know better by reflecting on what he does himself, when he . . . thinks, than by any discourse of mine. . . . if he does not reflect, all the Words in the World, cannot make him have any notion of it" (2.9.2). That what he thus finds is not peculiar to the observer's experience he also "knows," but this "knowledge" is indirect and less secure than the immediate awareness which the observer has of the workings of his own mind. That Locke takes there to be such indirect knowledge is evident from the same response to Stillingfleet: "I think the intellectual faculties . . . operate alike in most men." The ground of this knowledge is the reaction of friends; those to whom he showed the account of his "observations" agreed that it was a correct description of the way in which their intellectual faculties also operate. This is not the only ground. The best books mankind has produced support this extrapolation. The very structure of their arguments and expositions bears witness to its correctness. Thus we find that Locke asserts the universality of the method of reduction and composition in the same sentence in which he emphasizes that "knowledge" of it comes primarily from observation of processes to which he takes each observer to have private access: "I can but speak of what I find in my self, and is agreeable to those Notions; which, if we will examine the whole course of Men in their several Ages, Countries, and Educations, seem to depend on those foundations which I have laid, and to correspond with this Method, in all the parts and degrees thereof" (2.11.16). Nevertheless, lest we should read too much into the second part of this statement, the very next paragraph warns us, "These are my Guesses concerning the means whereby the Understanding. . . ." The knowledge attained is not general knowledge; the generalization is not characterized by certainty and truth. Neither, of course, should we overstress that these are guesses. Locke holds what he portrays as his mind's working to be most likely that which any human being would portray if a person were to observe and report the operations of his or her own mind.[6] He therefore takes the portrait he draws to be a picture of reasoning wherever it occurs. He believes the principles of his method to be a functional definition of reason.[7]

But strictly speaking, Locke makes no pretension to general knowledge of the method to be used in the pursuit of general knowledge. The question of infallibility is therefore limited to the following. Whenever he *believes* himself to be so engaged, how does Locke *infallibly know* that he is engaged in those mental processes which constitute discursive reasoning about universals, that is, in the kind of reasoning whose products he holds are always characterized by certainty and truth?

To this question I can find only two answers, both of them in the *Essay concerning Human Understanding*. The answers are more implicit than explicit. The one draws on both reflection and intuition, the other is in terms of intuition alone. The answers are related in that both involve the notion of immediacy, namely, the immediacy of reflection and the immediacy of intuition. The immediacy in question is not fully identical in the two answers. If I use the phrases "epistemic immediacy," "temporal immediacy," and "logical immediacy," then reflection and intuition share epistemic immediacy, but temporal and logical immediacy belong to intuition alone. What I mean by these uses of "immediacy" will become clear in the course of the exposition. I begin with (a) the answer that focuses on epistemic immediacy. Stating and discussing it will constitute the next part of this chapter. We will see that it cannot provide support for the doctrine of the infallibility of reason, and that Locke was possibly aware of this for there are indications that he felt uneasy about this sort of

6. In the first generation after Locke's death, those whom he influenced tended to remove the limitation on this point. Many of them no longer spoke of "guesses" but of knowledge of the universal sameness of reason's workings, a knowledge available to each individual from the contemplation of his or her own mind's activity because this contemplation was itself carried out by universal (or divine) reason present in each individual. As Sir Richard Blackmore put it, "Turn on it self thy Godlike Reason's Ray, / Thy Mind contemplate, and its Power survey" (*The Creation, a philosophical poem demonstrating the existence and providence of God* (1712), 8: 202–3).

7. Also in this respect Locke followed Descartes's lead. See my *Descartes and the Enlightenment*, chap. 1, section 1.

answer. That places the weight of the doctrine of infallibility on the second answer, (b) the one which introduces the notions of temporal and logical immediacy. I deal with this in the third section. It will become clear that this answer too is incapable of bearing so much weight. Locke seems to have been totally unaware of this fact, for, as we saw at the beginning of this section, he continues with absolute assurance to speak of the infallibility of reason in the works he wrote after the *Essay*. Since neither answer provides support for the doctrine and since there are (as far as I know) no hints at any alternative support, I must conclude that the doctrine of the infallibility of reason is a dogmatic assertion. We shall see that there are restrictions on the doctrine in addition to those already noted. But in however restricted a form it makes its appearance, as long as it is presented as an item of incontrovertible knowledge, it remains a dogmatic assertion.

2. The Epistemic Immediacy of Reflection and Intuition

"By REFLECTION . . . I would be understood to mean, that notice which the Mind takes of its own Operations, and the manner of them" (2.1.4). It is achieved when the mind "turns its view inward upon it self, and observes its own Actions about those Ideas it has" (2.6.1). Locke holds that through reflection, each person has an immediate awareness of the operations of his or her own mind. Although he speaks of "Ideas of reflection," what we are "being conscious of, and observing in our selves" when we "reflect" is "Perception, Thinking, Doubting, Believing, Reasoning, Knowing, Willing, and all the different actings of our own Minds" (2.1.4). Thus in awareness of mental operations, it is not as if there are three distinct entities: the mental operation, the idea of the mental operation, and the mind which has the idea of the mental operation. The orthodox reading of Locke is that he did have such a three-entity view of our awareness of physical objects: there is the physical object, the idea of that object, and the mind which has the idea of that object. It is the idea which represents the object to the mind, and it is the idea of which the mind is immediately aware. Of the object it has a mediate awareness, an awareness mediated by the idea. This doctrine of representational realism presents a problem for those holding it, namely, how do they know that the idea is a true or adequate representation of the object? Whether or not Locke is a representational realist in his philosophy of perception—a case has been made for denying that he is[8]—he does not hold that position in

8. Among others, Yolton and Woozley have argued that even with respect to the perception of physical objects Locke is not a representational realist. At first, I found their

his account of reflection. That at least is how I shall interpret what he writes about "reflection." A passage such as 4.21.4 provides strong support for this reading (although it at the same time contains at least prima facie evidence that with respect to our awareness of physical objects Locke was a representational realist: "the Things, the Mind contemplates, are none of them, besides itself, present to the Understanding"). This reading allows him the strongest position from which to justify the claim that he knows reason to be infallible. I shall, then, take him as saying that when we reflect on what we do when we reason, the activity perceived is the mind's procedure in its successful pursuit of general knowledge. The doctrine of the immediacy of reflection is one to the effect that when I reason, or remember, or doubt, I do not have an idea which represents to me that I am reasoning or remembering, or doubting, but the reasoning, remembering, or doubting in which I am engaged is itself what I am immediately aware of. This doctrine of the immediacy of reflection would rule out the problem inherent in that of representational realism.

To speak of the epistemic immediacy of reflection is to articulate only part of the ground of Locke's answer to the question of how he knows reason to be infallible. The full ground is taken to be that this immediate reflective awareness of the operations of the mind coincides with intuitive knowledge of these operations. Hence this reflective awareness may be called *intuitive* reflective awareness. Intuitive reflective awareness is taken to be infallible.[9]

Let me come to this statement of the full ground in a different way. Locke holds that there is intuitive knowledge of reasoning. Intuition, he assumes, allows each of us to claim knowledge of the fact that we reason

arguments plausible. But it now seems to me that Woozley's have been seriously undermined by Charles McCracken and Yolton's by considerations like those of Eric Matthews. See John W. Yolton's most recent statements of this issue in his *Perceptual Acquaintance from Descartes to Reid* (Minneapolis, 1984), especially chap. 5; also *Locke: An Introduction*, pp. 122–23, 145–48; A. D. Woozley's edition of *An Essay concerning Human Understanding* (New York, 1974), pp. 27–35; Charles McCracken, *Malebranche and British Philosophy* (Oxford, 1983), pp. 132–33; and Eric Matthews, "Mind and Matter in the 18th Century," *The Philosophical Quarterly* 36 (1986): 420–29, especially pp. 422 and 426–27.

9. Commentators tend to present this doctrine of the infallibility of reflective awareness without remarking on it. See, for example, Yolton's *Locke: An Introduction*, the top of p. 30; although Yolton focuses on the subject rather than on the subject's activity of perceiving, the doctrine of infallible knowledge of that activity through reflective awareness is implied. There is a long tradition of conformity to this doctrine, beginning with writers including Sir Richard Blackmore in literature and Isaac Watts in philosophy. In Blackmore's *The Creation* we read "The Mind proceeds, and in Reflection goes, / Perceives she does Perceive, and knows she Knows" (7: 253–54). And Watts contrasts "Inward Consciousness and Intelligence [i.e., reflective awareness], as well as Divine Faith and Inspiration" with "Sense or human Faith" because the latter "are often fallible" (*Logick: Or, The Right Use of Reason in the Enquiry after Truth*, p. 184).

when we reason. In addition, each person can claim intuitive knowledge of the procedures in which reasoning consists. Each of us is capable of certainty on these points because we can know them through immediate intuitive awareness of the internal operations of our mind. Since (as we saw) by "reflection" Locke means "that notice which the Mind takes of its own Operations, and the manner of them," this intuitive awareness is taken to be intuitive reflective awareness. Hence one Lockean answer to the question of how we know that reason is infallible would be that we know it through intuitive reflective awareness.

In view of this answer, we must read the passages in which Locke speaks about the infallibility of reason with one more qualification in mind. The first was that, strictly speaking, Locke's knowledge of the infallibility of reason is limited to his own reasoning and does not extend to the reasoning of others. The additional qualification is that even with respect to his own reasoning, this knowledge strictly speaking concerns present activity only. Anything said about the absolute trustworthiness of reason which transcends the grasp of present intuition is extrapolation. It may be well-grounded extrapolation, but no result of extrapolation can be characterized as an object of intuition, as "irresistable," as that which "forces it self immediately to be perceived, as soon as ever the Mind turns its view that way; and leaves no room for Hesitation, Doubt, or Examination" (4.2.1). Before we examine whether Locke possesses the grounds for even this reduced claim, a few more comments are in order about intuitive knowledge and reflective awareness.

For Locke, intuitive knowledge always involves epistemic immediacy. It does so when the object of intuition is an idea or a set of ideas (in that case the epistemic immediacy pertains by definition; cf. 2.8.8) but also when the object is an activity or thing, as in the intuitive knowledge we possess of our own existence (cf. 4.9.2). In the latter case, there is what I called the immediacy of intuitive reflection. This overlap of reflection and intuition is not limited to our knowledge of our existence. Reflection and intuition also coincide in the reflective act which reveals that we are intuiting something; of such acts, Locke holds they give intuitive knowledge of the fact that we are intuiting.

Locke does not teach that all intuitive knowledge is reflective awareness. For example, Locke would not take as instances of reflective awareness the intuitive knowledge that white is not black, or that a circle is not a triangle. But he does seem to hold that all acts of reflective awareness are to be identified as instances of intuitive knowledge.[10] Even if, in terms of

10. One implication of work done by D. J. Rabb on Locke's notion of reflection is that for Locke all acts of reflective awareness present us with instances of infallible knowledge. I

Locke's position, it makes sense to speak of a coincidence of reflective awareness and intuitive knowledge when what one is aware of is an act of intuition, this does not imply that there is such a coincidence when one is aware of other modes of thought. It seems that Locke believed there to be such an implication. At least, the first answer to the question of how he knows that reason is infallible assumes the existence of that implication. It will soon be clear why making that assumption is a mistake.

First, I must show that Locke in fact makes the claim that there is intuitive reflective awareness of reasoning; it is present in passages such as 2.9.2 and 4.9.2–3. The latter is the more explicit of the two. It reads in part as follows:

> We have the Knowledge of our own Existence by Intuition; of the Existence of GOD by Demonstration; and of other Things by Sensation.
>
> As for our own Existence, we perceive it so plainly, and so certainly, that it neither needs, nor is capable of any proof. For nothing can be more evident to us, than our own Existence. I think, I reason, I feel Pleasure and Pain; Can any of these be more evident to me, than my own Existence? If I doubt of all other Things, that very doubt makes me perceive my own Existence, and will not suffer me to doubt that. For if I know I feel Pain, it is evident, I have as certain a Perception of my own Existence, as of the Existence of the Pain I feel: Or if I know I doubt, I have as certain a Perception of the Existence of the thing doubting, as of that Thought, which I call doubt. Experience then convinces us, that we have an intuitive Knowledge of our own Existence, and an internal infallible Perception that we are.

One difficulty to which this passage may seem to give rise can quickly be shown to be spurious. If "nothing can be more evident to us, than our own Existence," it might be implied that anything else is less evident, hence not perfectly evident and therefore not intuitively certain. The question "can any of these be more evident to me?"—a question asked about thinking, reasoning, doubting, feeling pleasure and pain—might then seem to imply that certainty pertains to knowledge of existence, but not to knowledge of thinking, reasoning, etc. However, just because these are not more evident, they need not be less so. They could be equally evident. That, it appears, is Locke's intention, for he writes that "if I know I doubt, I have as certain a Perception of the Existence of the thing doubting, as of that Thought, which I call doubt." The knowledge of that which I call thinking, reasoning, doubting, feeling pleasure or pain, is

---

argue that this Lockean view is mistaken. See Rabb's "Reflection, Reflexion and Introspection," the *Locke Newsletter*, no. 8 (1977): 35–52; as well as his *John Locke on Reflection: A Phenomenology Lost* (Lanham, Md., 1985).

therefore taken to be as evident as that of my existence. Locke believes that all of these are items of intuitive knowledge, that each is a case of reflective awareness in which one knows with unshakeable certainty and truth that of which one is aware.

So let us take this passage as saying that the knowledge I have of my thinking or reasoning is as certain as that of my existence. We can now ask whether Locke can legitimately say that he has the same kind of knowledge of his own reasoning as he has of his own existence and that the knowledge in the first instance is as certain as that in the second.

Reasoning, for Locke, is one of the modes of thinking. Another mode of thinking is remembering (2.6.2). We are therefore assumed to gain knowledge about the activity of remembering in exactly the same way as we get to know about that of reasoning, namely, through intuitive reflective awareness. Now suppose we introduce *remembering* into the passage quoted from 4.9.3, as follows: "I think, I reason, [I remember] . . . ; can any of these be more evident to me, than my own Existence?" In view of some of the things he writes elsewhere, Locke need not give a different answer from that offered before. For usually (though, as we shall see in a moment when we look at a passage like 4.2.7, not invariably) Locke uses "to remember" as an "achievement verb." As he writes, "He remembers, i.e. he knows (for remembrance is but the reviving of some past knowledge)" (4.1.9). Thus if I say "I remember" when what I claim to remember is not the case, then I misuse the word "remember." The problem with this is that whether my memory claim is veridical or not, there is no difference in my mental state when I say "I remember." I may be immediately aware of my mental state, but this reflective awareness does not give me infallible knowledge of whether or not I am remembering when I believe that I am remembering. Which is to say that Locke is wrong, at least in this case, to hold that there is a coincidence of reflective awareness and intuitive knowledge. I can only know that I am remembering when I have evidence external to what I claim to be a memory experience.

Of course, the main point of 4.9.3 is not that "we have intuitive knowledge of our own Existence, and an internal infallible Perception that we are" because we *correctly* identify the experience of which we are reflectively aware as one of reasoning or remembering or feeling pain. Locke's argument is like Descartes's in the Second Meditation. Because I am aware, therefore I exist, and the fact that I am aware provides me with an "infallible Perception" that I exist. But for establishing the existence of the one who is aware the awareness need not include a correct identification of the mode of awareness in question. For the purpose of establishing existence there need be no coincidence of reflective awareness and intuitive knowledge of a certain mental activity. Intuitive knowledge of existence is possible regardless of whether the mental act of which one is reflectively aware is correctly identified.

Nevertheless, the passage also states it as Locke's doctrine that the reflective awareness of thinking (that is, of activities like reasoning or remembering) and of feeling pain is as "infallible" a "Perception" as the perception that one exists. That is, it states that the perception tells me that I in fact exist, reason, remember, feel pain. I have "as certain a Perception of" the existence of reasoning as of the existence of the reasoner; and the perception is explicitly stated to be intuitive perception. When we substitute "remembering" for "reasoning" it becomes clear why Locke cannot be right in saying that through reflective awareness I am assured that a certain mental state is really one in which I remember rather than just believe I remember. It is because there is no discernable relevant difference in mental states regardless of the correctness or incorrectness of their identification. There may be reflective awareness of the mental state but, since intuition is held to be infallible, there can be no reflective *intuitive* awareness of it.

Sometimes Locke himself comes close to making this point explicitly, as when he writes about the role of memory in deduction.

> This intuitive Perception of the Agreement or Disagreement of the intermediate Ideas, in each Step and Progression of the Demonstration, must also be carried exactly in the Mind, and a Man must be sure that no part is left out; which because in long Deductions, and the use of many Proofs, the Memory does not always so readily and exactly retain: therefore it comes to pass, that this is more imperfect than intuitive Knowledge, and Men embrace often Falsehoods for Demonstrations. (4.2.7)

The implication would seem to be that people accept falsehoods because they believe them to be conclusions of demonstrations, that is, they believe they accept a truth. This belief is based on the conviction that in what they take to be a demonstration, memory has served them well (else they would not take it to be a demonstration). The conviction in this case does not differ from what they would have had if what they take to be a demonstration really was a demonstration, if memory had in fact served them well. Locke here implicitly admits that reflection on the activity of the mind called "deduction," as that activity runs its course, does not provide knowledge that what one claims to remember is actually remembered.

That is part of the conclusion which may be drawn from a passage such as 4.2.7. The other part is that reflection on the activity taken to be that of deduction does not provide knowledge of whether one is actually deducing. Because of the necessary presence of memory in deduction, we do not know whether (and if so, when) reflective awareness coincides with intuitive awareness; and epistemic immediacy alone does not provide grounds which make incontrovertable Locke's claim about the infallibility of deducing or reasoning.

Some passages in the *Essay* may well indicate that Locke was aware of the fact that, if he were to base his claim of infallible knowledge of the infallibility of reason on claims about epistemic immediacy, these would be too weak at least as far as the deductive aspect of reasoning is concerned. Passages such as 4.2.1, 4.2.6, 4.2.7, and 4.17.14–15 state that deductive knowledge is less certain than intuitive knowledge. The explicit ground given for this lesser certainty is the presence of memory in deduction and its absence in intuition. The presence or absence of memory would not lead to a difference in certainty if we could infallibly know that we remember when we take ourselves to be remembering. That is, there would be no problem if such claims were based on reflective awareness which coincided with intuitive knowledge. Passages such as 4.2.7 and 4.17.15 are therefore not just implicit admissions that we do not infallibly know the veracity of a memory claim through reflective awareness. They are, in addition, Locke's implicit admission that the epistemic immediacy of reflection alone is an insufficient ground for the claim that we can possess infallible knowledge of reason's infallibility, that is, of the process of deducing. One may legislate that both "to remember" and "to reason" are achievement verbs, but that does not preclude unwitting misuse of the phrases "I remember" and "I reason." No reflection on a single mental state or activity can identify that state or that activity as one of remembering or of reasoning.

Discussion of these few passages does not make the accusation of dogmatism inescapable. But the least we must say is that they give us no grounds for justifiably holding reason to be infallible.

3. The Temporal and Logical Immediacy of Intuition

Can such grounds be found if we focus once again on the intuitive power of reason and introduce the notions of temporal and logical immediacy? We shall find the answer to be negative. In fact, the introduction of temporal and logical immediacy provides two paths leading us to the position from which the charge of dogmatism becomes unavoidable. They are these.

First. The difference which distinguishes all acts of intuition from all acts of deduction is that temporal and logical immediacy are said to characterize the former but not the latter. The conclusion of a deduction follows with necessity from the various steps of the argument. The image of "steps" points at the fact that a deduction does not take place all at once, that there is no temporal immediacy. Locke also speaks of deduction as being a chain with links. This indicates that in deduction the relation between the conclusion and that on which it rests cannot be one of logical immediacy; some, perhaps many, "ideas" or "proofs" play a mediating role.

Locke holds that there is a threefold immediacy which characterizes intuition. There is epistemic immediacy; this it shares with deduction. And there are temporal and logical immediacy, neither of which it shares with deduction. There is temporal immediacy because the act of intuition is said to occur all at once. (No doubt, there are all sorts of problems with the notion of an instantaneous act; but I will not let them detain me here). There is logical immediacy because the object of the act consists of single ideas (as in 4.1.4, 4.7.14, and 4.8.2) or of ideas which stand in a direct or unmediated necessary relationship to one another (as in 4.7.19). Of course, if I am to intuit "that White is not Black, that a Triangle is not a Circle" (4.7.19), I must be able to handle concepts such as "white," "black," "triangle," "circle"; and both the formation and retention of concepts involve memory (e.g., 2.11.9). But the act of intuition by which I know the essential dissimilarity of the ideas in these two sets of ideas is taken to occur all at once. In it, there is room for neither "steps" nor intervening "links," and in that respect there is no role for memory to play.

This implies that Locke's position would allow him to say that he knows intuitively that he is intuiting when he is intuiting, but not that he knows intuitively that he is deducing when he is deducing. Which is to say that he has intuitive or infallible knowledge neither of the fact that he is demonstrating or reasoning nor of the manner of demonstration, that is, of the method of reasoning. Let me state the grounds for this conclusion more explicitly.

Demonstration is a process involving various stages, activities, and faculties. Besides intuition, deduction, and memory, there are intrinsic to it the activities of the "intellectual Faculties" of "Sagacity and Illation." ("By the one, it finds out, and by the other, it so orders the intermediate Ideas, as to discover what connexion there is in each link of the Chain, whereby the Extremes are held together"; 4.17.2.) To know that one is deducing does not require knowledge of the entire deduction. But it does require knowledge which extends beyond an instantaneous act of grasping an idea that is relevant to the deduction, or an instantaneous act of grasping that one idea stands in an immediate and necessary relationship to another idea. It requires knowledge which exceeds what intuition can deliver. To know that one is deducing requires knowledge of more than two contiguous "links" of the chain: knowledge of the nature of these links, and knowledge of the activities which produced these links. The intellectual grasping of this group of entities and activities is inconceivable apart from memory. Memory is therefore intrinsic to this act. Hence the act cannot be that of intuiting. Consequently, there is no intuitive knowledge of the "Operations, and the manner" of deduction; there is no intuitive or infallible knowledge of (the method of) reasoning—even when what we are talking about is the individual's own reasoning.

Second. What we claim to be deductive reason's activity and what we claim to be the products of that activity, we cannot know to be that activity and we cannot know to be such products in terms of just that activity or just those products. The activity presupposes that which reduces initially obscure complex items to items which are clear and distinct and, ultimately, self-evident. Deductive activity itself must then be exposed as of the kind which creates clear and distinct complex items on this self-evident foundation. Its final products must be revealed to be the kind of clusters of ideas in which all the ideas are "seen" to be clear and distinct and all the relations between or among them as necessary. Unless the product of what is claimed to be a deduction is "seen" as in all respects characterized by clarity and distinctness, it cannot be claimed to be a product of deduction. Because of the complexity involved this "seeing" goes far beyond intuitive insight. If the product is in fact that of a deduction then the characteristics of clarity and distinctness do of course belong to it (this is just as much a tautology as saying that truth belongs to the veridical memory). The point is that no single act of intuition can reveal that a product of deduction is characterized by clarity and distinctness.

This second way of making the point contains an element which reinforces the charge that the doctrine of the infallibility of reason amounts to no more than a dogmatic assertion. This element is found in the criterion of clarity and distinctness. The foundations from which we reason must be clear and distinct or self-evident. Resolution of the contents of our sentient states is supposed to lead to the absolutely simple general ideas which are the simplest or the foundational universals; and intuition is the intellectual faculty through which we are to grasp these universals. Clarity and distinctness are therefore the critera which determine what kind of product of mental activity is characterized by certainty and truth, and what kind of mental activity leads to possession of such a product. Hence these criteria help to determine what we mean when we say that reason is infallible. But what justification is there for applying these criteria? The only justification Locke hints at is that unless we appeal to the self-evidence of the intuition of simple universals, we are led into an infinite regress (4.7.19). Even if we were to grant that without some sort of criteria there is an infinite regress, hence no foundation for and thus no possibility of general knowledge, how could Locke know that clarity and distinctness are these criteria? To claim purely intuitive insight for this doctrine (assuming such a claim could be made without begging the question) is claiming too much, for the doctrine itself is far from simple. It embodies the complex assertion that at the foundation of one's systematic general knowledge there are contextless items of knowledge, items known per se rather than per aliud. I can see no intuitive—or for that matter any other satisfactory—justification for this doctrine.

One may speculate and say that Locke espouses this doctrine because of his acceptance of an ideal characteristic of his age. His is, after all, a philosophy of mastery. From the mid-seventeenth century on, thinkers hankered after mastery or power.[11] They all accepted the Baconian dictum that "knowledge is power." If knowledge is power, complete knowledge might be full mastery. Items known clearly and distinctly are items known completely.[12] Self-evident items, items known per se, are known clearly and distinctly. Hence the imposition of these criteria at the foundations was to allow complete mastery of these foundations. And the use of these criteria throughout general knowledge (nothing would count as general knowledge unless it was known to be clear and distinct) would extend this mastery to all of general knowledge. The application of general knowledge to life itself, for example, as "morals" in the realms of ethics and politics, was then expected to lead to the achievement of mastery in everyday life.[13]

But these comments are speculative; I shall leave them for the time

11. See my *Descartes and the Enlightenment* for a substantiation of this statement in terms of both Descartes and several of the eighteenth-century philosophes.

12. Locke adopted these criteria from Descartes. For Descartes an item is clear if all of it is before the mind and distinct if nothing but it is before the mind. See *The Principles of Philosophy*, 1: 45. Locke's change of terminology in the second edition of the *Essay* (to "determined" and "determinate") in no way constituted a break with Descartes' doctrine on this point.

13. In his *Understanding Locke* (Edinburgh, 1983), pp. 195–205, John J. Jenkins also argues that Locke is unable to support the position that one can know certain claims to knowledge to be veridical through reflection on one's mental states. He concludes that Locke's "thought is particularly untidy at this point" because it is influenced by a dogmatic belief. Whereas I speculatively relate Locke's dogmatism to acceptance of the ideal of mastery, Jenkins relates Locke's "untidiness" to "one of the presuppositions" of Locke's "ontology," namely, that God exists. (I remember John Jenkins with gratitude for discussion of an earlier version of this chapter with him.)

being. What is not speculative is that Locke has no rational justification for holding reason to be infallible. One may then ask whether it is fair to say (as I did) that the doctrine of the infallibility of reason is a dogmatic assertion? Dogmatism, after all, goes against the grain of the philosopher I have so far presented. I have presented Locke the revolutionary, for whom nothing may be accepted on trust, for whom whatever is accepted without the authoritative stamp of reason constitutes an espousal of prejudice. If by "dogma" we refer to a fundamental principle or tenet which guides our action, and if by "revolutionary" we refer to a person who holds that nothing may be accepted as a principle except that which comes from the crucible of the individual's reductionistic reason, then we now see a deepseated tension in Locke's position. For in it, the only principles which are non-dogmatic are those which infallible reason makes available to a person. That, however, is itself a principle containing elements of which reason cannot be the source. Hence it is fair to characterize that principle as a dogmatic assertion. Locke's belief that reason is its source I have shown to be mistaken. It is no minor mistake for, at the heart of the Lockean position, it creates the tension of incoherence: Locke the revolutionary is also Locke the dogmatist.

The question raised at the beginning of this chapter was: How does Locke know—know infallibly—that reason is infallible? The answer is that, whether as an item of general or of intuitive knowledge, he does not know it. There was also another question at the beginning of the chapter: In view of the doctrine of the infallibility of reason, how does Locke account for the existence of error in matters where reason is supposed to be able to give us certainty and truth? That question will lead us directly into the next chapter, into discussions of prejudice and passion. Now it may not be clear why or even that it does so. It might be said that Locke holds reason to be infallible and that he puts the blame for error on memory. To say so would be correct in part but would not go far enough.

It would be correct to blame memory for error in what is asserted to be demonstrative knowledge because, as we have seen, Locke himself does so. But to explain error entirely in terms of the often unbearable burden placed on memory in long deductions is not a good enough explanation. That this is so can be easily shown. First, if there is disagreement between two persons about the conclusion of a lengthy demonstration, the argument can be rethought and, through careful and frequent rethinking, the burden on memory can be lightened. But rethinking of an argument does not always lead to agreement as to which conclusion is to be drawn. It may well be that neither of the disputants has grounds for suspecting the other (or themselves) of misremembering, that neither is in fact misremembering, yet disagreement persists. Second, there is often strong disagreement about conclusions of arguments which are very brief, so brief that it is implausible to blame divergence of opinion on the weakness of memory. In the *First Treatise of Government* one argument against the doctrine of the divine right of kings goes as follows. If God had appointed Adam, and the eldest son in succession, to be king over mankind, then at least all but one of the various present rulers of mankind are usurpers; and since we do not know which (if any) of them is in Adam's most direct line of succession, we cannot be obliged to submit to any one of them. In the *Second Treatise* one argument for limiting the power of the sovereign is this. Since each human being is autonomous, the sovereign can have only such powers over other human beings as these human beings have themselves decided to delegate to the sovereign. Both of these arguments are brief, yet the conclusion of each was sufficiently controversial that wars were fought over which of them would prevail in the practice of life. It was not because of weakness of memory that wars were fought and nations torn assunder. The disagreements which led to quarrels, to attempts at suppression, and finally to large-scale violent conflict, had to do far more with the presence of prejudice and passion than with weakness of memory. That this is Locke's position is one of the points that the following chapter will clearly establish.[14]

14. In his "Locke and the Ethics of Belief" (*Proceedings of the British Academy* 64 [1978]: 185–208), Passmore (in a more round-about way than I do) reaches the same conclusion. "And so in the end Locke is led to conclude that men can believe falsely, not as the result of having inadequate evidence, but as a result of being dominated by powerful inclinations" (208).

～ 4

"Infallible" Reason, Prejudice, and Passion

1. Reason, Prejudice, and Passion

For Locke, to be human is to be rational. He also holds that all human beings are creatures of desire or passion and that their passions lead them to all sorts of prejudices. Human beings are born to be masters but, says Locke, prejudice has till now frustrated the achievement of that mastery.

Prejudice takes on many forms. Sometimes it presents itself as majority opinion, sometimes even as "universal Consent" (1.3.26). But in whatever guise it appears, it can never be a person's guide to life if one wants to lead a truly human life and achieve the mastery one is capable of. To become a master requires walking the path of reason. Any human being can achieve at least a degree of mastery. But no one can achieve mastery to a high degree except through overcoming prejudice, that is, except through ceasing to accept what one's reason has not authorized as true or good. Locke says that "natural reason" is the "touchstone" "every man carries about him . . . to distinguish truth from appearances"; but he adds that "the use and benefit of this touchstone . . . is spoiled and lost . . . by assumed prejudices, overweening presumption, and narrowing our minds"(*Conduct*, §3).

That sentence provides the general answer to a pressing question: if Locke takes reason to be infallible, how does he explain what may appear to be reason's failures as they manifest themselves in our errors, quarrels, unhappiness, and misery? The answer is that although reason is infallible, the person capable of being rational is not. Locke never tires of pointing this out to his adversaries, as when he accuses Jonas Proast (his persistent opponent in the controversy about toleration) of laboring under the "insupportable presumption" of a pretense "to infallibility" (*Toleration*, 532).

People acquire "presumptions," "prejudices," or, to use another of Locke's favorite phrases, people become "partial," because they have a "feeble passionate Nature" (2.21.67). To understand Locke correctly at this point we must be careful to insist on a distinction I described earlier. Although it is correct to say that all prejudice stands in the way of mastery, it would be incorrect to assert the same about passion. Locke holds that mastery can be achieved only if we give full reign to what I called the "master passion": a person's passion for mastery. This master passion must be sharply distinguished from natural human passion. Whereas reason stands in judgment over all objects of natural passion, reason serves the master passion. Once the master passion holds full sway in a person's life, prejudice in all its forms is in the process of being vanquished and mastery is in the process of being achieved.

It is the relationships between reason, prejudice, and passion that I want to explore further: those between reason and prejudice in this section, and between reason and passion in the next. Before I focus on these relationships let me make more explicit the relevance of this chapter to both the preceding and following parts of this study.

Prejudice is the most serious cause of the apparent failings of reason. In a sense we may say it is human to be partial. However, we must remember that "it is human" in the phrase "it is human to be partial" has a meaning which differs from its use in "it is human to be rational." Here we must keep the discussion of the second chapter firmly in mind. There we saw that a newborn child is neither actually prejudiced nor actually rational; a human being is liable to become prejudiced and has the potential to become rational. But the liability to prejudice is not a part of human nature in the way that the potential for rational action is. Prejudice is evil and, for Locke, no evil is originally natural to a human being. That is, a human being possesses no natural ability which when actualized would, as it were automatically, lead a person into error or evil—an important point, which I will substantiate and develop in Chapter 7, section 3. Human beings are not prejudiced at birth but they are all, to a greater or lesser degree, prejudiced by their upbringing. Since all become prejudiced to at least some extent, we may say that to be prejudiced is human, that is, it is part of the human condition. But a being does not become truly human, does not actualize the potential of human nature, except by overcoming prejudice. Our upbringing, education, and general social context saddle us with the prejudices that would thwart the development of our rational nature. The development of our rational nature therefore goes hand-in-hand with rejection of potential and overcoming of acquired prejudices. It has been rightly observed that, for Locke, "men are rational to the extent that they master partiality."[1]

Thus it is not difficult to see how these discussions of reason and prejudice relate to the idea of mastery. Mastery is achieved to the extent that a person overcomes prejudice and submits to the dictates of reason. Neither is it hard to understand how freedom and right education are relevant to the achievement of mastery: freedom is potentially related to vanquishing prejudice, education to initial shielding from prejudice. An original measure of freedom is required for the very possibility of resisting and overcoming prejudice. And one needs the right kind of cultural milieu, especially the right kind of education, to reach the best possible position for use of one's freedom to resist, or to shake off, prejudice and to submit to the dictates of one's reason. There is more to the roles of both freedom and education than the preceding sentences indicate. But enough has been said to make it clear that, for doing full justice to the discussion of mastery, the topics of freedom and education require the careful attention they will receive in the following two main parts of this book.

Born potentially rational, human beings tend to become trapped in the web spun by "fashion," "common opinion," "custom," and "education"—a web of "wrong notions" and "ill habits" (2.21.69). Each person has to destroy this web of prejudice in which we are all caught; and each has the power or freedom to do so. This act of annihilation is the first crucial step of progress on the road to full mastery. The subsequent acts of using reason to attain "just values" and of submitting to reason's dictates are further crucial steps that advance a person toward full mastery; they are acts which extend our control over our destiny. But how do we overcome prejudice and whatever else is a cause of making reason appear as if it fails us? The answer to that question presupposes clarity on major aspects of the relationship between reason and prejudice.

2. Reason as Destroyer of Prejudice

Two points about the relationship between prejudice and reason are of special importance for my purposes in this section. The *first* concerns

---

1. That phrase is Philip Abrams's, from *John Locke: Two Tracts on Government* (Cambridge, 1967), p. 96.

Locke's doctrine that this relationship is asymmetrical. Although the power of prejudice is very strong it cannot corrupt, let alone destroy reason. Whatever prejudice may do, reason remains as the infallible "touchstone." Although it can prevent the light from shining brightly, prejudice lacks the power to quench the candle of the Lord. Reason, in contrast, can destroy prejudice. The *cause* of the asymmetry in this relationship is central to the *second* point. This point concerns the doctrine that the understanding plays a role in both prejudice and reason. The understanding is, as it were, the bridge from prejudice to rational action. Its presence helps to create the opportunity for the triumph of reason over prejudice. I consider these two points in turn.

First. In the twentieth chapter of Book 4 of the *Essay* Locke deals with the "causes" of "Contrariety of Opinions." In view of his doctrines concerning reason—its universal sameness and its infallibility—it is not surprising to learn that Locke holds that wherever there is contrariety of opinion there is prejudice. Contrariety is therefore an illegitimate state. Wherever it is found, at best one of the opinions can be the correct one. And since contrariety tends to persist, this reveals that the prejudice involved is at least stubborn (how else could it persist in the face of truth?) or stubborn and infecting all parties (why should one prejudice give way in the face of an attack by other prejudices?) Dealing with what Locke takes to be the causes of contrariety will make it clear that the relationship between prejudice and reason is asymmetrical. I devote several pages to this chapter.[2] As I do so I follow Locke's argument in the order he presents it.

The very organization of this twentieth chapter is instructive. Locke identifies and discusses four causes of "Contrariety of Opinions." They are "1. Want of Proofs. 2. Want of Ability to use them. 3. Want of Will to use them. 4. Wrong Measures of Probability" (4.20.1). The first two deal with "wants" that have as their cause *lack of opportunity*; the third and fourth are "wants" that stem from *lack of examination*. Lack of examination is a voluntarily contracted cause of contrariety; in contrast, lack of opportunity is not self-willed.

Lack of opportunity pertains to many a person, primarily in the form of either preoccupation with eking out the means of subsistence, or with

2. Because of the stress on probability throughout 4.20, one might come to think that Locke is dealing only with fields other than that of general knowledge. Such a conclusion would be mistaken, for the chapter's doctrine is at least as much about general as about other forms of knowledge (cf. 4.20.16). Also here, general knowledge includes the area of a person's greatest concern: "Are the current Opinions . . . sufficient Evidence and Security to every Man, to venture his greatest Concernments on; nay, his everlasting Happiness, or Misery?" (4.20.3; see also 4.20.6 and 4.20.10).

natural intellectual limitations. The necessities of life simply make it impossible for many to spend much time in thought (4.20.2–4); and the universality of reason does not preclude differences of ability in the actual use of reason (4.20.5). But in neither case does lack of opportunity eliminate the need, ability, or responsibility to examine and, if called for, go against current opinion in matters of a person's most basic concerns. It is not this involuntary cause that demands most of Locke's attention. He is far more concerned with (and gives much more space to) the voluntary cause, that of lack of examination.

On an initial reading it may seem as if Locke gives short shrift to the self-willed cause, to lack of examination or want of will to use proofs; it may appear as if he reserves only a single paragraph for its discussion (namely, 4.20.6). This appearance is deceptive. In actual fact the cause of want of will is an underlying cause of all wrong measures of probability. And to these wrong measures Locke devotes the rest of the chapter (4.20.7–18). Hence we may take that part of the chapter, which is its largest part by far, as a discussion of specific limitations that flow from lack of examination. It is self-willed when people refuse to examine their own and their society's beliefs and practices. Those who lack opportunity (the ones discussed in the first five paragraphs of the chapter) are not solely culpable for holding at least some of the unexamined beliefs to which they cling; but those who fail to examine are doubly blameworthy. They are responsible for their own prejudices and co-responsible for at least some of the prejudices of others, namely, when they set themselves up as their teachers and guides. Let me now turn to this larger part of the chapter, to the presentation of what Locke writes about this culpable group; it is here (beginning with the sixth paragraph) that we come to see the asymmetrical nature of the relationship between prejudice and reason.

Those who "will not use Proofs" have both the opportunity and the intellectual wherewithal to gain rational insight. They "have Riches and Leisure enough, and want neither Parts nor other helps." But they fear the upheaval that, they rightly suspect, would result from rational inquiry. They want to retain "those Opinions, which best suit their Prejudices, Lives, and Designs, content themselves without examination, to take upon trust, what they find convenient, and in fashion." In other words, they refuse to be the revolutionaries that the life of reason demands. Consequently, they allow themselves to be "subjected" and "enslaved" in their "Understanding." "How Men, whose plentiful Fortunes allow them leisure to improve their Understandings, can satisfy themselves with a lazy Ignorance, I cannot tell." That Locke does not mean what he writes in the last phrase of this statement from 4.20.6 is clear from the following paragraphs, which consist in "telling" "how" this irrational satisfaction comes about.[3] In colorful vignettes the passages relate why people can become "content . . . without examination, to take upon trust" what they find "convenient, and in fashion," or why they refuse to examine what they recognize as having been accepted on trust.

The first tale (4.20.8–10) is about those who as children have become subject to wrong education. They suffered the fate of having been "principled": unexamined propositions were "insinuated into their unwary, as well as unbiass'd Understandings." While children, they were never given the chance to act as a rational being ought to act: "to beware what he admits for a Principle, to examine it strictly, and see whether he certainly knows it to be true of it self by its own Evidence." Propositions that would show up these principles for prejudices, no matter "how clearly soever proved," are likely to meet with a very cool reception from such people when, as adults, they inadvertently come face to face with them. That is because these principles are "riveted" to their understanding "by long Custom and Education beyond all possibility of being pull'd out again." The last part of that sentence is an overstatement that presses home the power of prejudice. It is echoed in the next paragraph: "Whoever therefore have imbibed wrong Principles, are not, in Things inconsistent with these Principles, to be moved by the most apparent and convincing Probabilities." That these are overstatements and are not to be read as freeing such persons from responsibility in these cases, is evident from the continuation of that sentence: "till they are so candid and ingenuous to themselves, as to be persuaded to examine even those very Principles, which many never suffer themselves to do." "Many" refuse reason's call to revolution; many continue to accept what their reason has not authorized. The implication is that none of them *has* to act that way. They all possess the power to free themselves from their bondage to prejudice; none—regardless of the tenacity of the "riveted" prejudices—has had his or her reason destroyed. They all still have the opportunity to be revolutionaries, to be rational, to be (more fully) human.

The second story (4.20.11) is the vivid portrayal of the "learned Professor." This is the kind of person who is in the grip of "a received Hypothesis," that is, of current opinion that has the backing of tradition. The situation of the learned professor is not much different from that of the person who was principled at a very early age. Both tend to be unwilling to examine the principles or hypotheses which rule their

---

3. And much more was already said in the *Essay*, particularly when in 2.21 Locke discussed human freedom.

thought and action. For the bane of the learned is that, once laborious uncritical study of the traditional authorities has led them to accept their principles, all else is to be judged in terms of these principles but these principles themselves are beyond the pale of evaluation. Such principles thus usurp the role of reason: they guide action and their guidance is not to be questioned. Hence the learned professor is unwilling to reason, to be methodical in the rational, revolutionary sense: "And who ever by the most cogent Arguments will be prevailed with, to disrobe himself at once of all his old Opinions, and Pretences to Knowledge and Learning . . . and turn himself out stark naked, in quest a-fresh of new Notions?" But here as well unwillingness is not to be identified with inability. Locke's own experience witnessed to the possibility of "a learned Professor" disrobing himself of "all his old Opinions . . . he hath all his Time been labouring for," of a person confessing that "what he taught his Scholars . . . was all Errour and Mistake." Within six years he himself had switched from the conservative position of his *Two Tracts of Government* to the revolutionary stance that came to be expressed in the *Essay* and the *Two Treatises*, from the scholastic atmosphere of Oxford University to the subversive environment of Shaftesbury's London household. (It is no idle speculation to say that he made the switch through the influence of Descartes's works).[4]

An unwillingness to examine the principles also is evident in the third illustration (4.20.12–16). This is the case of people who, because of especially prevailing passions (for example, being covetous, or in love), either face clear arguments but refuse to submit to their cogency, or refuse to face arguments altogether. In the first instance they escape the force of the arguments by introducing the ruse of "there may be a Fallacy," or of "not yet all that may be said on the contrary side" is known. Either move leaves them uncommitted to the truth and allows them continuation in their old and familiar ways. To remain uncommitted they must deliberately turn their backs on certain arguments. When faced by what is intuitively certain, or what is clearly and briefly demonstrated, or is evidently highly probable, the understanding has no choice but to assent to truth or probability. Once we have been compelled to assent, not to change our ways becomes more difficult (though, as we see in the third part of this chapter, not impossible). But people can avoid the situation of being compelled to assent to the truth because they have "a Power to suspend and restrain" their enquiries and "not permit a full and satisfac-

---

4. See my "Critical Notice of Richard Ashcraft *Revolutionary Politics and Locke's Two Treatises of Government*," part 3 (ii, c; and iii).

tory examination" or not permit any examination at all, "not imploying" their "Faculties in the search of any Truth." All of these stratagems are inspired by "prevailing Passions." All have a single aim: continuation in our accustomed ways based on familiar but uncritically held beliefs. All are inspired by passionately held prejudices. None can be adopted without strenuous exertion of our freedom.

The last of Locke's presentations (4.20.17–18) is more a summation than a new case. It is the widespread submission to various forms of "authority," primarily to the "authority" of one's culture and tradition. What keeps most people "in Ignorance, or Errour," is "the giving up our Assent to the common received Opinions, either of our Friends, or Party; Neighbourhood, or Country." But as we were shown from each of the earlier portrayals, no tenets are ever to be accepted on trust, whether that trust be inspired by the learnedness or honesty of those who promulgate them, or by the fact that they are backed by "the Vote of the Multitude," or that they have enjoyed "the attestation of reverend Antiquity." To assent on any such ground is to abdicate our responsibility as rational beings. That responsibility is: never to be uncritical, always to examine whatever is advocated for acceptance. And as we saw before, rational examination dictates initial rejection.

If we now step back from this chapter of the *Essay*, what stands out clearly is Locke's belief that the power of prejudice is very strong. In addition, what begins to reveal itself is Locke's conviction that the relationship between prejudice and reason is asymmetrical: prejudice does not penetrate or subvert reason, but overshouts the voice of reason, or stops the ears to reason's dictates, or prevents reason from speaking at all. Prejudice cannot penetrate reason and, as it were, make it decay from within. The rational person fears prejudice because prejudice tends to curtail the efficacy of reason. But the prejudiced person fears reason because reason can destroy prejudice and shake the comfort of the uncritical life to its very foundations. The prejudiced person is therefore preoccupied with inventing ruses to prevent the confrontation of prejudice and reason. We see Locke's conviction that there is this asymmetrical relationship illustrated time and again in that part of the *Essay*'s 4.20 where he deals with the self-willed cause of lack of examination as the ground of "Contrariety of Opinions." It is this conviction that leads him to hold individuals responsible for their prejudices. It helps to account for his optimism that impartiality and eventually mastery are within each person's grasp.

The doctrine that prejudice cannot destroy reason, that partiality cannot fully quench "the Candle of the Lord," is not peculiar to this fourth

Book of *Essay*. It appears in its first Book as well. The "candle" can always again be made to shine "bright enough for all our Purposes" (1.1.5), "bright enough" for us to "find out those Measures, whereby a rational Creature . . . in this World, may, and ought to govern his Opinions, and Actions depending thereon" (1.1.6). And it appears in other chapters of Book 4. Locke always acknowledges the power of prejudice to be very strong. He always acknowledges that people often have a passionate interest to adopt and retain certain biases: it is "the desire of Esteem, Riches, or Power" that "makes Men espouse the well endowed Opinions in Fashion, and then seek Arguments . . . to . . . varnish over, and cover their Deformity" (4.3.20). And because "the Parties of Men" often have an unholy interest in cramming "their Tenets down all Men's Throats, whom they can get into their Power, without permitting them to examine their Truth or Falsehood" therefore "the Subject part of Mankind, in most Places, might . . . with Ægyptian Bondage, expect Ægyptian Darkness"—were it not for the indestructability of reason! Humanity might expect the night of lack of liberty and want of mastery "were not the Candle of the Lord set up by [God] himself in Men's minds, which it is impossible for the Breath or Power of Man wholly to extinguish" (ibid.).

The doctrine that prejudice cannot douse the light of reason appears throughout Locke's works. Although important nuances are added elsewhere, basic to whatever further details Locke provides there remains the distinction between the involuntary and self-willed causes of lack of mastery. What remains are the following beliefs: the limitations flowing from the self-willed rather than from the involuntary causes bar the way of human progress toward mastery; that everyone possesses the ability to overcome these limitations; and people always possess freedom sufficient to effect their liberation from bondage to prejudice and sufficient to work at the realization of their rational nature and so to progress on the road of mastery.[5]

Second. We must now become clear about why it is that the relationship between prejudice and reason is asymmetrical, and why prejudice cannot corrupt reason but reason can destroy prejudice. Locke holds that reason has the opportunity to triumph decisively over prejudice because the *understanding* is involved in both prejudiced and rational action. Whenever there is understanding there is at least the flicker of the light of reason; and wherever there is the flicker of that light the possibility exists that it be

5. This last sentence clearly portrays Locke as an Enlightenment thinker. It just as clearly (though this is less often recognized) depicts him as sharing also on this point the position of Descartes. For corroboration of the second point, see my *Descartes and the Enlightenment*, especially chaps. 1, section 2; 2, section 1; 3; and 5, section 1.

blown into full blaze. This function of the understanding as a bridge between prejudiced and rational action now demands our attention.

In order to get this function into clear focus, there is one reminder and one preliminary point to be made. The reminder is this. It is not understanding alone which plays its role in the passage from prejudiced to rational action, since human freedom is equally involved; nevertheless, because freedom is the main topic for the next two chapters, I continue to keep it as much as possible in the background. The preliminary point concerns an important distinction between understanding and reason. It can be drawn by assigning different meanings to the phrases "human understanding" and "human reason."

This distinction, present throughout Locke's works, is not always consistently reflected in the way Locke himself uses "understanding" and "reason." The strict terminological distinction in the remainder of this chapter is therefore mine rather than Locke's. That I have not introduced it before and will sometimes disregard it in following chapters is because Locke frequently uses understanding and reason interchangeably. Had I tried to be terminologically pure before this point, I would only have unnecessarily complicated my exposition; and were I to insist on purity in following chapters, that would often result in awkwardness rather than in clarity. But at this point my exposition demands that I make, and observe, this distinction.

To some extent Locke's own use of "understanding" and "reason" warrant drawing the distinction. For he often speaks of "understanding" when he refers to a mind functioning within the confines of prejudice, and of the activity of reason when he refers to an impartial mind. A person who "has blindly given himself up to the Authority of any Opinion in it self not evidently true" has "a strong biass put into his Understanding" (4.20.8). And "by long Custom and Education" children have unexamined "Propositions . . . insinuated into their unwary, as well as unbiass'd Understandings" (4.20.9). The understanding need not, but can, be infected with prejudice. There are passages where the understanding is spoken of as "impartial," "unbiass'd," and "unprejudiced"; there are, in addition, many where "prejudice" is said to be "riveted" to the understanding, in which the understanding is anything but impartial. I do not know of any passages in which Locke speaks of "prejudiced reason." Sometimes, as in 2.21.53, Locke speaks of "reason unbiased," a phrase that may seem to imply that reason can be either biased or unbiased. I think this type of passage should be read as saying that because of prejudice we sometimes take as pronouncements of (necessarily) unbiased reason what are in actuality deliverances of prejudiced understanding.

Hence although Locke often uses "understanding" and "reason" inter-changeably, there is strictly speaking not meant to be synonymity because the interchangeability holds only in the passages where "understanding" refers to an impartial or unprejudiced mind.

Thus the distinction I want to be observed is that reason is by its nature always unprejudiced while the understanding is sometimes free from prejudice but often not. There is a bit more to the distinction. Employ-ment of the understanding free from prejudice will lead to truth. It is in such employment that "to understand" is often replaced by "to reason." But even then it is not the case that the sentence "I am an understanding being" is interchangeable with "I am a rational being." Knowing the truth through unprejudiced understanding does not necessarily lead to action in accordance with the truth because for Locke truth by itself does not compel one to action. But rational beings know the truth and conform their actions to that knowledge. One might say that, for Locke, rational action incorporates the truth obtained through unprejudiced understand-ing. It is in this way that the understanding is present in rational action. But—in a manner to be explicated in a moment—it is the understanding, and not reason, which is involved in irrational action. This full statement of the distinction between "understanding" and "reason" is to be kept before our minds throughout this section.

We may now turn to the importance of the presence of the understand-ing in prejudiced action. Specifically, we are ready to see how the under-standing can serve as a bridge from prejudiced or irrational to impartial or rational action. This discussion will in part be an elaboration of the distinction just drawn between "understanding" and "reason."

A human being has the choice of only two kinds of action, namely, rational and prejudiced. In either case the behavior in question evinces the presence of the understanding. Apart from the understanding's involve-ment there is no human action at all. This can be quickly established in two ways. (*a*) Only action for which we can be held responsible is human action; we cannot be held responsible if we lack the freedom expressed in the ability to choose between courses of action; the exercise of choosing involves weighing of alternatives, and weighing alternatives is an act of understanding (cf. 2.21.67). (*b*) All human action is willed action, and a person's will is "always determined by that, which is judg'd good by his Understanding" (2.21.56). Either way, we see it as Locke's position that without the understanding there is no human action at all.

There is rational action when people allow their understanding to "consider thoroughly, and examine fairly" (2.21.53) possible courses of action and when they then conduct themselves in accordance with the result of that examination. Prejudiced or irrational action results in part from inadequate use of the understanding. In the case of prejudiced action it still holds that the person's will is "determined by that, which is judg'd good by his Understanding," but the work of the understanding in judgment is then precipitate. The precipitation tends to be caused by prejudices already in place, and leads to an increase in prejudice: "by a too hasty choice of his own making, he has imposed on himself wrong measures of good and evil" (2.21.56).

Because the choice is "of his own making" the implication is that a person need not be imposed upon by prejudice. If insufficiently examined beliefs do inform action, this is ultimately because a person allows or wants them to do so. Thus since no beliefs (whether true or false, adequately or inadequately examined) by themselves compel to action, no one needs to live irrationally. But more important for my argument is that, because the understanding is also necessarily involved in action informed by insufficiently examined beliefs, there is (I can now make clear) always the chance for reason to break through.

In 2.21.67 we read, "How much sloth and negligence, heat and passion, the prevalency of fashion, or acquired indispositions, do severally contribute on occasion, to . . . wrong Judgments, I shall not here farther inquire." We have seen that Locke did inquire further in 4.20, and that the outcome is that whether it is negligence, heat and passion, or fashion, in all these cases what contributes to wrong judgments and hence to partiality in action is something one has adopted. And what has been acquired through adoption can be jettisoned. In the attempt to clear the deck of adopted prejudices, method plays a dominant role. The method in question is that whose articulation we have (in the first chapter) recognized to be a functional definition of reason. To be more precise, it is a functional definition of that part of rational procedure which consists in the analytic and synthetic activities a person must perform to attain knowledge; it does not include that part of rational procedure which consists in acting on the results obtained through analysis and synthesis. That is, method is for Locke a functional definition of the procedure of reason or of *the understanding unfettered by prejudice*. Recognition of this point allows the exact indication of why, in the presence of the understanding, we always have the promise of the breakthrough of reason.

To the extent that the understanding functions at all, it must begin with analysis. Full analysis requires rejection of the truth or bindingness uncritically believed to pertain to whatever confronts the understanding. Such rejection amounts to doing away with whatever initially confronts a person. To the extent that there is analysis at all, there is some degree of rejection. Wherever such rejection occurs there is, by definition, removal of prejudice. And Locke believes that to the extent that we are free from prejudice, we will be able to discern (and hence have the opportunity to act on) truth or goodness. Therefore, adopted prejudice stands in danger of being jettisoned whenever the understanding is brought to bear. For the activity of understanding is the application of the *Essay*'s revolutionary logic.

Any attempt to understand at all threatens some of the prejudices with which the understanding itself may well be infested. Any attempt to free the understanding from prejudice, to allow it to function in an unfettered manner is, to the extent that it is successful, a breakthrough of reason. When we considered the *Essay*'s 4.20, we saw that it is an understanding being who refuses to examine prejudices, who invents ruses in order not to have to confront and "yield to manifest Reasons," who clings tenaciously to "received hypotheses," who suspends and restrains enquiries into what carries the conviction of truth, who "gives up . . . Assent to the common received Opinions." In each of these instances it is an act of will which protects the understanding's prejudices through preventing it from adequate examination. It is an act of will which expresses itself in not yielding, clinging, suspending, restraining or giving up. It is only as a being possessing freedom and understanding that a person can be prejudiced. For prejudiced behavior is deliberate action on the understanding's precipitate judgment; and precipitate judgment results from intentional inadequate use of the understanding. Similarly, it is only as a being possessing freedom and understanding that a person can be rational. For rational behavior is deliberate action on well-considered judgment, and well-considered judgment results from intentional adequate use of the understanding. No free being is absolutely forced to cling tenaciously to received hypotheses. If we so will, we are capable of submitting our opinions to further inquiry, to give them a second (this time more searching) look.

In a sense life itself is against this second look because human beings have become prejudiced from a tender age and their prejudices receive daily reinforcement. There is, however, a sense in which life is also on its side. For there are situations in a person's life which of themselves encourage a second look. For example, as understanding beings, people can hardly fail to notice that "there is nothing more common, than Contrariety of Opinions" (4.20.1). Awareness of this phenomenon may lead them to wonder whether they themselves are prejudiced, whether the action that they believe will lead to their greatest possible happiness does in fact lead there.[6] It is therefore as understanding beings that they can work at the removal of prejudice through allowing their understanding to have a second look at the principles which govern their actions. Since no human action takes place without the involvement of the understanding, a second look is always a possibility. Hence at any point in a person's conscious life reason may break through.

Of course, just because life's vicissitudes encourage a more searching examination, it does not follow that reason's breaking through the bonds of prejudice is a matter of accident. There are two conditions that must be met to attain the state in which we can "consider thoroughly, and examine fairly." Or in words from the *Conduct*, there are two conditions to be met if one is to achieve the "freedom of the understanding which is necessary to a rational creature" (§12). Life's vicissitudes may prompt a person to comply with these conditions. The two conditions—which were at least implicitly with us throughout this section—are (i) "the love of [truth] as truth" rather than as something held dear by our society, and (ii) "the examination of our principles, and not receiving any for such, nor building on them, till we are fully convinced, as rational creatures, of their solidity, truth, and certainty" (ibid.). The first condition requires that we be determined to become epistemically autonomous; the second includes positive action on that determination. The result of that action is the "mastery of mind" which is "freedom of the understanding" (cf. 2.21.53).

The second of these conditions requires not merely an examination of "principles." Whatever comes before the mind needs to be examined. Ultimately, the examination is complete only when whatever is before the mind, is perceived clearly and distinctly. For when, in a later passage of the *Conduct*, Locke restates these two conditions he articulates them as, first, "perfect indifference" and, second, "to fix in the mind clear and distinct ideas of the question stripped of words" (§42). Preoccupation with words (rather than with what these words signify) tends to befuddle the understanding and to lead a person into prejudice. In that position a person is at best impotent, but more often a crusader in an evil cause. When, in contrast, a free understanding attains clear and distinct knowledge, the action based on such knowledge is taken to be action filling genuine needs. Such knowledge therefore gives a person the key to the

6. Hence Locke advises that young Englishmen visit continental Europe. They are to do so at an age when they can benefit from such travel, when they cannot but notice that the sacred doctrine of one place is the heresy of another, and hence can hardly refrain from questioning their own cherished beliefs. See the parallel to this in Descartes's *Discourse on Method* (CSM1, 113–14; AT6, 6).

passage of progress. Right education, though not a sufficient condition for it, can be one part of the process in which these two conditions may be met. For right education places a person in a position which is advantageous for him to become "fully master of his own thoughts" (*Conduct*, §45).

Once fully master of their thoughts, people are no longer subject to prejudice. Their understanding then functions without hindrance and, in the analytic phase of its procedure, refuses to accept anything on trust but attempts to reduce whatever it confronts to clear and distinct terms. Once they are fully master of their thoughts, rational action has the chance of a complete breakthrough and decisive victory. They can then come to see their way as clearly in ethics, politics and religion, as in mathematics (4.3.20). If they then act on the clear precepts that their understanding holds before them, reason triumphs in all of life. Locke believes that it is through this triumph that a human being obtains the full inheritance of mastery.

A person can become "fully master of his own thoughts." The quoted phrase is from the penultimate paragraph of the *Conduct of the Understanding*. It continues with the sentence: "This liberty of mind is of great use both in business and study, and he that has got it will have no small advantage of ease and despatch in all that is the chosen and useful employment of his understanding." Freedom—from prejudice, from mere habitual association of ideas, and from natural passion—is to allow for mastery in theory and in practice.

3. Reason as Servant of Passion

There is, then, an asymmetrical relationship between prejudice and reason in that prejudice can prevent reason from speaking but reason can destroy prejudice. Because prejudiced action always involves the understanding, it is possible for reason to break through and triumph over prejudice. The insight which we have gained on the relationship that Locke believes to exist between reason and prejudice goes some way towards answering the question raised at the end of the first part of this chapter: According to Locke, how do we lay aside prejudice and whatever else is a cause of reason's "failure"? The largest part of the answer is, however, still missing, and most of that cannot be supplied until the discussion of freedom in the next chapter.

But before I focus exclusively on the freedom that allows for the life of reason and for mastery through reason's victory over prejudice, we first need to pause at Locke's doctrine that reason is the servant of passion. This doctrine is of critical significance, for Locke believes that reason by itself is not efficacious because it is passion or desire rather than reason or knowledge that is the motive for action. Instead of stating that we have to be in a position of freedom from passion, this doctrine declares that nothing will be accomplished—no prejudice overcome, no mastery achieved—unless reason serves passion.[7]

This doctrine appears to run counter to what I have said about the relationship between reason and passion. Up to this point it has been freedom from passion that was to allow for mastery. But there are two sets of statements in Locke's writings, and only one of these supports the assertion that he holds freedom from passion to be a condition for the achievement of mastery. That set comprises statements of the kind that our "feeble passionate nature" is an obstacle to the exercise of reason (2.21.67). Such statements occur throughout his works. And since the kind of mastery Locke envisages cannot be attained unless reason is free to play a decisive role, it is statements such as these that warrant the assertion that Locke holds freedom from passion to be a condition for the attainment of mastery.

The first step to be taken in an attempt to remove this apparent conflict is to focus on Locke's distinction between *natural passion* or desire, and *the master passion*. Once that distinction is clear, we can see how there is freedom of the understanding and hence the opportunity for achieving mastery *only while* reason serves passion. One way towards this clarification is to begin with parts from two paragraphs of the *Essay*'s chapter on freedom, namely, 2.21.45 and 46.

> The ordinary necessities of our lives, fill a great part of them with the uneasiness of Hunger, Thirst, Heat, Cold, Weariness with labour, and Sleepiness in their constant returns, etc. . . . absent good, though thought on, confessed, and appearing to be good . . . is jostled out, to make way for the removal of those uneasinesses we feel, till due, and repeated Contemplation has brought it nearer to our Mind, given some relish of it, and raised in us some desire; which then beginning to make a part of our present uneasiness, stands upon fair terms with the rest, to be satisfied. . . . And thus, by a due

---

7. Although, for Locke, passion does not, as it did for Hume, select or decide what is right, nevertheless he is far closer to Hume than is often believed to be the case. See Hume's *Treatise*, II, iii, 3. Once we recognize this, statements such as the following can no longer stand without qualification: "Reason is not and never should be, as Hume was to call it, the slave of the passions. Morality for Locke lies in reversing this relation." (These statements are from John W. Yolton and Jean S. Yolton, eds. *John Locke: Some Thoughts concerning Education* (Oxford, 1989), p. 21.

consideration and examining any good proposed, it is in our power, to raise our desires, in a due proportion to the value of that good.

Human beings are always subject to natural desires aroused by "ordinary necessities." In addition, they tend to be subject to the "acquir'd" or "adopted" desires which Locke calls "fantastical" desires. These are, for instance, the "itch after Honour, Power or Riches . . . which acquir'd habits by Fashion, Example, and Education have settled in us" (2.21.45). For a reason I shall state in a moment, I want to call the master passion an acquired passion. But at the same time I want to distinguish it from both Locke's "natural" and "fantastical" desires. Hence there is an initial terminological problem that will lead to confusion if it is not taken in hand from the outset. I deal with it by arguing that there are grounds for classifying as "natural" the desires which Locke calls "fantastical" and which he characterizes as "acquir'd" or "adopted"; and that on these same grounds the master passion cannot be called "natural" but must be taken to be an "acquired" desire.

When hungry, it is natural for us to be uneasy with the desire for food. It is then natural to be subject to the passion of hope, or fear, or despair: of hope when we believe it likely that we will soon eat, of fear when we think it improbable that food is available, and of despair when we know that food is and will remain unattainable (cf. 2.20.9–11). The circumstances in which we find ourselves cause us to have this hope or fear or despair. No great exertion of freedom and understanding is required to obtain these beliefs and their accompanying passions. They are the results of awareness of our bodily state coupled with awareness of certain relevant conditions in our environment. These beliefs and passions may be called "natural" because they arise more or less automatically.

But the same may be said about the fantastical desires for honor, power, or riches. These desires are natural in the sense that they can come to arise just as near-automatically as the passions of hope or fear or despair when we are hungry. Although the former are "acquir'd habits by Fashion, Example, and Education" they have (says Locke) become habits "which custom has made natural to us" (2.21.45). Because of our upbringing certain desires have become natural to us in the sense that, given a particular situation (for example, one that presents the opportunity to increase power), hope or fear, joy or sorrow, arise without further exercise of freedom or understanding. We then hope because there is power to be grasped or we fear because others may grasp it before we do; we then experience joy because we feel assured that the power is ours for the grasping, and we sorrow because we see others beat us to it (cf. 2.20. 7–10).

Because both these natural and fantastical passions arise as it were automatically, without due, and repeated contemplation of the object of desire that aroused the passion, and without a due consideration and examining of the appropriateness of the passion in this instance, I call both sets "natural." They are "natural" as opposed to "rational." That is to say, they are natural in the sense that they occur without much (if any) exertion of our moral and intellectual powers. Our understanding does of course play its role, for no passions arise unless we are aware of certain irritations or uneasiness. But our awareness is not a thoroughly critical awareness and hence our understanding does not rise to the level of reason. When, insufficiently critical, we act on our "natural" desires, we live a life where our action is determined by the most pressing desire that circumstances happen to arouse in us. We cannot then be said to be in control of our own destiny for we are then ruled by desires that our reason has not authorized.[8]

Contrary to these "natural" passions (in the broad sense in which I now use "natural") there is the master passion. It is not "natural" either in the sense that we are subject to it from the moment of our birth, or in the sense that we come to experience it, as it were, automatically as a result of our physical situation or cultural conditioning. It is an acquired passion whose acquisition demands great exertion of our moral and intellectual powers. Since the master passion is the passion for being in control of our destiny, it is the passion for being ruled only by desires of which our reason has approved. The acquisition of this passion calls for suspension of action on all "natural" desires, for examination of the objects of these desires, and for comparing these objects with that which reason judges to be good. If the desired objects fall short of this good then there must be contemplation of this good until desire for the good comes to displace the "natural" desires so that, as a result, we commit ourselves to action on desires approved by reason. Once this complex process of suspension, examination, judgment, contemplation, and commitment to action on desires approved by our reason has become a process that we carry out as a matter of course in all the vicissitudes in which daily life places us, then we are firmly on the way to establishing ourselves as masters. Then the attitude of a master has become a habit to us. This is a hard-won habit. Our cultural context usually militates against its adoption. For which parent or teacher or institution encourages suspension of action on inculcated desires for the sake of criticism of the objects of these desires, criticism of what they hold dear or true or sacred?

---

8. In fact, we cannot then really be characterized as a "person." Development of this point, too, is better left for the following chapters.

I discuss details of this complex process in the two following chapters. Further details about the precise nature of the master passion can wait till later as well. All I need to establish now is the distinction between natural desires or passions and the master passion. What I now call the "natural" desires are desires of which an individual's reason has not approved. This is not to say that reason could not come to approve of them—perhaps it can, perhaps not. Locke's point is that "natural" desires are desires that have not been before the bar of the individual's reason. In contrast, when we are subject to the master passion, our desires are authorized by reason and we know that it is rational for us to pursue fulfillment of these desires. We know that pursuit of the object of these desires leads to true and lasting happiness. Since the happiness we then procure for ourselves is lasting, this pursuit is an exercise in mastery: it gives us control over our destiny.

We can now see why to say it is passion or desire rather than reason or the understanding that is the motive for action, is not to deny that action necessarily involves reason or understanding. There is no conflict between the doctrine that without the rule of reason there cannot be the kind of action which results in mastery, and the position that reason is not a sufficient motive for action. Locke holds that what motivates one to action is the desire to attain pleasure or avoid pain rather than knowledge of truth or of goodness.[9] That is to say, what motivates one to action is desired happiness. For happiness "is the utmost Pleasure we are capable of, and Misery the utmost Pain: And the lowest degree of what can be called Happiness, is so much ease from all Pain, and so much present Pleasure, as without which any one cannot be content" (2.21.42). In such desire, and in the action it motivates, either (unprejudiced) reason or (more or less prejudiced) understanding is necessarily involved. Whichever it is, its role is that of servant rather than of master. It serves in the attempt to discern where happiness lies, that is, it serves the motivating force of desire or passion for happiness.

It is happiness, rather than the good, that "every one constantly pursues, and desires what makes any part of it" (2.21.43). In practice, therefore, what is known as good is neglected if what is taken to lead to happiness conflicts with action constituting pursuit of the good. Individuals "may have a clear view of good, great and confessed good, without being concern'd for it, or moved by it, if they think they can make up their happiness without it" (ibid.). "For all that we desire is only to be Happy" (2.21.71). It is this "general desire of happiness" which "operates con-

---

9. An exploration of implications of this statement that I leave undiscussed may be found in John W. Yolton's "Action and Agency," the sixth chapter of his *Locke and the Compass of Human Understanding* (Cambridge, 1970).

stantly and invariably in us" (ibid.). Locke calls it a general desire because it operates constantly and invariably; but as the rest of his sentence makes clear, this general desire can manifest itself only through particular desires. To make use of my earlier terminology: this general desire should not be called a "natural desire" as distinct from an acquired "rational desire." For it sometimes manifests itself as "natural desire" while at other times it expresses itself in the form of "rational desire."

This dominant, general desire for happiness ought to have reason (rather than prejudiced understanding) for its servant. Locke makes it clear that it is not a matter of course that reason is in fact its servant. Once reason does serve it, the general desire of happiness has become the master passion. Only once the general desire of happiness has become the master passion can this general desire come to its highest degree of satisfaction. For only true and lasting happiness can fully satisfy this desire, and only reason is capable of finding the path to this greatest good of true and lasting happiness. When our passion is served by our reason, we live a morally upright life and achieve a high degree of mastery. We then have a good deal of control over our destiny, for we then cannot fail to acquire lasting temporal happiness and we are assured of eternal bliss (cf. 4.12.11).

This high degree of mastery presupposes the mastery of our mind that allows us to consider thoroughly, and examine fairly alternative desires and courses of action. It demands, in other words, freedom from prejudice. When that demand is not met, mastery is beyond reach. Locke is well aware of the fact that many of his contemporaries fail to meet that demand: he writes about those who "think they can make up their happiness" "without being concerned for" "great and confessed good." The distinction between understanding and reason, as well as that between natural passion and master passion, helps us to see what is at stake in actions such as theirs. In such actions it is the understanding which plays the servant's role. The understanding is then necessarily involved because unless one believes that a course of action will diminish pain or augment pleasure, it will not be consciously pursued. But this understanding is not the unfettered understanding or reason; some prejudice or other is allowed to prevent it from thorough and fair examination. In such actions we are not fully master of our own mind. We then achieve at best limited, ephemeral satisfaction of our desire for happiness because our understanding then guides passion along a path which (more likely than not) diverges from that in which the greatest good may be successfully pursued.[10]

10. The distinction between understanding and reason only helps to see in part why a person can come to believe that pursuit of "great and confessed good" conflicts with achievement of happiness. Again, it is the account of freedom which is needed to complete the picture.

Locke takes the general desire of happiness to be an original aspect of human nature. He believes that without it there would be nothing that would identify a creature as peculiarly human. In various places Locke refers to the doctrine that lies behind this feature of his thought. The phrase "this desire operates constantly and invariably in us" is itself a hint at it. There is a reference to it as well when, apropos his definition of "desire" ("The uneasiness a Man finds in himself upon the absence of any thing, whose present enjoyment carries the Idea of Delight with it, is that we call Desire") he says that "uneasiness" is "the chief if not only spur to humane Industry and Action" (2.20.6). The doctrine is stated most clearly in the *Essay's* 2.7.2–4:

> Delight, or Uneasiness, one or other of them join themselves to almost all our Ideas, both of Sensation and Reflection. . . . By Pleasure and Pain, I would be understood to signifie, whatsoever delights or molests us; whether it arises from the thoughts of our Minds, or any thing operating on our Bodies. . . . The infinite Wise Author of our being . . . has been pleased to join to several Thoughts, and several Sensations, a perception of Delight. If this were wholly separated from all our outward Sensations, and inward Thoughts, we should have no reason to preferr one Thought or Action, to another; Negligence, to Attention; or Motion, to Rest. And so we should neither stir our Bodies, nor employ our Minds; but let our Thoughts (if I may so call it) run a drift, without any direction or design; and suffer the Ideas of our Minds, like unregarded shadows, to make their appearances there, as it happen'd, without attending to them. In which state Man, however furnished with the Faculties of Understanding and Will, would be a very idle unactive Creature, and pass his time only in a lazy lethargick Dream. . . . Pain has the same efficacy and use to set us on work, that Pleasure has.

This passage ought not to lead us to the conclusion that, for Locke, any pleasure is as good as another, so that the distinction between "natural desire" and the desire for mastery would be of little or no importance. Locke does not take the human being to be the kind of hedonic creature who lives for, and by, the avoidance of any pains and the pursuits of any pleasures which any particular thoughts and sensations might afford. If such a conclusion were to be drawn from it, this passage would make nonsense of Locke's talk of freedom of the understanding, of not being captive to the opinions in fashion. For at least in the short run it is often if not always risky or painful rather than profitable or pleasurable to go against the opinions in fashion. Little if anything would be left of the freedom of the understanding if all the understanding is called upon to do is to determine in any one situation which action maximizes its particular pleasure or minimizes its particular pain. What Locke has to say about happiness should quickly dispell all suspicions that he might be propounding a doctrine of individualistic, relativistic hedonism. He holds that our greatest satisfaction results from the pursuit of "real Happiness" (2.21.49–52) and that we can never achieve real happiness except through the pursuit of the true good. His view of real happiness and of its pursuit requires the role of reason. Given Locke's view of reason (its universal uniformity and infallibility) the role of reason as servant precludes advocacy of relativistic hedonism. Such hedonism would fit Locke's position only if he allowed that a biased understanding could adequately serve the passion for mastery.

We can now see how Locke relates reason, passion, and the ideal of mastery. We can be successful at achieving mastery only to the extent that we are free from prejudice. The constant presence of the desire to gain pleasure and avoid pain coexists with a rational nature that demands a critical stance to all proffered pleasures and threatening pains in any particular situation. The only life a human being can live is that of a passionate, constantly desiring creature. But the only desires of which a truly human life allows satisfaction in the course of the particular situations that constitute such a life, are those authorized by reason. Thus Locke's stress on ubiquitous desire does not abrogate his position that people ought to live compelled by reason.[11]

Locke holds that it is in a life compelled by reason that the ideals of both autonomy and mastery come to their proper expression. A life compelled by reason is a life free from prejudice. Freedom from prejudice is one expression of autonomous existence. It is existence directed neither by unexamined traditional or contemporary beliefs, nor by the unexamined immediate desires that arise from particular pleasures or pains experienced at the moment. It is existence in which beliefs and desires are examined by each individual's unprejudiced understanding, by the intellectual power whose revolutionary procedure is that articulated in the "logic" of the *Essay*. We know that, in its analytic phase, the understanding's examination of beliefs requires their reduction to the simplest possible elements and that this reduction is tantamount to their initial rejection. Prior to the examination of a desire, action on the desire must be suspended, so that the desire does not at that time constitute a motivating force. In either

11. We met this position at the end of Chap. 2, section 3. It is a position hardly peculiar to Locke, for it is one he shares with Descartes as well as with thinkers of the eighteenth century. The position is, in fact, typically part of the Enlightenment stance.

case—that is, both in the rejection of belief and in the suspension of desire—individuals have the chance to start de novo. They have the opportunity to accept as true only such beliefs as their own reason authorizes, and to be motivated only by such desires as their own reason has sanctioned. Hence Locke's belief that the ideal of autonomy comes to its proper expression in a life compelled by reason.

In a life compelled by reason the ideal of mastery is to come to expression through implementation of individual autonomy. It is mastery over prejudice and over the particular hedonic pressures of the moment that are to allow us mastery of our fate through presenting us with the opportunity of adopting only rational beliefs and allowing only rational desires to motivate us to action. Such mastery is to procure for us the greatest possible temporal happiness as well as eternal bliss.

The story is far from complete. What I have presented in these three chapters on "Reason and the Nature of a Master" is Locke's position on the nature and role of reason, with special focus on important relationships that are said to hold between reason on the one hand and prejudice, passion and mastery on the other. Particularly significant was the notion of freedom of the understanding or mastery of one's mind. But nothing has so far been said on how, precisely, this freedom can come about. Yet upon its very existence depends the possibility of human autonomy, of a life compelled by reason, of achievement of the ideal of mastery. We may be born to be masters, but it is becoming more and more clear that there is nothing automatic about our achievement of mastery. It is therefore time to turn to Locke's doctrine of freedom. The idea of "freedom of the understanding" will be found to be an important dimension of this doctrine.

B

Freedom and the Nature of a Master

Apart from reason and freedom we cannot achieve mastery. That reason plays so crucial a role has been established in the three preceding chapters. In the process we often came across assertions that freedom occupies a place as important as that of reason. Thus I have claimed that throughout his works Locke characterizes human beings as, no matter how beset with prejudice, always possessing sufficient freedom to liberate themselves from prejudice, to work at the realization of their rational nature, and so to progress on the way of mastery. It is now time to support the statement that human freedom plays this necessary role.

We became acquainted with Locke's doctrines that human beings are creatures of desire and that to act on inadequately examined desires or on mere natural passion traps them in the web of prejudice. My support for the statement that freedom plays as crucial a role as reason will take the form of discussing the statements that human beings possess an original freedom that enables them to deny themselves the satisfaction of such desires as their reason has not authorized, that they can replace their natural passion with a passion for mastery. In the process of these discussions I will have opportunities to augment what I have said about the role of reason. Hence the next two chapters will allow me to complete my discussion of the joint necessity of freedom and reason for the achievement of mastery.

To the extent that they are hampered by prejudice people fail to secure mastery. No mastery is achieved except in a life whose acts are authorized by reason. One important question of Part A was: How does a person lay aside prejudice, the cause of reason's "failure"? To this question the two following chapters give a fuller answer than I could so far provide. We shall see that this question leads to another one: How do we keep ourselves from the kind of behavior which gives prejudice power over us, that is, how do we keep from acting on our natural passions, on unexamined or inadequately examined desires? That is the major question of the first of these two chapters. In the second, discussion will be guided by a more basic question yet: Is a person in fact able to lay aside prejudice and hence capable of keeping from action on unexamined or inadequately examined desires?

In these two chapters my major source of Locke's views is the *Essay*'s 2.21, the chapter on freedom. Whenever I refer to or quote from it in these chapters, the reference gives simply the paragraph rather than the book, chapter, and paragraph (e.g., "§70" rather than "2.21.70").

∾5

Freedom and Unobstructed Action

There is much confusion about Locke's position on freedom. Perhaps the most important source of this confusion is Fraser's copious footnotes to Locke's discussion of freedom in the *Essay*'s chapter 21, "Of Power." For a long time Fraser's edition of the *Essay* was the complete edition most readily available to the twentieth century; and even today we sometimes find it listed in bibliographies of recent books as if it were still the only complete text on the market.[1] For decades readers were confronted with footnotes to "Of Power" which "clarified" the text in a way which depicted Locke as a "naturalist," as a "determinist" for whom talk of freedom only obscured the fact that human beings are in all their actions determined by material causes.

Fraser is hardly alone in portraying Locke as a determinist. He is joined by authors such as Berlin and Passmore. I believe them to be wrong on this point. Since their writings continue to be influential, I need to state some of the details of their view in the first part of the chapter.

Careful attention to Locke's text reveals his position that a human being can be free, that a person can be the author of decisions and need not merely be "the locus of causal summation for external influences," that

---

1. See, e.g., Daniel C. Dennett, *Elbow Room: The Varieties of Free Will Worth Wanting* (Oxford, 1984), p. 179. Fraser's edition was first published by Oxford University Press in 1894. A Dover edition came on the scene in 1959. It ought to have been made redundant by the far less tendentious edition of John W. Yolton (Everyman's Library, London and New York, 1961) and should certainly have been totally eclipsed by that of Nidditch (Oxford, 1975).

there are areas in which choice is not determined by biological, psychological or other natural causes. However, Locke denies that a person's physically unobstructed behavior that is not directed by reason is an instance of free action (he would, as we shall see, object to the words "person," "free" and "action" in that sentence). He also denies that a person's unobstructed action that is guided by the outcome of an inadequate examination carried out by a prejudiced understanding is an instance in which freedom comes to full expression. In the latter situation, as a result of prejudice, there are elements of subjectivism and relativism which, Locke believes, keep a person from full freedom. I am concerned with these denials in the second and third sections of this chapter. These denials point to what Locke affirms to be the case, namely, that a human being can be free, and is free when there is unobstructed action guided by reason. I state some of the implications of this doctrine in the fourth part.

1. Man Is "A Part of the Mechanism of Nature"

"How can a person be an author of decisions, and not merely the locus of causal summation for external influences?" This is one of the questions on Daniel Dennett's list of "questions composing the free will problem."[2] Dennett's question is central to Locke's "Of Power." And Dennett's answer, which gives "the libertarians the materials out of which to construct an account of personal authorship of moral decisions," is a part of Locke's answer. Moreover, his path to that answer coincides for at least some distance with the way Locke traveled. Dennett writes that

> the model I propose points to the multiplicity of decisions that encircle our moral decisions and suggests that in many cases our ultimate decision as to which way to act is less important phenomenologically as a contributor to our sense of free will than the prior decisions affecting our deliberation process itself: the decision, for instance, not to consider any further, to terminate deliberation; or the decision to ignore certain lines of inquiry.[3]

It is at this level of "prior decisions affecting our deliberation process itself" that Locke also places some of the weight of his argument.

Dennett has been influenced by Locke.[4] This kind of influence (one

2. See Daniel C. Dennett, "On Giving Libertarians What They Say They Want," which is the fifteenth chapter of his *Brainstorms: Philosophical Essays on Mind and Psychology* (Hassocks, U.K. 1978), reprinted 1981. My quotations are from pp. 286–87 and 298.

3. *Brainstorms*, p. 297.

4. In his later work *Elbow Room*, this influence (and some more of its details) becomes explicit. See pp. 36 and 86.

leading to the defense of libertarianism) though not unique is nevertheless surprising. There is a barrage of opinion that would (and no doubt often does) prevent a correct understanding of Locke because it places him among those who deny that a person can be "an author of decisions" and who assert that a person is "merely the locus of causal summation for external influences." Among writings which perpetuate this view are those of Berlin, Fraser, Passmore, Aaron, and Clapp.[5] In order to be able to remove this barrier we should be somewhat familiar with its details. I therefore present what is said about Locke on freedom by the first three of these: by Berlin (because he epitomizes much of the current often off-handed presentation of Locke as a determinist), by Fraser (because he believes that "Of Power" provides sufficient grounds for reading Locke as a determinist), and by Passmore (because he applies this deterministic interpretation to Locke's educational writings).

Before I present their critiques and my attempts to show that these do injustice to Locke's text, I should state how, in these two chapters, I approach "Of Power." Locke revised this chapter of the *Essay* for each of the four editions following the first. When Molyneux objected that the brief account of freedom in the first edition was unsatisfactory Locke agreed and expanded the chapter to incorporate a doctrine that, though restated with greater clarity in subsequent editions, remained basically unchanged. This is the doctrine of libertarianism. In my exposition, I will not state Locke's original position of the first edition and show how the second edition goes beyond it. Neither will I retard the progress of my exposition through details about how subsequent editions subtly clarify the second one. Instead, I will use what Locke left us as his considered and final presentation in the form of "Of Power" as it is now before us in the text Locke wanted us to read when he prepared the fifth edition. That text I will read as sympathetically as possible, throughout attempting to do justice to Locke's intention that—so, I believe, a careful reading of this text will reveal—was to present a consistent libertarian doctrine. As opposed to Fraser's reading (or for that matter, to a forthcoming nuanced and sophisticated version of it such as Vere Chappell's) I find no incompatibility between Locke's early-stated doctrine of a "determined will" and his subsequently introduced tenet of a "power of suspension." A prima facie ground for the plausibility of my reading is the fact that Locke did

---

5. Aaron holds Locke to be a determinist in both the first and second editions of the *Essay*. See his *John Locke*, 3d ed., pp. 268–89. J. G. Clapp, in the *Encyclopedia of Philosophy*, ed. Paul Edwards (New York, 1967), asserts that Locke leaves the issue of freedom and determinism unresolved; see his "Locke, John," 4: 495. Both these treatments are inadequate but, if only because of their ready accessibility, they help to spread the mistaken view of Locke as a determinist or, at least, as one who could not escape determinism.

allow both doctrines to stand together from the second through the fifth editions. I intend to show that the text supports my reading of the joint assertion of these doctrines without contradiction. It is not as if in this venture I tread new ground: as Chappell has pointed out, some of Locke's earliest followers read him in precisely this way.[6]

In his *Four Essays on Liberty*[7] Berlin advances his own view in juxtaposition to that of the determinist when he writes:

> If my choice is itself the result of antecedent causes, I am, in the relevant sense, not free. Freedom to act depends not on absence of only this or that set of fatal obstacles to action—physical or biological, let us say—while other obstacles, e.g. psychological ones—character, habits, "compulsive" motives, etc.—are present; it requires a situation in which no sum total of such causal factors wholly determines the result—in which there remains some area, however narrow, within which choice is not completely determined.

The "determinists" who particularly incur Berlin's wrath are the "British empiricists . . . and their modern followers," for their views make "the concept of worth and desert" contentless. Berlin places Locke on his list of British empiricists and, without argument or textual support for this inclusion, identifies him as one of those to be held culpable:

> The majority of determinists . . . hold that I normally praise or blame a man only if, and because, I think that, what occurred was (or might at any rate in part be) caused by his choice or the absence of it; and should not praise or blame him if his choices, efforts, etc., were conspicuously unable to affect the result that I applaud or deplore; and that this is compatible with the most rigorous determinism, since choice, effort, etc., are themselves causally inevitable consequences of identifiable spatio-temporal antecedents. This (in substance the classical "dissolution" of the problem of free will by the British empiricists—Hobbes, Locke, Hume, and their modern followers Russell, Schlick, Ayer, Nowell-Smith, Hampshire, etc.) does not seem to me to solve the problem, but merely to push it a step further back.

6. For V. C. Chappell's reading of this chapter of the *Essay* see his "Locke on the Freedom of the Will," *British Journal for the History of Philosophy* 1 (1992). The early followers he mentions as seeing "no conflict between the doctrine of suspension and the rest of the Lockean theory of freedom" are Anthony Collins (*Philosophical Inquiry concerning Human Liberty*, in J. O'Higgins, *Determinism and Freewill* [The Hague, 1976], pp. 73–74) and Jonathan Edwards (*Careful and Strict Enquiry into the . . . Freedom of the Will . . .* , ed. Paul Ramsey [New Haven, Conn., 1957], p. 210).

7. Isaiah Berlin, *Four Essays on Liberty*, (Oxford, 1969). My two quotations are from the lengthy strategically situated footnote on pp. 64–65, and from p. 146.

The problem is pushed back to the spatio-temporal antecedents, to up-bringing, education, social status, character, and habits. At this level the question about freedom must be asked once again. And the answer is that, although all of these may be contributing factors to choice and subsequent overt action, none of them alone nor all of them together fully explain choice and action: "there remains some area, however narrow, in which choice is not completely determined." That is Berlin's position. Un-known to him, it is a position that he shares with Locke. Both of them are libertarians; thus neither of them is a determinist, not even a "soft deter-minist" or "compatibilist," that is, a thinker for whom actions are both necessary and free—even though this is precisely Berlin's reading of Locke.[8] Their communality of outlook exists not just in the abstract statement, "choice is not completely determined"; it includes some of the important details which give concreteness to this statement.

One theme of Locke's *Essay* is that freedom is to be realized in the progressive elimination of arbitrariness from human action through the rejection of behavior that is determined by purely fortuitous pleasure. In "Of Power" this theme is expressed in the thesis that freedom calls for the elimination of obstacles when these obstacles consist in the resistance of a person's passions not approved by reason. This theme finds its reflection in the *Second Treatise*. Peter Laslett (who is not one of those imputing determinism to Locke) has written about this treatise that in it "Locke's theory of freedom" can be defined "positively as the progressive elimina-tion of the arbitrary [that is, the non-rational] from political and social regulations."[9] These more concrete statements about freedom come close to what Berlin says the "rationalist" (rather than the "empiricist") means by "freedom." And this "rationalist" view is one for which Berlin has considerable sympathy. The "rationalist," he writes, sees freedom as "self-mastery, the elimination of obstacles to my will, whatever these obstacles may be—the resistance of nature, of my ungoverned passions, of irrational institutions, of opposing wills or behaviour of others."

8. In "Locke on the Freedom of the Will," Chappell discusses this view of Locke as "compatibilist," arguing that for Locke "all human actions are causally determined, and hence all free actions are." In these two chapters, I intend to show that underlying the actions discussed by Fraser and Chappell there can be, according to Locke, actions which are absolutely undetermined, that it is their presence which characterizes other actions as "free" in an "incompatibilist" non-determinist sense and that it is their absence which precludes such freedom and results in ("hard" not "soft") determinism, i.e., that their presence is co-extensive with the existence of a (for Locke) truly human being and that their absence results in this being's loss of its humanity through the resulting incorporation in the "mechanism of nature."

9. "Introduction" to *Two Treatises*, p. 125.

Berlin is here still caught in the traditional but (as is now widely accepted) largely indefensible juxtaposition of "rationalist" and "empiricist." That is one cause of his not recognizing the affinity of his own position with Locke's. Perhaps another factor is the assumption that offspring resembles the parent in all important respects. Even if it were true that Locke is the father of British empiricism and philosophers such as Russell and Ayer are his distant progeny, this is insufficient ground for concluding that Locke's view on freedom closely resembles that of later thinkers whom he influenced in many other respects.

The authority enjoyed by statements such as these from Berlin, most likely derives at least in part from Fraser's edition of the *Essay*,[10] an edition that may have been one of the sources of Berlin's attitude toward Locke. Its annotations to "Of Power" certainly set the stage for Berlin's pronouncement to be accepted as non-controversial. In these notes Fraser presents Locke as a vacillating[11] thinker who dearly wanted to preserve human freedom but who found himself forced into half-hearted determinism by the tendency of other doctrines to which he was already committed.

According to Fraser, Locke is thoroughly deterministic in the first half of "Of Power." Notions such as "uneasiness," "pleasure," "pain," and "desire" are all applied to the agent in such a way that "the so-called 'agent' is himself, in each particular 'act' of willing, ultimately the passive subject of a natural necessity consequent upon 'uneasiness'; he is merged in nature, and is not the agent of the action that is nominally his" (note to §29). All desire, says Fraser, is purely natural, and volition is nothing but "the natural effect of the *dominant* uneasiness or desire of the moment. Volition is *victorious* desire"; "volition however deliberate, is . . . *desire* only." Hence Fraser concludes that Locke makes "volition an issue of the physical system, and man, even in the deepest root of his being, a part of nature" (notes to §§30, 31).

---

10. References to and quotations from Fraser's notes are all to the Dover edition of 1959.

11. "Naturalism, or the universal applicability of physical causation, as an adequate account of the voluntary determinations of spiritual agents, equally with events in the material world, notwithstanding his vacillations, is Locke's *implied* principle." Note 1 to §74 (p. 372). In "Locke on Freedom of the Will" Chappell takes the position that if Locke was "vacillating" in the second through fourth editions of the *Essay* he certainly made up his mind when he prepared the fifth edition for publication, for he then "repudiated" his earlier determinism and, through accentuation of "the doctrine of suspension," took up the position of the libertarian. My argument in these two chapters will be that, from the second edition through the fifth, because he was a libertarian throughout, there was neither "vacillation" nor "repudiation" on this score—which is of course not to say that there was no progressive clarification, sometimes through deletions and more often through additions.

In view of the contents Fraser gives to these various concepts and of the way he relates them, it becomes clear that he will run into difficulty with passages in the second half of "Of Power," especially with those where Locke relates "the deepest root" of human beings to their ability to suspend action on desires. Locke there argues that it is through suspension of desire that merely natural desire can come to be replaced by rational desire. What Fraser refuses to admit is that, because it is authorized by reason, the desire which then comes to determine action is a new desire which must be taken as different from the merely natural desire which we at first experienced. Fraser does not allow the distinction between natural and rational desire. Hence he cannot admit Locke's doctrine that it is only once our "victorious desires" are desires that reason has sanctioned that we have escaped the realm of natural necessity and live the life of moral beings. Fraser anticipates passages in which this doctrine appears and attempts to cover his position against their force:

> "Freedom" in willing would thus consist in a man being naturally deter-
> mined to will by his desire or feeling of uneasiness, guided by his judgment,
> and volition is based upon capacity for being made uneasy. He afterwards
> qualifies this (§§48–53) by *inconsistently* claiming for "free agents" power to
> "suspend" volition, pending deliberation, thus mixing the natural passivity
> with a *semblance* of moral superiority to this. (Note to §31, in which I have
> substituted my italics for Fraser's.)

There is, then, according to Fraser, only a semblance of human freedom in the *Essay*. The explicit admission in this passage is important: the second part of Locke's account in "Of Power" is inconsistent with the first. Since Fraser takes the first part to be thoroughly deterministic, one may venture the guess that if the second part were separate from the first, Fraser would there find an incomplete account that, as far as it goes, does justice to what he takes to be necessary to human freedom because it allows for an area in which choice is not determined by natural causes.

From the mid-point in "Of Power" Fraser has two options. The one is to reconsider his interpretation of the first half in view of the fact that it produced a reading he recognizes to be inconsistent with the doctrine of the second half. The other is to bring the second half in line with what he takes to be the naturalism of the first half. It is the latter option which he adopts. And so we read in his notes to paragraph 48:

> Free agency with Locke thus consists at last in "power to suspend" volition.
> But unless in this man rises above a merely natural causation of motives, he is
> no more ethically free in suspending the voluntary execution of a desire than

in any other exercise of will. A power to suspend volition, necessarily thus dependent, leaves man still a part of the mechanism of nature.

This recognition of power in the agent to "suspend" conversion of desire into will is the nearest approach Locke makes to recognition of the spiritual freedom that is supernatural. But after all, on his premises, the suspension must be the natural issue of uneasiness.

Even by themselves these notes betray the forced reading of Locke's text. The reason why suspension "must" be the "natural" result of uneasiness is that what Fraser takes to be Locke's premises (that is, the first half of "Of Power") dictate it. That they do not really do so we shall see in the next chapter. In the course of its argument I shall be able to do justice to the parts of the text (particularly those about suspension and self-determination) that Fraser either neglects, gives a forced reading, or pronounces to be inconsistent with Locke's "premises."[12]

If we take Locke to be a determinist and then read his works on education with this belief in mind, the resulting picture is one of Locke as holding that nurture is of ultimate importance, that habituation accounts for a person's moral worth (or lack thereof), and that achievement of mastery in all domains of life depends entirely on proper training. This, as we have seen, is Passmore's view of Locke. It fits well with his belief that, for Locke, "man has no nature at all," that neither reason nor freedom are in any way original to the individual, that it is education which makes a human being both rational and free. When we examined these beliefs to the extent that they concerned human reason,[13] we already found that the passages from Locke's *Education* on which Passmore based them were unable to bear their weight. A few additional comments are now in order especially about freedom.

Passmore gives it as Locke's position that "we become free, capable of resisting our desires, by habituation, we are not born free by nature."[14] Habituation or education becomes all-important also in the realm of morals: "education is the secular equivalent of supervenient grace, in that it creates in us the will to be good."[15] This "freedom," this "will to be good," totally embedded as it is in the habits which scientifically designed education has inculcated, is a freedom that is scientifically explicable as a freedom acquired through a certain kind of natural development. All that

---

12. For a partial substantiation of these charges, see Fraser's notes to §49, n. 3; §52, n. 1; §53, nn. 1 and 2; §57, n. 5; §72, n. 3; §73, n. 1; §74, n. 4 on p. 369–70, and n. 1 on p. 372.
13. See Chap. 2, section 3.
14. In "The Malleability of Man," p. 23.
15. Ibid., p. 26.

is original, says Passmore, is "Ultimately no more than this: the human tendency (the only innate tendency) to avoid pain and pursue pleasure."[16]

It is certainly correct to say that Locke holds the pursuit of pleasure and the avoidance of pain to be natural and original tendencies. With respect to them, to speak about freedom makes little sense, for these natural tendencies humans share with animals. If we here speak of "freedom" at all, it is the "freedom" that consists merely in the fact that there is physically unobstructed behavior. What Locke holds to be peculiarly human is the *rational* pursuit of happiness. It presupposes both reason and freedom as powers innate to the individual. These are powers that can be developed (or stifled) only in human beings; animals do not possess them. They can be developed, not created, in a person: one cannot "create in him the will to be good"—at least not in the sense of a creation where there is at first nothing within so that all of it comes from without.

Passmore's reading of Locke on freedom would gain plausibility if Locke had conflated "original" and "initial." It is true that Locke does not hold a human being to be free from the time of birth.[17] But in the "moral" sense (which is the sense here intended by both Passmore and myself) a creature is, strictly speaking, not even human at birth. For a human being in the moral sense is a corporeal rational being (again, see *Essay* 3.11.16). In the moral sense the creature is born only potentially human: initially it is neither rational nor free. But it is so originally, in the sense that Locke holds reason and freedom to be original to each individual: they come from within, not from without. Apart from this original freedom Locke holds that it makes as little (or as much) sense to call a human being's unobstructed behavior "free" as it is to speak of the "freedom" of the untethered horse to amble across a common.

We have now met three writers who hold that Locke is a determinist or at the very best a "compatibilist": Berlin, who without argument places Locke in the ranks of those for whom "choice" and "effort" are "causally inevitable consequences of identifiable spatio-temporal antecedents"; Fraser, who argues that in Locke's "Of Power" a human being does not "rise above a merely natural causation of motives" and hence is "a part of the mechanism of nature"; and Passmore, whose assumption that Locke is a determinist helps to explain his mechanistic interpretation of Locke's educational theory. In each case, I have given some reason for my belief that their positions are wrong. Whether I am correct in rejecting their views will now have to be more firmly established through careful atten-

16. Ibid.
17. This we saw well enough in Chap. 2, section 3.

tion to what Locke actually says in "Of Power." This part of my exposition is important for countering those who hold Locke to be a determinist, but it is also needed because, although the most recent well-known studies (those of Dunn and Yolton) present Locke as a libertarian, they (much like Berlin) do not attempt to establish the correctness of that assumption either.[18]

As I now turn to "Of Power" we must keep in mind my limited aim for this chapter. It involves consideration of the question: How according to Locke do we keep ourselves from behaving merely naturally? Berlin, Fraser and Passmore either fail to ask, or fail to do justice to, this question because they believe its antecedent—*that* we can keep ourselves from mere natural behavior—not to be a part, or not to be a legitimate part, of Locke's position. In the remainder of this chapter both this question and its antecedent will occupy center stage. But the critical issue of whether, given Locke's doctrine, a person is in fact able to transcend mere natural behavior will be left for the next chapter.

2. Unobstructed Action Not Determined by Reason

Attentive reading of Locke's discussion of freedom reveals his conclusion that a human being is naturalistically determined unless guided by reason; or more positively, that there is freedom, truly human action, whenever a person's reason guides. But if "Of Power" is read with less than the great care it demands, then it may leave the impression that a human being is always naturalistically determined, never free. This impression then arises because Locke writes repeatedly of "uneasiness" or "desire" as the only stimulus to action. The headings of paragraphs 35, 36 and 37, for example, respectively state that "The greatest positive good determines not the will, but uneasiness," "Because the removal of uneasiness is the first step to happiness," "Because uneasiness alone is present." In these headings (as in their corresponding paragraphs) there is no mention of reason as a determining force. Hence they may seem to imply that freedom beyond that which naturalists would allow is not a part of Locke's view.

18. See John Dunn's *Locke*, pp. 64 and 69. Although in Yolton's *Locke: An Introduction*, it is assumed throughout that Locke is a libertarian, the closest Yolton comes to arguing for this assumption is on p. 115, where he simply quotes Locke's "characterization" of "freedom" in the "terms" of 2.21.8. This "characterization" is then followed by the statement that the "power . . . of persons to be free agents . . . turns out to be an important ingredient in Locke's account of the world."

Statements from other parts of the *Essay* may well reinforce this impression. For example, echoing passages I discussed in the preceding chapter,[19] Locke writes in 2.20.6 that "the chief if not only spur to humane Industry and Action is uneasiness." Hence when he asks "What determines the Will?" the answer presents no surprise: "The motive to change, is always some uneasiness: nothing setting us upon the change of State, or upon any new Action, but some uneasiness" (§29). Locke's doctrine may thus seem to contain only the following as its elements: no human action occurs without the stimulus of uneasiness or desire; the kind of action pursued depends on the kind of desire present; the desire itself comes about through awareness of something lacking that if it were obtained would "carry the Idea of Delight with it" (or in other words, desire is aroused by an expectation of "happiness and that alone") (§41); happiness "in its full extent is the utmost Pleasure we are capable of, and Misery the utmost Pain" (§42); and "what has an aptness to produce Pleasure in us, is that we call Good, and what is apt to produce Pain in us, we call Evil, for no other reason, but for its aptness to produce Pleasure and Pain in us, wherein consists our Happiness and Misery" (ibid.). They easily fit the view we just met: Locke has no room for a situation "in which choice is not completely determined"; his doctrine leaves one "a part of the mechanism of nature."

I have now introduced the following as key concepts of Locke's doctrine: (*a*) will, (*b*) uneasiness or desire, (*c*) pleasure and pain, happiness and misery, good and evil. An attempt to become clear on how, for Locke, these concepts function in their interrelationships with one another, will introduce concepts which have not yet come into their own in this context. Once they come to play the role Locke intended for them, we will see that Locke means his position to be neither that of the "hard" determininist nor of the "soft" compatibilist.[20]

(*a*) *Will*. The mind or the agent (in this context, these terms are synonymous for Locke) has the power "to order the consideration of any Idea, or the forbearing to consider it; or to prefer the motion of any part of the body to its rest, and *vice versa* in any particular instance" (§5). It is this power "we call the Will."[21] If there is any freedom at all for Locke, then it

19. I refer to passages such as 2.7.2–4; see Chap. 4, section 3.

20. This is as far as the present chapter will take us for, as I said earlier, I will leave the question of how (if at all) Locke in fact escapes determinism for the next chapter.

21. Locke regularly uses the words "will" and "volition" interchangeably, but in the paragraph in which he gives this definition he distinguishes between will and volition as between the power and its use: "The actual exercise of that power, by directing any particular action, or its forbearance is that which we call Volition or Willing." I follow

is the agent but not the will that is free. The will is always determined simply because there is no motivation to action unless the agent experiences uneasiness or desire. It is uneasiness or desire that in each particular instance of volition has motivated the agent and thus determined the will. To the question "What determines the Will?" Locke therefore answers "The mind, . . . the Agent itself"; and to the question "What moves the mind?" he replies that "The motive, for continuing in the same State or Action, is only the present satisfaction in it; The motive to change, is always some uneasiness." Hence he concludes it is uneasiness that is "the great motive that works on the Mind to put it upon Action, which for shortness sake we will call determining of the Will" (§29).

The phrase "for shortness sake" is of crucial importance. It is meant to remind us that in human action uneasiness does not directly or immediately determine the will. Determination of the will is always mediated because it is the *agent's* uneasiness and it is the agent who allows determination of the will. In that sense the agent is the immediate cause of the determination. The agent has the powers of both will and understanding, and no uneasiness or desire comes to determine the will unless it is consciously experienced, that is, unless it is at least to some degree noticed and understood. This is the major reason for Locke's insistence that "will" and "desire" "must not be confounded." When Fraser comments on this passage that all Locke is saying is that "volition is victorious desire" he introduces a phrase which is felicitous in well-defined circumstances. But as we shall see later, Fraser's use of it violates Locke's intentions.

(*b*) *Uneasiness, desire.* "That which in the train of our voluntary actions determines the Will . . . is some present uneasiness, which is, or at least is always accompanied with . . . Desire."[22] Desire, in turn, "is always moved

---

Locke's usual lead and use the two terms interchangeably, employing either one or the other depending on which fits a particular context best. It is clear from this definition that the will functions in an area broader than that circumscribed by the word "moral." Locke's discussion of will in fact constitutes his theory of action rather than just of moral action. Although I primarily focus on moral action in this chapter it will, on occasion, be natural to make certain points about the broader area in which the will functions.

22. It may be more correct to say that uneasiness "is always accompanied with" desire than to say that uneasiness "is" desire. Locke often uses the terms interchangeably. His justification is that "Desire is a state of uneasiness" (§32), that "desire" is "nothing but an uneasiness in the want of an absent good" (§39). Desire is thus taken to be a species of uneasiness: "The uneasiness a Man finds in himself upon the absence of any thing, whose present enjoyment carries the Idea of Delight with it, is that we call Desire" (§6; see also 2.20.6). Again, I follow Locke's usual lead and use the two terms interchangeably. Leibniz worried about the interchangeability of the two: "wherever there is desire there will be disquiet; but the converse does not always hold, since one is often in a state of disquiet without knowing what one

by Evil, to fly it: Because a total freedom from pain always makes a necessary part of our Happiness" and "all that we desire is only to be Happy" (§71). Whenever there is the experience of uneasiness there is desire to be rid of that uneasiness. Except when uneasy, no one desires. Hence "The motive to change, is always some uneasiness" or desire (§29). Both the absence (or potential absence) of pleasure and the presence (or potential presence) of pain cause uneasiness. For Locke, pleasure goes with happiness, pain with misery. Hence the motive to change is desire for happiness. As we read in paragraph 62, "I lay it for a certain ground, that every intelligent being really seeks Happiness, which consists in the enjoyment of Pleasure, without any considerable mixture of uneasiness." Locke says it is basic to human nature to seek pleasure and avoid pain. As a consequence Locke holds that, in principle, while conscious a human being is always uneasy, and the will is always determined by "some (and for the most part the most pressing) uneasiness a Man is at present under" (§31).

"At present," at *any* conscious present, a person is uneasy. For one is either aware of discomfort or pain and desires to be rid of that; or of an "absent positive good" or of the fact that the good now enjoyed may not be there tomorrow, and also both of these awarenesses create uneasiness. Since at any "present" a person can conceive of a situation better than the one which now prevails or can dread the loss of the pleasurable situation now enjoyed, a person is always uneasy, always desiring. One might say that, for Locke, to be human is to be in a state of desire.[23] Which is to say that desire is insatiable.

To speak of "insatiable desire" is not to overstate the case. As we saw in the preceding chapter, Locke himself writes that "We are seldom at ease, and free enough from the solicitation of our natural or adopted desires, but a constant succession of uneasinesses . . . take the will in their turns" (§45). His point here is not that we are sometimes, though seldom, "at ease." Instead, it is that we are seldom sufficiently at ease from the solicitation of "a constant succession" of desires aroused in us through the vicissitudes of daily life, to be "free to the attraction of remoter absent good." And once attracted by "remoter absent good" we are, of course,

---

wants, in which case there is no fully developed desire." (See *New Essays*, p. 192, ed. and trans. Peter Remnant and Jonathan Bennett [Cambridge, 1982].) But surely Locke is right in that whenever there is uneasiness there is the desire to be rid of that uneasiness; hence Leibniz's worry seems unnecessary.

23. This conclusion has been drawn as well by Pamela Kraus. See her "Locke's Negative Hedonism" in *The Locke Newsletter*, no. 15 (1984), pp. 43–63, pp. 56–57. Kraus, incidentally, also points out that Locke borrows from Descartes his thesis that "desire is the chief if not only spur to . . . Action." See her pp. 49 and 62, and *Descartes' Passions of the Soul*, 2: 86–87.

no longer at ease either, but desire it. Hence a person is never at ease, is always desirous.[24]

Because a person is always propelled by desire to increase or at least maintain present happiness, or to eliminate or at least decrease present misery, therefore he or she is never at ease but is always subject to passion, either to natural or to rational passion. Locke says as much himself in the theological language of 2.7.5:

> God hath scattered up and down several degrees of Pleasure and Pain, in all the things that environ and affect us; . . . that we finding imperfection, dissatisfaction, and want of complete happiness, in all the Enjoyments which the Creatures can afford us, might be led to seek it in the enjoyment of him, with whom there is fulness of joy, and at whose right hand are pleasures for evermore.

(c) *Pleasure and pain, happiness and misery, good and evil.* All of these concepts are intimately related. Pleasure and pain appear as definitions of good and evil; and happiness consists in the experience of pleasure, misery in that of pain. (See §42; and for a similar statement, 2.20.2.) Equally intertwined with these concepts is that of desire. For desire fills the role of prompting us to make the presence of pleasure or the absence of pain into

---

24. When Jean Le Clerc wondered whether really all human actions are instigated by uneasiness, Locke replied that even such "indifferent things" as first to put on the right or the left shoe, or "whether he should sit still or walke . . . whilst he is in a deep meditation" involve uneasiness. The uneasiness or desire is minor and indirectly related to the actions in question: it is the uneasiness "of dispatch," that delay about trifles will not hold up action on more important matters. (See *The Correspondence of John Locke*, 5:159–60.) Some commentators deny this aspect of Locke's doctrine. John Colman, for example, writes: "Of course, there may be times when an agent is content with his present situation and therefore does not suffer any uneasiness" (*John Locke's Moral Philosophy* [Edinburgh, Scotland, 1983], p. 217). Locke's point would be that alongside the predominant state of satisfaction one suffers in some manner the uneasiness called fear, for one fears the loss of the situation which gives contentment. Colman adds that "At these times he will continue in whatever course of action he happens to be following" (ibid.). That is generally correct—although that action may then come to be expanded to include precautionary moves so that the dominant state of satisfaction remains intact. Colman then quotes from §29: "The motive, for continuing in the same State or Action, is only the present satisfaction in it"; and he concludes that "Strictly speaking, what uneasiness brings about is a change in the direction of the will" (ibid.). But that does not follow. A less truncated quotation from §29 indicates as much: "The motive, for continuing in the same State or Action, is only the present satisfaction in it; the motive to change, is always some uneasiness: nothing setting us upon the change of State, or upon any new Action, but some uneasiness." "Uneasiness" can set us upon the "change of State," or "upon *any* new Action." Clearly, there are more actions than those which lead to "a change of State." Some actions are designed to *preserve* the present state. Those actions too we are set upon by uneasiness—by the uneasiness we call fear of losing that state.

a reality. Desire helps to mediate between experience and action: if we experience pain, desire prompts us to act in such a way that we become free from pain and experience pleasure; if we experience pleasure, desire prompts us to action which increases or at least maintains that pleasure. This is one of the points Locke makes in paragraph 43. From this paragraph it is clear as well that the root of a human being's insatiable desire is to be found in pleasure and pain, happiness and misery. Without pain there is no uneasiness or desire. Similarly, there is no desire apart from the fear of loss of pleasure, or without the knowledge that a greater pleasure still eludes us. In these situations there is no action apart from desire. Once again the statement from 2.20.6 comes to mind: "the chief if not only spur to humane . . . Industry and Action is uneasiness." The uneasiness in question is desire for happiness.

Reinforced at this point is a theme from my preceding chapter: it is not reason, not knowledge of the good, which motivates to action. Instead, the motive for action is passion or desire. "For whatever good is propos'd, if its absence carries no displeasure nor pain with it; if a Man be easie and content without it, there is no desire of it, nor endeavour after it" (2.20.6). It is "Pleasure and Pain, and that which causes them, Good and Evil," that "are the hinges on which our Passions turn" (2.20.3).

The kind of action pursued depends on the kind of uneasiness or desire to which a person is subject, and the nature of the desire is itself determined by the particular "Modifications or Tempers of Mind" (ibid.) caused by experiences of pleasure or pain. The different kinds of desires we call our various passions: love, hate, joy, sorrow, fear, despair, anger, and envy. For the passions are nothing but different kinds of uneasiness to which we can be subject; they "depend on different Modifications of Pleasure and Pain" (2.20.5). So, for example, sorrow "is uneasiness in the Mind, upon the thought of a Good lost, which might have been enjoy'd longer; or the sense of a present Evil" (2.20.8). In love and hate, anger and envy, human beings' unobstructed actions are overt reactions to the situations in which they find themselves. They are reactions determined by the experiences that these situations caused in them. In other words, they are overt reactions ultimately caused and determined by the objects or situations that affect persons to begin with. In that sense it is "Pleasure and Pain, and that which causes them" which "are the hinges on which our Passions turn."

We have now seen that the concepts of will, uneasiness or desire, pleasure, pain, happiness, misery, and good and evil are central to Locke's account of human action. Does it not now appear as if human action is naturalistically determined? In spite of the fact that neither *reason* nor *freedom* have as yet made their appearance, does not the account of human action seem at least in outline complete? Since it is action not guided by reason, human action appears as naturalistically determined behavior. It is small wonder, then, that Locke is widely perceived as a determinist. Or is it?

Agreement with the statement that my report of Locke's doctrine of human action is complete in outline would be prompted more by what some of the standard commentaries would lead one to believe than by what Locke's text in fact warrants. Commentators such as Fraser and Aaron, although they make mention of other concepts, allow only those so far introduced to play the decisive role. Once they make that move there is little chance of their seeing Locke's as other than a deterministic account. For Locke himself holds that persons are not free if their unobstructed action is not guided by their reason.

There are, however, many points at which this report is incomplete. Let me get to some of the important ones by way of a minor detour. It consists in drawing attention to two of the ways in which Locke uses the term "indifference." The first is this. When I am standing still because I determined myself to stand still, I can at a later time determine myself to run. In either case such determination leaves the body "indifferent." Standing still has not destroyed the body's ability to run, and running has not made it impossible to come to a standstill. Either ability remains intact although only one of them is (and at any particular time can be) exercised. In this context Locke speaks of the "indifferency . . . of the operative Powers of the Man, which remaining equally able to operate, or to forbear operating after, as before the decree of the Will" (§71). Unless there is a disease (as when afflicted with St. Vitus Dance, one does not have the power to stop one's body from moving) such powers are to be characterized as "indifferent." This indifferency is a good thing. In contrast, a second sense of "indifferency" is meant to mark a bad situation. That is the indifferency in which the mind is not determined by its own judgment, in which it is indifferent about truth and falsehood, good and evil. This sense of "indifference" is used in paragraph 48 where it is juxtaposed to the "indifferency" of the first sense. It is the indifferency in which the agents, not determined by their own judgments, act in whichever way their fortuitous desires happen to push them. Such indifferency Locke considers to be an evil thing. To possess it is akin to not possessing the indifferency of the first kind, for to be in either state is to be abnormal. A human being ought not to be in the state of such a "perfect Indifferency in the Mind, not determinable by its last judgment of the Good or Evil, that is thought to attend its Choice" (§48). For "were we determined by any thing but the last result of our own Minds, judging of the good or evil of any action, we were not free, the very end of our Freedom being, that we might attain the good we chuse"(ibid.). If we are not determined by our own judgment, our intellect is not rightly involved in our action. In that case of indifferency there is not really human action. The behavior in question does not differ essentially from that which occurs "if my Hand be put into motion by a Convulsion"(§71). In either case the behavior can be accounted for in naturalistic terms. In neither case is there freedom.[25]

Via this detour we arrive at Locke's doctrine that unless the intellect is active in relevant ways, there is neither human action nor human freedom. When their unobstructed action is not guided by reason, human beings are naturalistically determined. In words from paragraph 48, they then suffer "want of liberty" because they are "under the determination of some other than" themselves, of something other than their "own Thought and Judgment."

Thus, for Locke, the will is always determined. Either it is determined by immediate desire of a particular but possibly only apparent good, by a "good" we happen to run into and by a desire we therefore happen to have aroused in us, a desire the possession of which was itself initially beyond our control. Or it is determined by desire which follows reflection on the "good" we encountered, a "good" judged relative to the standard of what is really good. In the first situation the agent is not free and, strictly speaking, the action does not qualify as human action. In the second, there is freedom and human action, in part because the understanding entered into examination of the particular good to establish whether it is an instance of real good. (There is more to why rational action is free action, but that is not relevant to the present argument.)

This is Locke's position in "Of Power." It is a doctrine implicit in the *Essay* from its first Book onwards. In Book I, Locke states it as his view that beings whose action is not guided by their reason are creatures whose behavior is determined by factors that belong to the realm of natural causation. He writes if you "take away . . . all Moral Rules whatsoever" then you deny "freedom to Mankind" and "thereby" make "Men no other than bare Machins" (1.3.14). Moral rules unknown to human beings are of no use to them. So the implication is that action determined by knowledge of moral rules—of true good—is action in which a person is "other than" a "bare Machin." Which is to say that persons cannot be free in action which is not determined by their reason.

That doctrine is at least implicit in the material already introduced from

---

25. A third use of "indifference," that of e.g., 4.3.20, where "indifference" is synonymous with "impartiality," has already presented itself in earlier chapters and will come to the fore again later on.

"Of Power." It is implicit especially at those points where I kept my report incomplete. In the following paragraph, I list two such points (*a* and *b*).

We have seen that in human action it is not as if uneasiness directly determines the will: Locke warns us that whenever he writes as if there is this immediate relationship, that it is "for shortness sake." It is the agent who is the immediate cause of the determination of the will. The agent can stand between desire and action on desire. This aspect of his doctrine led Locke to introduce certain expressions which (although I have quoted them) I have so far neglected. (*a*) One of them is that a person's will is always determined by "some (and for the most part most pressing) uneasiness a Man is at present under." Why the phrase "*for the most part* most pressing?" If Locke's account of motivation were purely mechanistic, it would always be "the most pressing" desire which would win over other desires and thus determine the will. It is only because the agent can stand between desire and action on it, can rationally evaluate the desire which would prompt to action, that it is not always the initially most pressing uneasiness that wins out. (*b*) The will is constantly determined by some desire or other, and that makes human beings creatures whose desire is insatiable. At any particular time an agent can conceive of a situation better than the one which now exists, or fear the loss of a pleasure currently enjoyed. There is no present in which the agent does not suffer some uneasiness, hence in which some action is not contemplated. A peculiarly human capacity is at work here, namely, the intellectual capacity called "foresight." Without foresight, one might rest content in the pleasures one has. One might even be reconciled to the suffering of present uneasiness. Without foresight, how would a creature know that better states of being are possible? Without foresight, therefore, how could there be action at all? At best there would only be uneasiness. There would be uneasiness when, for example, memory presents a past state as more pleasurable or less painful than that which pertains at the moment. There could then be the passion of sorrow, "the uneasiness in the Mind, upon the thought of a Good lost, which might have been enjoy'd longer" (2.20.8). But human action requires two conditions. There must be the psychic factor of uneasiness, and the intellectual factor of foresight. Without the two jointly operating there would be no insatiable desire resulting in constant contemplation of action.

A human being is always uneasy, always desires, and always contemplates action to satisfy this desire. That is because human agents are *intellectual* beings. As intellectual beings they know the fear of loss of present pleasure and the envy of pleasures they do not at present enjoy but might through effort obtain. Their minds search for ways in which present pleasures can be increased or at least maintained, and for means by which present pains can be removed or at least minimized. They can search for true and lasting pleasures. That search necessitates comparison of present with other possible pleasures, of present pains with other possible experiences. That search, in other words, demands that apparent good be examined to determine whether it is real good, and apparent evil to see whether it is real evil. Because persons can stand between their desires and action on these desires, because they can examine present pleasure and pain, present good and evil, they can be free. For it is Locke's position that agents are free if their unobstructed action is guided by their reason.

3. Unobstructed Action Guided by Inadequate Understanding

If there is to be action (or freedom) rather than mere behavior (or causal determination) then, says Locke, the intellect must play a decisive role: "Where-ever Thought is wholly wanting . . . there Necessity takes place" (§13), and "as far as this Power reaches, of acting, or not acting, by the determination of his own Thought preferring either, so far is a Man free" (§21). What is not immediately clear is that Locke holds as well that not all unobstructed thought-directed behavior qualifies as free action. There is freedom if unobstructed action is guided by reason. To the extent that it is guided by another form of thought, by a prejudiced understanding, unobstructed behavior fails to qualify as free action. I next focus on the last of these assertions, on the point that although all human action involves thought, not all of it involves adequate understanding and hence not all of it is fully free. Its exploration will lead us to recognize that it is because human action is often guided by inadequate understanding of desires and their potential consequences, that it tends to be determined by principles of a relativistic and subjectivistic nature. We see that because Locke believes that a person ought to be guided by reason, he rejects subjectivism and relativism as well in "morals." (That he does so in epistemology we saw in the first chapter.)

All human behavior that is not mere reflex action involves thought to some extent. All action is motivated by uneasiness and is intended to reduce or eliminate pain or to introduce, preserve, or increase pleasure. Hence there is no action apart from consideration of consequences. And whereas consideration of consequences is typically the work of the understanding, there is no human action apart from involvement of the understanding. As we just saw, human beings are endowed with an understanding that has the power of foresight. Apart from foresight, uneasiness is not a force which motivates to action.

Some behavior may look as if it is human action while in reality it is not. Human beings behave subhumanly when they allow themselves to be guided immediately by whatever desires their physical contexts happen to arouse in them. They then no longer stand between desire and action on desire. In such circumstances there is not really human action but only natural necessity. In such cases behavior is sub-human: there is no control over one's destiny, and no enjoyment of freedom except that of unobstructed motion—a freedom shared with the untethered horse ambling across a meadow led on from place to place only by awareness of tasty tufts of grass. There is neither human action nor human freedom as long as the understanding leaves desires in their "natural, uncultivated" state.[26]

In the preceding chapter we saw that not all understanding is adequate. Freedom does not come to full expression if a person's unobstructed action is guided by the result of the understanding's inadequate examination of desires and their potential consequences. Inadequate examination sometimes involves a wrong estimate of the extent of the evil of certain consequences; or if we judge rightly of their evil, it sometimes groundlessly involves the assumption that subsequent action (repentance, for instance) can undo this evil (§66). Inadequate examination often leads us too quickly to believe that the consequences of a certain action will increase our happiness, and so we often precipitously deem a certain action to be good. It is Locke's stress on this latter fact of life—that precipitous judgments lead different people to take different things as good—which has led some commentators unjustly to accuse him of moral subjectivism and relativism.

Of course, Locke does say that although everyone pursues what they consider to be good, "the same thing is not good to every Man alike" (§54). But these words (nor those of a similar kind which follow them in paragraph 55) cannot be used to brand Locke as a relativist. They are meant as a statement of fact: wrong though it is, it is the case that "the same thing is not good to every Man alike." His condemnation of the kind of thinking that gives rise to (or would approve of) such relativism stands

26. The phrase "natural, uncultivated" is Marwyn Johnson's, who correctly observes that "In relation to the natural, uncultivated desires working on him, a person is passive, reacting to his environment and those forces which produce uneasiness in him" (*Locke on Freedom* [Austin, 1977], p. 78). As we shall see, to the extent that Johnson implies that all that is needed for activity or freedom to be on the scene is the mere "cultivation" of "natural" desires, he fails to appreciate the radical thrust of Locke's doctrine. In that failure he is far from alone.

out clearly for the attentive reader. For Locke adds that only if "all the Concerns of Man terminated in this Life" can we possibly hold to the relativity of "good." Since he does not take that to be the way things are (or at least not the way things are beyond reasonable doubt) it is his position that all ought to choose the same good and that although all need not choose the exact same path to it[27] all ought to choose a path that, upon examination, others can see as leading to true happiness. "If . . . Men in this Life only have hope . . . 'tis not . . . unreasonable, that they should seek their Happiness by avoiding all things, that disease them here, and by pursuing all that delight them" (§55). Only if this counterfactual were to express the true state of affairs would it be the case that "Men may chuse different things, and yet all chuse right" (ibid.). Relativism and subjectivism, Locke concludes, become plausible as correct attitudes only if we "suppose" that human beings are "like a Company of poor Insects . . . which having enjoyed for a season, they should cease to be, and exist no more for ever" (ibid.).

Fraser's comment on this passage reveals a drastic misreading, a misinterpretation shared by (or passed on to) others.[28] "This scepticism about the *summum bonum* illustrates Locke's indifference to ideals, and implies that ends cannot be chosen because they are in themselves, or absolutely, good, but only that they are 'good' because the individual finds them by experience to be pleasurable." What Locke is saying, on the contrary, is that the lives of those who submerge themselves in the unexamined or even inadequately examined pleasures offered by each moment, are really beastly and insectlike. Contrary to what some would have us believe, Locke's position is that "the principle of all virtue lies in a power of denying ourselves the satisfaction of our own desires, when reason does not authorize them." I have used some of these words from *Concerning Education* (§38) regularly in this book. We really need not go beyond the *Essay*, or even beyond "Of Power," to find the doctrine these words express. In "Of Power," it is stated in the paragraph following that in which Locke pronounces some who appear as belonging to the human race to be no better than "poor Insects."

Locke rejects subjectivism about happiness and relativism about the good. If it were right to believe that "Men in this Life only have hope," then "taste" and "pleasure" can be seen as equally relative since neither concerns "things themselves." That is, neither then concerns things as

27. This is one point at which Locke's doctrine of toleration would enter the scene.
28. Perhaps the most celebrated instance is that of Leo Strauss. See his *Natural Right and History* (Chicago, 1953), p. 249.

they really are, apart from the idiosyncracy of a particular person dominated by the pleasure or pain of a particular moment. This is the doctrine
of paragraph 55. Paragraph 56 expands on it. While in a state of desire
with respect to a particular pleasure, or in a state of aversion with respect
to a particular pain, "a Man may suspend the act of his choice from being
determined for or against the thing proposed, till he has examined,
whether it be really of a nature in it self and consequences to make him
happy, or no." Locke then adds:

> And here we may see how it comes to pass, that a Man may justly incur
> punishment, though it be certain that in all the particular actions that he
> wills, he does, and necessarily does will that, which he then judges to be
> good. For though his will be always determined by that, which is judg'd
> good by his Understanding, yet it excuses him not: Because, by a too hasty
> choice of his own making, he has imposed on himself wrong measures of
> good and evil; which however false and fallacious, have the same influence
> on all his future conduct, as if they were true and right. He has vitiated his
> own Palate, and must be answerable to himself for the sickness and death that
> follows from it. The eternal Law and Nature of things must not be alter'd to
> comply with his ill-order'd choice.[29]

Human beings, subject as they are to prejudice and hence liable to be
precipitate and to act irrationally, also have the opportunity to examine
thoroughly and to be guided by their reason. This implies no justification
for relativism, for a person ought to go the latter rather than the former
path. Because they can suspend the determination of their will until they
have carried out a "due and mature examination," an examination that
does justice to "the weight of the matter, and the nature of the case" (§51),
human beings are responsible when they choose to go wrong. Each is able
to conduct an investigation which includes judging of "the thing proposed . . . in itself and consequences" (§56) in view of ultimate good. Each
is capable of this investigation because human beings are equipped to
grasp "the eternal Law and Nature of things." In paragraph 70 Locke
restates this position unambiguously:

29. Dennett's affinity with Locke is clear: "by a too hasty choice of his own making." For
both Locke and Dennett, freedom is related to "the decision, for instance, not to consider
any further" (see note 3 of this chapter). But the difference between the two is implicit here as
well. For Dennett (who is neither a reductionist nor a foundationalist) it holds that "However much one considers and evaluates and reflects, there is always logical room for more";
hence "we are . . . inevitably confronted with the need for a limited and incomplete survey of
considerations" (*Elbow Room*, p. 86). For Locke (who is both a reductionist and a foundationalist) freedom is misused at this level of deliberation unless "consideration" has been
"complete" that is, has led the intellect to items which are clear and distinct.

Whatever false notions, or shameful neglect of what is in their power, may put Men out of their way to Happiness, and distract them, as we see, into so different courses of life, this yet is certain, that Morality, established upon its true Foundations, cannot but determine the Choice in any one, that will but consider: and he that will not be so far a rational Creature, as to reflect seriously upon infinite Happiness and Misery, must needs condemn himself, as not making that use of his Understanding he should.

For Locke, human beings have no right but to impose upon themselves invariant truth and goodness. They are culpable unless they employ their understanding adequately and then submit themselves to the compulsion of their reason.

As we read in paragraph 53, we are not "Masters of our Minds" when, through bias or precipitation, we keep the understanding from an adequate examination. And, so Locke here implies, when we lack such mastery we are neither fully free nor truly human. It is, he continues, our duty to be "Masters enough of our Minds to consider thoroughly, and examine fairly."

But the forbearance of a too hasty compliance with our desires, the moderation and restraint of our Passions, so that our Understandings may be free to examine, and reason unbiassed give its judgment, being that, whereon a right direction of our conduct to true Happiness depends; 'tis in this we should employ our chief care and endeavours.

As we saw in preceding chapters, Locke holds that, strictly speaking, reason is neither fallible nor biased. What is therefore at stake in this passage is that the understanding's bias, or the person's precipitancy, hinders or even prevents the work of reason. Denying the presence of both prejudice and haste, people then rashly take as pronouncements of reason what are in fact deliverances of an understanding that has not run the full course of an adequate examination.

It is, Locke believes, only action based on desires authorized by reason that, without fail, lead to true happiness. Sometimes, action based on inadequate understanding may, fortuitously, result in true happiness. But since it was achieved more or less accidentally, this happiness is not a manifestation of mastery of one's fate. In general, the degree of mastery and the measure of happiness persons are capable of achieving are directly proportional to their exercise of reason.[30] The more adequate the under-

30. This statement echoes one of Aarsleff's. See Aarsleff, "The State of Nature and the Nature of Man in Locke," p. 102.

standing's examination, the more responsible the judgment and the more perfect the liberty of the ensuing act.[31]

Unobstructed behavior not guided by reason tends to incorporate us into the mechanism of nature. To the extent that we are so incorporated we lack reason and freedom. Since these are the two aspects that characterize a corporeal being as human, then, to the extent that we lack them, we resemble the "Company of poor Insects."

Both God and humankind are "under the necessity of being happy" (§50). Whatever this may imply for God, for human beings "the necessity of being happy" does not automatically provide the experience of happiness. They are under "the constraint . . . to act for it"; they must prevent action until they have adequately examined. And "the more any intelligent Being is so"—that is to say, the more it unbiasedly examines its desires and the potential consequences of the actions to which they would impel—"the nearer is its approach to infinite perfection and happiness" (ibid.). Locke believes this "approach to infinite perfection and happiness" to lie within each person's power. For "when, upon due Examination, we have judg'd, we have done our duty, all that we can, or ought to do, in pursuit of happiness" (ibid.). A "due Examination" is everybody's "duty." Throughout his writings Locke holds that if persons have a duty they also have the ability to act as their duty prescribes.

I leave discussion of the nature of this duty for the next chapter where we shall see that this aspect of Locke's doctrine is hardly unproblematic. Before we turn to it, further reflection on action guided by reason is still in order.

4. Unobstructed Action Guided by Reason

Three of the major tenets of Locke's theory of action are that those guided by reason (i) act in accordance with a universal rule, (ii) are truly free and enjoy lasting happiness, (iii) are masters of their fate. These points came to the fore in the preceding pages, but some of them require amplification. In addition they need to be more explicitly connected with each other. Doing so allows me to draw an important conclusion, one that closely relates this chapter to the preceding ones and demonstrates the coherence of Locke's thought. This conclusion is that, for Locke, a cor-

---

31. This statement incorporates phrases from R. Polin's "John Locke's Conception of Freedom," p. 3.

poreal rational creature can be human only if it is as revolutionary in "morals" as in epistemology.

(i) Unobstructed action determined by unexamined desire exemplifies no freedom and does not qualify as human action. However, since (apart from reflex action) there is no human action except upon some consideration of consequences, there is, strictly speaking, no unobstructed human action determined by wholly unexamined desire. Although the desire is often insufficiently examined, some examination must have been carried out for, as we saw, without some foresight of consequences there would be no action at all. This allows the introduction of a conclusion from the preceding chapter: the necessary presence of the understanding in all human action guarantees the possibility of the breakthrough of reason, of fully human action perfectly free.

We have seen that it is through stress on the understanding's ability to foresee consequences that Locke makes the point that no human action can be accounted for in terms that exclusively relate to the particularity of the moment of action. He writes, "the present moment not being our eternity, whatever our enjoyment be, we look beyond the present, and desire goes with our foresight, and that still carries the will with it" (§39). Because we are creatures of foresight, no single state or experience affords us complete satisfaction. Especially important here is Locke's denial that "Men in this Life only have hope." Reason tells us that there is at least a possibility that God exists; that there is, consequently, at least a possibility that life eternal is our destiny; that the quality of this eternal life is determined by the nature of our actions from one present moment to the next; that therefore not just any action is rationally responsible; and that responsible actions are those that conform to some invariant decree. The invariance of this decree can be explained either in terms of God's or human reason's nature. Neither God nor reason change. Hence God's decrees bind His creatures forever. And "Mankind . . . knew, by the light of nature" whether "they transgressed the rule of their nature, reason, which dictated to them what they ought to do" (*Paraphrase*, note to Romans 5:13).

Foresight coupled with reason forces Locke's position away from relativism. And so we read that "we . . . impose on our selves" when "the future loses its just proportion, and what is present, obtains the preference as the greater" (§63), when we allow a "present Pleasure" to occupy "the whole Mind" so "that it scarce leaves any thought of things absent" (§64). In cases such as these, present pleasure or pain "lessens in our Thoughts, what is future; and so forces us, as it were, blindfold into its embraces"

(ibid.). The imposition upon ourselves is here explained but neither con-
doned nor presented as inescapable. Although we are said to be "forced"
to act as if we have no foresight, no situations (except possibly those of an
extreme kind, as when one is tortured—see paragraph 53) can force us to
do so with ineluctable necessity. In each of the various acts that together
constitute the totality of their earthly lives, human beings, characterized
by foresight and reason, are confronted with the responsibility to form
themselves into creatures fit for divine approval. They cannot avoid the
responsibility for mastery.

(ii) The acts that make one master of one's fate for time and, if there be
such, for eternity, are acts of freedom which guarantee both lasting freedom and happiness. The possibility of such acts is conditional upon
adequate examination of each particular desire and of its potential consequences. Locke writes:

> As therefore the highest perfection of intellectual nature, lies in a careful and
> constant pursuit of true and solid happiness; so the care of our selves, that [in
> any particular situation] we mistake not imaginary for real happiness, is the
> necessary foundation of our liberty. The stronger ties, we have, to an unalter-
> able pursuit of happiness in general . . . the more are we free from any
> necessary determination of our will to any particular action, and from a
> necessary compliance with our desire, set upon any particular, and then
> appearing preferable good. (§51)

In the rest of this paragraph Locke makes it clear that the "care" to be
taken consists in suspending action on a particular desire and in adequately
examining that desire; in addition, it consists in the subsequent determination of the will by the now well-informed agent rather than by unexamined or insufficiently examined desire. The possibility of lasting freedom and happiness requires both this examination and determination.

It is not as if all forms of subjectivity are banned; it is the subjects' own
nature that places them under "the necessity of preferring and pursuing
true happiness" (§71), and it is for the sake of their personal happiness that
they are "obliged to suspend the satisfaction" of their own "desires in
particular cases" (ibid.). But this centrality of the individual is not meant
to introduce subjectivistic relativism. For (as we just saw in the statement
from paragraph 51) Locke juxtaposes the "particular" to the "general": the
particular pleasure or pain of each moment is to be judged in terms of
what makes for "real happiness." Only an understanding free from prejudice, that is, only reason, is capable of guiding in terms of "real happiness." Once reason guides action, we act in accordance with the "eternal

Law and Nature of things" (§56). We are then free from the natural causal determination that is coincident with indiscriminate fulfillment of desires aroused in us haphazardly in the course of daily experience. It is not when more-or-less biased understanding serves natural passions, but when reason serves a person's master passion, that action is fully rational and free and happiness truly lasting.

(iii) In the situation where reason serves the master passion, human beings are still characterized by desire. But there is then nothing haphazard about the desire, and nothing accidental when action on it procures lasting happiness. In that situation persons are masters of their fate. The particular desires that then prompt them to action are no longer "natural" desires, not even (as some would have it) "cultivated"[32] natural desires; for it is now clear that Locke is profoundly distrustful of all natural passion. Instead, the desires that then prompt to action are desires of which agents are themselves the origin. This last point can be supported as follows.

The will is always determined. Persons are not free when their will is immediately—that is, without intervening suspension—determined by a particular "good." They are then determined by a "good" that happens to "offer itself," by a desire they just happen to have aroused in them, that is, by a desire whose possession is beyond their control. Persons are free when their will is determined by the right kind of desire. One can have such a desire only subsequent to adequate examination of the pleasure or pain which offered itself, and this adequate examination requires that the "particular" be judged in terms of the "general." An adequate examination can take place only when action on the original desire is suspended. Suspension and examination lead to arousal of another desire that may then become the one determining the will. This desire differs from the original desire in that the person has aroused it through acts of suspension and examination, which leaves it nothing of a haphazard nature. That it is a different desire is clear enough in those cases where the new desire does not even resemble the original one. Such a desire comes about when examination of the original desire makes clear that nothing like it can be authorized by reason, because action on nothing like it could possibly lead to true and lasting happiness. But the desire adopted after suspension and examination of the original desire is also genuinely new even if it resembles the original desire. Apart from the fact that it is no longer haphazard, it is no longer natural, but rational. For it is one authorized by reason, and

---

32. See note 26 above.

no natural desire is characterized by reason's authorization. Even if some-one else's reason has given a certain desire its authorization, Locke's individualistic epistemology dictates that such an authorization can carry no weight for me. Thus whether the desire appears to be like the original desire or not, in either case it is a new desire. In the end, in either case it is the authorization by the individual's reason which makes the individual the origin of the desire that then comes to motivate to action. Thus the will is always determined, but the agent can become fully autonomous or self-determined.

The parallel between Locke's theory of action and theory of knowledge is striking at this point. In both he shows himself to be a revolutionary. As an epistemologist Locke teaches that no one may begin by accepting as knowledge what others claim to be knowledge. One cannot acquire general knowledge unless one first completely sweeps away whatever tradition would have one accept, and then start anew from a foundation of "general ideas" that each has obtained through analysis of what first-person experience has provided. In epistemology, if general knowledge is to become a reality, no trust is to be placed in what is initially given.[33] Similarly in action theory: no freedom (and hence no truly human action) is possible if one enjoys without question the pleasures that offer them-selves, or if one avoids without examination the pains one meets. Free-dom is possible only if action on all initially experienced desires—i.e., on all natural desires—is suspended. Freedom becomes a reality only once one acts on desires that one's own reason has authorized. "The result of our own judgment upon . . . Examination is what ultimately determines the Man, who could not be free if his will were determin'd by any thing, but his own desire guided by his own Judgment" (§71). At the root of both his epistemology and his theory of action there is Locke's insistence on revolutionary, strictly individual autonomy.

33. See Chap. 1, section 3.

～6

Self-Determination

A person avoids being incorporated into the mechanism of nature through the complex act that includes suspension of natural desires, examination of these desires and their potential consequences, contemplation of true good, judgment of the suspended desires in terms of the good contemplated, and submission to the outcome of that judgment. I made this point in the preceding chapter but only as an assertion. It now remains to be shown that, according to Locke, the acts of suspension, examination, contemplation, judgment, and submission are, none of them, in turn to be explained through the kind of uneasiness that would make these acts manifestations of the mechanism of nature. And it remains to be established as Lockean doctrine that, in these acts, a person experiences pure self-determination. I deal with these issues in this chapter's first section.

Locke teaches that persons are wholly free if their action is guided by their reason. He also holds that freedom consists in pure self-determination. But is there not some form of determination when action is guided by reason? How, if at all, can Locke reconcile the need for authorization by reason with the idea of pure self-determination? Discussion of that question begins in the second part of this chapter. One aspect of its answer is that, according to Locke, there is no conflict between self-determination and authorization of actions by reason because people cannot be compelled to act in accordance with pronouncements of their reason unless they determine themselves to be so compelled.

Is such an act of determination an instance of pure self-determination or is it prompted by a person's master passion? The issue to be explored in the third and fourth parts of this chapter is that of the relationships among self-determination, reason, and the master passion. Here we will deal decisively with statements we met in the preceding chapter (but which I passed over without comment) and which begin to play an important role in the first two sections of this chapter. I have in mind statements to the effect that human beings are under the "constraint" to act for happiness, that they are "under the necessity of being happy" and therefore under the "constraint" not to act in precipitous and unpremeditated ways.

Before I continue there are two related points to which I must direct attention. The first concerns the nature of the mind or agent or self— terms that, as we have seen, Locke uses interchangeably in this context of his discussion of freedom. When we consider Locke's doctrine of self-determination, what is the nature of this self which determines itself? The second concerns passages from "Of Power" about the relation of freedom and "Thought and Judgment" in acts of self-determination.

The first can perhaps be approached best through three statements from the *Essay* (the last of these has functioned before in my account).

> Self is that conscious thinking thing, (whatever Substance, made up of whether Spiritual, or Material, Simple, or Compounded, it matters not) which is sensible, or conscious of Pleasure and Pain, capable of Happiness or Misery, and so is concern'd for it self, as far as that consciousness extends. (2.27.17)

> Person, as I take it, is the name for this self. Where-ever a Man finds, what he calls himself, there I think another may say is the same Person. It is a Forensick Term appropriating Actions and their Merit; and so belongs only to intelligent Agents capable of a Law, and Happiness and Misery. (2.27.26)

> For as to Substances, when concerned in moral Discourses, their diverse Natures are not so much enquir'd into, as supposed; v.g. when we say that Man is subject to Law: We mean nothing by Man, but a corporeal rational Creature. . . . And therefore, whether a Child or Changeling be a Man in a physical Sense, may amongst the Naturalists be as disputable as it will, it concerns not at all the moral Man, as I may call him, which is this immoveable unchangeable Idea, a corporeal rational Being. (3.11.16)

Locke's "Of Power" is not a "moral Discourse." Instead, it presents the framework within which moral discourse becomes possible. The three passages just quoted augment this framework. They tell us something positive and something negative. Positively, they tell us that there is a moral self, a person, or an agent, when there is conscious, law-directed activity concerning happiness or misery. Negatively, they tell us that "in moral Discourses" we need not settle certain questions about spirituality or materiality. It is true that a moral being is a "corporeal rational Being" and that without corporeality there would be no consciousness of pleasure or pain, of happiness or misery. And it is true that the desires that would immediately compel the will, obtain their strength from bodily states. But moral beings are not to be identified with their bodies or desires or will. From the preceding chapter we know that—whatever the bodily states—there are neither desires, nor determinations of the will, for which the self is not held to be responsible. The present chapter will make it clearer that Locke intends to be read as neither determinist nor indeterminist; he does not hold that human action is caused by natural events, nor does he hold that it is caused by nothing. What will become more clearly established is that Locke's doctrine is that of the voluntarist: the cause of human action is the agent or the self. This immediately tells us something about the nature of the self. It tells us that, because our actions are neither determined by events or states nor by nothing, selves "have a prerogative which some would attribute only to God: each of us, when we act, is a prime mover unmoved."[1] That it is this kind of self that, for Locke, pertains to "moral man," is one of the points that will become firmly established in this chapter.

The second point connects directly with what I just said about the agent. There are passages in "Of Power" (for example, paragraph 71) in which Locke rules out the existence of freedom "antecedent to the Thought and Judgment of the Understanding"; it is ruled out because "no Agent" is "allowed capable of Liberty, but in consequence of Thought and Judgment." This passage ought not to be taken as saying that agents experience freedom only in submission to reason (where, as we know, the dictates of each person's reason are expressions of the universal Law of Nature and, as such, might be taken to submit agents to conditions which, transcending their individuality, are in that respect external). This chapter will firmly establish it as Locke's position that agents are free when they are guided by their reason. But it will become equally clear that freedom manifests itself prior to its manifestations in action guided by reason, because agents can freely refuse to submit themselves to reason "in consequence of" the kind of "Thought and Judgment" which is not

---

1. I have borrowed these last phrases from p. 23 of Roderick M. Chisholm's "Freedom and Action." This article appeared on pp. 11–44 of *Freedom and Determinism* (New York, 1966), a collection of essays edited by Keith Lehrer. At many points, the article is a contemporary retelling of Locke's story.

rational "Thought and Judgment." Hence this passage does not conflict with the strain of extreme voluntarism which we will discover in Locke's position; and certainly this voluntarism allows for the view of the self as "a prime mover unmoved."

1. The Experience of Self-Determination

The question of freedom is in part to be settled in terms of the nature of the complex act that contains as elements the suspension of action on desires, examination of these desires and their objects and consequences, contemplation of the good, and sanctioning a desire because reason approves of it or replacing it with a quite different desire because reason disapproves.[2] As we already know, Locke believes it is in these acts of suspension, examination and judgment that we exercise our freedom.

To ascertain whether Locke's position in fact allows for the possibility of this freedom, we must answer the following question: What determines agents to suspend satisfaction of immediate desire for a particular pleasure or for avoiding a particular pain? This question may be put as follows: Is the "mind" or agent that directs or determines suspension of action on desire in turn itself directed or determined and, if so, by what? The question can also be put: Can agents ever free themselves from the influence of the "multitude of wants and desires" (§45) and so suspend a desire on which they are prodded to act, without being determined in that suspension by some other desire? If agents are determined in their acts of suspending, then it is difficult to see how there could be room left for freedom to enter the scene. Yet some of Locke's statements would seem to rule out freedom precisely at this stage.

Consider again, for example, these words from paragraph 29: "What moves the mind, in every particular instance, to determine [the will] . . . to this or that particular Motion or Rest? And to this I answer, The motive . . . to change, is always some uneasiness." It is, so this passage may seem to say, not just the will but also the "mind" or agent that is always "moved" "in every particular instance" by the "uneasiness" the agent experiences during that "instance." Such a reading would seem to do justice to Locke's belief that no action takes place unless there is desire.

---

2. From the preceding paragraph, it is clear that this is not the only way in which freedom manifests itself. There is an additional, crucially important act I discuss later in this chapter. That it is disregarded now does not invalidate any aspects of the present stage of my exposition.

Thus if no action takes place apart from desire and no desire is aroused apart from pleasure or pain, then must not the act of suspension (that is to allow for government of desire and hence for overt acts of freedom) itself be desired, and must not this desire in turn be aroused by pleasure or pain? The continuation of paragraph 29 supports this reading: "uneasiness . . . is the great motive that works on the Mind to put it upon Action." Where, then, does freedom enter the scene?

One might, at this point, reiterate the Lockean doctrine that it is the will and not the "mind" or agent that is "moved" by "uneasiness." Agents, one might say, are not thus moved, at least not necessarily, for they can suspend both the pursuit of particular pleasure and avoidance of particular pain, and thus cease whatever action there issued from the original uneasiness. But such a reiteration would be a retrogressive, irrelevant response because the question now is: What makes them suspend at all?

For Locke to be able to ascribe freedom to human beings, it would seem that the answer should be not in terms of externally caused pleasures or pains, satisfactions or uneasinesses, but in terms of pure self-determination, of a determination that has its cause solely in the agents themselves. Does Locke ascribe the possibility of such self-determination to agents? And if he does, what to do, then, with the words just quoted from paragraph 29 to the effect that *agents* are always determined by uneasiness? One way to answer these questions is through the short detour that leads back to "Of Power" via various Lockean doctrines not explicitly stated there. To broaden my discussion—and to give prominence to what might be taken as anti-voluntarist tendencies in Locke's position—I follow this detour.

Human beings live in a rational universe.[3] If they act irrationally, they act against their own nature as well as against that of the universe. At least in the long run such action is self-destructive.[4] Because of the inborn tendency towards self-preservation, human beings suffer irritation, uneasiness, or desire, when they do not act, or do not know whether they act,[5] in a way conducive to self-protection. The experience of uneasiness

3. The belief in a rational universe in one that plays its role throughout Locke's works, from the early *Essays on the Law of Nature* onward (see especially essays 2 and 7).

4. See, for example, paragraph 63 of the *Second Treatise*. This aspect of Locke's doctrine is widely acknowledged. Ruth Grant, for example, writes that "Nature is directed towards the preservation of life, and this is the standard for reasonable and rightful action" (*John Locke's Liberalism*, p. 71).

5. That lack of knowledge in this instance causes uneasiness, and that this uneasiness can lead to suspension of action, is clear from the continuation of a passage introduced before from paragraph 50. The part which I quoted earlier reads "That in this state of Ignorance we short-sighted Creatures might not mistake true felicity, we are endowed with a power to

is therefore a sign that their existence is, or may be, in jeopardy. In order to preserve themselves, they have to act in accordance with their nature, that is, they must act rationally. In order to act rationally they must examine each of their desires—which presupposes that action on them must be suspended. Since self-preservation ensues when we act on the results of such examinations (that is, when we act on knowledge of what is true pleasure or lasting pain) the inborn habit of pursuit of pleasure and avoidance of pain is really the natural (but by itself untrustworthy) inclination to self-preservation.

As is clear especially from the *Second Treatise*, self-preservation is a fundamental right as well as a fundamental duty. But this right cannot be enjoyed and this duty cannot be acted out except after examination and judgment of desires—which assumes the act of suspension. Without suspension, no one knows what is true pleasure or real misery. Cultivating the power of suspension to the extent that suspension itself comes to be a habit is, therefore, a duty more fundamental than even the pursuit of self-preservation, since it is a condition for the possibility of the latter.

Hence, for Locke, the most basic task for human beings is to arouse in themselves the right kind of desires, namely, those that enhance their preservation. In their preservation lies their true happiness. Many statements from "Of Power" find a fitting place in this account. For example: "we are by the necessity of preferring and pursuing true happiness as our greatest good, obliged to suspend the satisfaction of our desire in particular cases" (§51). The "necessity" accompanies the uneasiness that exists when self-preservation is, or may be, in danger. But human beings share this uneasiness with other corporeal sentient beings.[6] It would then seem as if human beings are as much a part of the mechanism of nature as are certain sub-human forms of sentient life. Hence this detour seems to have led us to the conclusion that there is no pure self-determination.

However, the sentence "It is the desire for true happiness which places us under the 'necessity' to suspend the satisfaction of our desires in particular cases" is meant to convey more than the statement "Sentient beings are led to suspension of particular desires by the 'necessity' which accompanies the uneasiness that exists when self-preservation is in dan-

---

suspend any particular desire, and keep it from determining the will, and engaging us in action." It continues with the statement that "This is standing still, where we are not sufficiently assured of the way." So here the agent suspends a particular action because of the uneasiness or the uncertainty that result from the lack of knowledge about whether the particular action leads to true good.

6. This aspect of Locke's position is also well known. Again witness Grant: "The natural law understood as a desire for preservation would not distinguish men from beasts" (*John Locke's Liberalism*, p. 93).

ger." If, in the notion of self-preservation, the latter points to an aspect human beings share with other corporeal sentient beings, the former implies one in which they transcend them. This aspect is that of "obligation" which we just met in paragraph 51: "We are by the necessity of preferring and pursuing true happiness as our greatest good, *obliged* to suspend." Corporeal sentient creatures other than human beings are under the *natural* necessity to act in ways that enhance self-preservation. For human beings this necessity is of a *moral* kind: they have a genuine choice whether or not to act in ways that enhance their preservation. Thus freedom reappears on the scene.

In his note to this passage from paragraph 51, Fraser remarks that "Human freedom means original power to act immorally and unreasonably, as well as in accordance with right reason or moral obligation." Locke, he implies, denies that human beings possess this "original power." Here lies the deepest source of Fraser's (and others) persistent misreading of the *Essay*'s teaching on freedom. These teachings are to the effect that human beings are not determined to the greatest good unless they want to be so determined, and that they are not determined to want to be so determined—although they are under the necessity to want to be so determined because they are under the necessity to act in accordance with their nature, that is, they are under the necessity to act in ways which enhance their preservation. But the necessity in question is the necessity of duty. It tells people what they ought to do if they want to live rationally, happily, in ways most conducive to their preservation. But it leaves them the power to refuse to do what they ought to do.

Precisely because acquiring the habit of suspension is a duty, any particular act of suspension that is a part of the process of acquiring this habit must itself be an exercise in freedom. Locke does not both call acts of suspension duties and consider them to be naturalistically necessitated. He writes:

> For the inclination, and tendency of their nature to happiness is an obligation, and motive to them, to take care not to mistake, or miss it; and so necessarily puts them upon caution, deliberation, and wariness, in the direction of their particular actions, which are the means to obtain it. Whatever necessity determines to the pursuit of real Bliss, the same necessity, with the same force establishes suspence, deliberation, and scrutiny of each successive desire, whether the satisfaction of it, does not interfere with our true happiness, and mislead us from it. (§52)

To use an example. I know that if I want to live uprightly I have to be honest in my dealings. Such knowledge does not necessarily make for honesty, for although I am able to act honestly I must decide to act with honesty in particular situations. I am under no ineluctable compulsion to live uprightly. If I were, no dishonesty would be possible and no decision about honesty would be necessary. The same holds for what Locke says about "obligation" and "necessity." Human nature inclines people to pursue happiness. In order to act in accordance with their nature, human beings are under the necessity of suspension, for only after suspension can particular proposed actions be examined and judged in terms of true good. But why should human beings act in accordance with their nature? Here, too, Locke attaches the concept of "necessity": the "inclination" and "tendency" "of their nature to happiness is an obligation and motive, to take care not to mistake . . . and so necessarily" makes them scrutinize "their particular actions." Also this necessity is a moral one; it is "an obligation and motive." Speaking theologically (in language medieval philosophers as well as modern ones such as Kant would have approved) we might say that God has given us the potential to be truly happy and each one of us is obliged to actualize this God-given potential. Speaking metaphysically and naturalistically (in language which would have been unobjectionable to Aristotle as well as to thinkers such as the philosophes) we might say that wherever there is a natural potential we must develop it, and therefore we are obliged to actualize our natural potential for happiness. In either case there exists an "ought," a demand (whether of God or of nature) which each must decide to heed or to disregard. Thus self-determination remains intact.

The paragraph from which I just quoted continues with the sentence: "This as seems to me is the great privilege of finite intellectual Beings." "This" refers to "suspence, deliberation, and scrutiny of each successive desire" so that action conducive to true felicity may be assured. As with self-preservation in the *Second Treatise* so also here is a duty as well as a right or privilege. And privilege, too, can be accepted or rejected. In a sentence in which "can" implies "ought" and excludes a naturalistically necessitated "must," Locke continues the paragraph with the words that human beings "can suspend their desires, and stop them from determining their wills to any action, till they have duly and fairly examin'd the good and evil of it. . . ." People can live irrationally and be on the road to utter misery, or they can live rationally and travel the path to utmost happiness. In either case the decision is their own. It is a decision to be taken in what appears to be a freedom of pure self-determination.

That such self-determination exists Locke takes to be a fact each of us can experience. "The mind" has "a power to suspend the execution and satisfaction of any of its desires," "as is evident in Experience" (§47; see also §52). No one ought to be determined by whatever pleasure or pain is immediately experienced; and although one ought to be determined by it, no one is immediately determined by the greatest good (not even by the greatest acknowledged good). For Locke, each person's task is clear: all of us ought to suspend action that consists in satisfaction of immediately experienced pleasure or in fleeing from immediately experienced pain. We then ought to examine that pleasure or pain to see whether it leads to true happiness. If it does not, we ought to contemplate absent good until desire for that good supplants the desire on which action has been suspended. It "is evident in Experience" that we can do all this. Locke is saying that we ought never to do what is evil or sinful and that, if we so will, we never need to act evilly or sinfully. He is saying that we ought always to act in a morally upright way and that if we so will we never need to act otherwise.

It is, says Locke, experience itself that reveals to each of us that whether we so will depends ultimately only on ourselves. Hence to each it is experience that brings home that there is no radical inability that results from, say, depravity, or insufficient rationality, or lack of opportunity. Experience vouches for the fact that to be truly human no one needs either divine grace, or divine inspiration, or a time and place different from that occupied. In spite of near-stifling dogmas, misguided education, or societal cajolement, experience reveals to all of us that we retain within ourselves the power to break through whatever conditioning would bind us into following willy-nilly the well-trodden paths.

It is experience rather than demonstrative argument which is to acquaint us with this unconditioned freedom. Indeed, demonstrative argument would persuade us otherwise. Like Descartes, Locke cannot see a way to reconcile this human freedom with divine omnipotence and omniscience.[7] Given the existence of God, demonstrative argument would rule out human freedom. For if human beings are really free, they might present God with the surprises of actions not foreknown. Human freedom would then set limits to the divine nature. Locke accepts both divine omnipotence and omniscience, and human freedom. In this instance he sets limits to the power of demonstration. And so he writes to Molyneux

---

7. In *Principles* I, 41, Descartes states, "We may attain sufficient knowledge of this [infinite] power to perceive clearly and distinctly that God possesses it; but we cannot get a sufficient grasp of it to see how it leaves the free actions of men undetermined." One year after its publication Descartes reiterated his belief in the co-existence of divine omnipotence and human freedom, but added that human freedom remains dependent on divine power, for if it were not, this would put a limitation on divine power and thus involve the "contradiction" of saying that God's "power is both finite and infinite" (to Elizabeth, 3 November 1645). A few weeks later Descartes attempted to illustrate the non-contradictoriness of his belief through an analogy. The attempt is not very convincing (to Elizabeth, January 1646). (For both letters, see Kenny's *Descartes: Philosophical Letters*, pp. 184 and 188.)

For I own freely to you the weakness of my understanding, that though it be unquestionable that there is omnipotence and omniscience in God our maker, and I cannot have a clearer perception of any thing than that I am free, yet I cannot make freedom in man consistent with omnipotence and omniscience in God, though I am as fully perswaded of both as of any truths I most firmly assent to.[8]

Throughout his works, and not the least in "Of Power," Locke teaches that it depends on each individual's action whether or not true and lasting happiness will be achieved. A person's happiness is founded on the ability to govern the determination of the will. This ability is fundamental for Locke. Its existence is known as a fundamental given. Even if there were not the complication of an omnipotent and omniscient God, Locke would not—because he could not—provide a *demonstrative* argument for its existence. For a thinker like Locke, if something in the realm of experience is truly fundamental, knowledge of it is through the immediacy of *intuition*. Locke agrees with Descartes[9] that here experience takes precedence over demonstrative argument, intuited fact over (in this case indemonstrable) conclusion. "I cannot have a clearer perception of any thing than that I am free," wrote Locke on Molyneux. And so he places the intuitive perception of his freedom on equal footing with the intuitive perception of his existence. (Cf. 4.9.3.)[10]

2. Self-Determination and Authorization by Reason

Experience acquaints us with the fact that we possess unconditioned freedom. Does that statement conflict with other important dimensions of Locke's position, specifically, with those concerning the role of reason and the extent of mastery? In what sense, if at all, can human freedom be called "unconditioned" if, as we have seen, Locke insists that there is freedom when a particular action is determined by a dictate of reason? And are there not limits set to the ideal of mastery if, as we have seen as well, it is Lockean doctrine that only when they tread the path of reason can individuals free themselves from the vicissitudes of fortune? Is there

8. 20 January 1693; *Correspondence* 4: 625–26.
9. See *Principles* I, 6, 32, 39.
10. Matthew Prior, one of Locke's contemporaries, missed at least part of Locke's point when, in his *Dialogues*, he had Montaigne address Locke as follows: "Why Mr. Lock, your own Definition of Liberty, is, that it is something, which You your Self must feel; what signifies it therefore to Define at all?" *Dialogues of the Dead and other works in Prose and Verse*, ed. A. R. Waller (Cambridge, 1907), p. 228.

not a more radical sense of "being master of one's fate" in the decision whether one wants to be guided by reason at all? Thus two issues remain for examination: that of the connection between self-determination and the authorization by reason, and that of the relationship among self-determination, reason and mastery. I devote this section to the first of these.

A person lacks freedom when "under the determination of some other than himself," of something else than "his own Thought and Judgment" (§48). Does Locke mean to say, in statements such as these, that people experience the freedom of self-determination only when their unobstructed action is guided by their own *rational* thought and judgment? There are passages which would seem to answer this question affirmatively, such as paragraph 50, in which the absence of thought and judgment is equated with the absence of reason, and the absence of reason with that of freedom. These passages therefore seem to conflict with a conclusion from the preceding section.

This conclusion was that Locke's position requires there to be a set of acts in which freedom manifests itself in situations that are prior to the rule of reason. These are the acts in which the satisfaction of particular desires is suspended in order that they may be scrutinized. I concluded that these acts (as well as those of determining oneself to examine, judge, and contemplate) appear to be instances of pure self-determination because they are determined by neither desire nor reason. They are acts neither of "choosing or doing the worse" (§50) nor of choosing or doing what reason pronounces to be good. Instead, they place a person in the position to choose either the worse or the better, either evil or good. Their occurrence is a necessary condition for the situation in which action can be characterized as either rational or irrational. These acts are to be situated in an area different from that of unobstructed action dominated by unexamined desire, as well as of unobstructed action ruled by reason. But can Locke consistently hold that there is such freedom in this different area? If further reflection now confirms the affirmative answer, it would appear that the purest form of self-determination, the experience of greatest freedom, lies in this area. For does not any determination at all, including determination by universally uniform reason, limit an individual's liberty?

Several of Locke's statements put it beyond question that he is aware of the requirements of his position, that he believes there exists freedom in this different area. He speaks about this freedom as both necessary and dangerous. It is necessary because without it there cannot be reason's authorization. It is dangerous because it can be misused. Both these aspects of it we have met; each now requires further comment. I will begin by describing the danger of it.

Its danger lies in its misuse. One case of the misuse of this freedom (it will be remembered) is that in which, after initial suspension of action on a desire, someone decides to cease focusing critical attention on the desire and its object before adequate examination has taken place, and decides to act before the desire has been judged in terms of the good. That is to say, there is a misuse of this freedom when, after initial suspension, persons act on a desire they know has not been authorized by reason. There is another instance of misuse when, after initial suspension of action on a particular desire, a person fixes attention on both the particular desire and the good, but refuses to fix attention on the good sufficiently long for it to become the dominant object of desire and proceeds to act on the desire initially suspended. That is to say, there is misuse of this freedom when persons act on a desire they know cannot be authorized by reason.[11]

Locke holds that when people misuse this freedom they act perversely. They then fail to determine themselves as they ought, because they do not arouse in themselves a desire for the good. At this stage, such failure is not because they are swept along by a desire that has "taken the will." The "failure" is deliberate: since the desire was initially suspended it no longer was in a position to "take the will"; it is only the agent who can deliberately restore it to that position. Locke speaks of this "very wrong, and irrational" (§66) misuse of freedom more than once—as in paragraph 47.

There he writes that the liberty employed in the power of suspension of action on desire can be misused and "from the not using of it right comes all that variety of mistakes, errors, and faults which we run into, in the conduct of our lives, and our endeavours after happiness." The implication is that we know, or at least can come to know, what the situation demands in length of suspension and in intensity of consideration, and that we can determine ourselves to continue our activity for the required length and intensity. We normally do not cease to pay attention out of inability. Inability can exist, but it is the unusual case as when, for example, we are tortured into revealing a secret. We know it is wrong to reveal a secret we have pledged ourselves to keep, but the pain of torture may become so overwhelming that action to make it cease (i.e., revealing the

---

11. The notion of paying attention or refusing to pay attention ("inadvertancy" is the term Locke uses for the latter—e.g., 2.13.27) as essential to human freedom is one that was widespread in the seventeenth century. Locke shared it with, for example, Descartes, Malebranche, and Norris. On Descartes, see my *Descartes and the Enlightenment*, chap. 4, part 2. On Malebranche and Norris, see Charles McCracken's *Malebranche and British Philosophy* (Oxford, 1983), p. 158.

secret) becomes inescapable; we are then forced to cease to pay attention to the knowledge by which we would normally guide our action. In such an unusual case "God, who knows our frailty, pities our weakness, and requires of us no more than we are able to do . . . will judge as a kind and merciful Father" (§53). The usual case is the one in which God would be neither kind nor merciful because we deliberately, without being subject to inescapable compulsion, acted precipitously or against what we know to be good. In this *misuse* of freedom, self-determination is clearly at work: given the conditions that pertained we could have done otherwise.[12]

Can the same be said about the *proper* use of this freedom? Instances of its proper use occur when a person suspends action on desire, fixes attention on the object of that desire and thoroughly examines it, and at the same time pays attention to the good so that it becomes an object of desire. As we saw, all of these are meant to be acts of self-determination. But now there enters the other part of Locke's story, namely, that of authorizing reason. For this freedom as self-determination manifested in these acts of suspension, examination and contemplation, issues in acts authorized by reason. One might say that self-determination exists for the sake of just these acts. Since no such authorization is possible except through self-determination, while at the same time no overt free action is possible apart from such authorization, what follows is this. For Locke, in order to be free in one's unobstructed behavior two conditions must be met: persons must be self-determined and their acts must be authorized by reason. These two conditions must pertain simultaneously.

They do not necessarily pertain simultaneously. For as we have seen,

12. This confirms a point made before, that, for Locke, the pursuit of evil is voluntary and, ultimately, the result of neither ignorance nor weakness. Locke follows neither Plato nor Aristotle: he holds no brief for Plato's ethical determinism nor (as some mistakenly believe) for Aristotle's theory of incontinence. (On p. 359 of vol. 2 of the *Encyclopedia of Philosophy*, Richard Taylor says the exact opposite to what I here say about the relationship between Locke and Aristotle on this point.) Isaiah Berlin was wrong in his criticism of Locke; he himself follows in Locke's footsteps when he says "Freedom . . . requires a situation in which no sum total of . . . causal factors wholly determines the result—in which there remains some area, however narrow, in which choice is not completely determined." And we can now see that Dennett, with whose defense of libertarianism I opened the preceding chapter, is equally in the line of Locke when his answer to the question "How can a person be an author of decisions, and not merely the locus for causal summation for external influences?" takes the form of an argument to the effect that "our ultimate decision as to which way to act is less important phenomenologically as a contributor to our sense of free will than the prior decisions affecting our deliberative process itself: the decision, for instance, not to consider any further, to terminate deliberation; or the decision to ignore certain lines of inquiry" (*Brainstorms*, pp. 287 and 297).

there are acts in which persons are self-determined but their behavior is not authorized by reason;[13] and Locke explicitly identifies them as acts of freedom. Must we now say that there is an inner freedom of the mind and an overt freedom of unobstructed action? (In the former the agent is fully self-determined while in the latter the agent acts in accordance with the dicta of authorizing reason). And would the second of these have to be called the lesser of these two forms of freedom?

Paragraph 48 is a good point of departure for an attempt to arrive at an answer to both these questions:

> To be determined by our own [rational] judgment is no restraint to Liberty. This is so far from being a restraint or diminution of Freedom, that it is the very improvement and benefit of it: 'tis not an Abridgment, 'tis the end and use of our Liberty [of self-determination]; and the farther we are removed from such a determination [by our own rational judgment], the nearer we are to Misery and Slavery. . . . Nay were we determined by any thing but the last result of our own Minds, [rightly] judging of the good or evil of any action, we were not free, the very end of our Freedom being, that we might attain the good we chuse. And therefore every Man is put under a necessity by his constitution, as an intelligent Being, to be determined in willing by his own [rational] Thought and Judgment, what is best for him to do: else he would be under the determination of some other than himself, which is want of Liberty.

A person can come "under the determination of some other than himself" through not submitting to reason at all. This is the case in which the (inner) freedom exercised in suspension, examination and contemplation is misused, with the result that one abandons oneself freely to either a desire that reason has not approved or a desire of which one knows that reason cannot approve. In either case the outcome of that free act tends to be loss of freedom. For once one has thus abandoned oneself to a desire, it will become ever more difficult in subsequent situations to suspend action on, examine, and judge similar desires. Habits are formed quickly, and habitual behavior (except that of habitual suspension and examination of desires) is dangerous. The desire will then become uncontrollable, irresistible, and the one subject to it will then tend toward incorporation in a set of merely natural and fortuitous events. Free abandonment to unauthorized desire is the first step on the road of "Misery and Slavery," the

---

13. There are also cases in which persons are not self-determined but, in some sense, their behavior is authorized by reason. We saw cases such as these in Chap. 4 ("Borrowed Reason"); they will receive further discussion in the chapters on education.

beginning of the loss of autonomy that ends in one being "driven up and down, as a bubble by the force of the wind" (§67). On the other hand, acting rationally is "the end and use of our Liberty" of self-determination; acting rationally is both a "benefit" and an "improvement" of self-determination.

Self-determination and authorization by reason are, then, the two conditions jointly necessary for the inner freedom of the mind, that is, for the possibility of continued existence of the first of these conditions, that of self-determination. Free abandonment to unexamined pleasure is habit-forming. And the habit formed is one that destroys a person's ability to suspend action on desires in order to examine these desires. That is, it destroys the possibility of self-determination—of self-determination to both evil and good, both irrational and rational action. Since it destroys the ability for rational action, it destroys a person's ability to achieve mastery.

Locke posits the necessity of this joint condition in the words "Without Liberty the Understanding would be to no purpose: And without Understanding, Liberty (if it could be) would signify nothing" (§67). Without the inner liberty manifested in acts of self-determination there would be no suspension and hence no opportunity for reason to play its role. On the other hand, without reason "Liberty . . . would signify nothing." This is so whether, because of insufficient duration of suspension and lack of thoroughness of examination, only the prejudiced understanding functions and reason cannot play its role; or because, in spite of the unprejudiced understanding's adequate examination, reason's pronouncements are left unheeded. In either case, the desires acted upon have not gained reason's approbation and the outcome of such deliberate action is bondage. Hence, "without Understanding, Liberty (*if it could be*)."

But why should people want to have their acts authorized by reason? Why should they want to achieve mastery? Why is deliberate abandonment to desire unauthorized by reason not as free and praiseworthy an act as deliberate placing oneself under reason's authority—indeed, why is it not more praiseworthy to do the former rather than the latter? Is not the advocacy of the latter and the condemnation of the former in conflict with the notion of individual autonomy?

Commentators who (unlike Berlin and Fraser) read Locke as propounding a coherent libertarian doctrine give short shrift to questions like these. Polin, for example, writes that "Far from limiting our freedom, the determination of it through good reasons and reasonable motivation exemplifies it." He adds, "It would be absurd to imagine that liberty would consist in acting according to whim, to shrug off the yoke of reason and not to submit to the constraint of reflexion and judgment." He then draws the conclusion, "This is . . . why Locke does not hesitate to present the power of freedom as associated with the power of reason."[14]

It is clear that Polin is neither explaining nor justifying but merely reiterating Locke's position. Polin does not raise the question why it would be "absurd" to "shrug off the yoke of reason." Hence he leaves vague both the nature of, and the motive for, this "association" of "freedom" and "the power of reason"; and he fails to raise the question whether there might not be a contradiction or, at the least, a tension in this association. Polin is aware of a tension in "Locke's theory of freedom," but this is the tension between freedom as conformity to rational order and freedom as rejection of that order. My concern is with the tension *within* the former, *within* the notion of "freedom as conformity to rational order." What is missing from a valuable account such as Polin's is proper consideration of the role of passion, particularly of the master passion.

We now know what is the nature of the association of "the power of freedom" and "the power of reason." We do not yet know whether this association can be posited without contradiction. Once we understand the importance of passion in this part of Locke's doctrine, we will be able to answer the question whether there is a conflict between self-determination and authorization by reason.

3. Self-Determination and the Master Passion

The importance of passion can be stated quite succinctly. In some of our doings we are driven by natural passion, in some by the master passion. (Whether the sum of these makes up the totality of our doings remains, of course, to be settled.) If by natural passion, then reason plays no role and hence the question of a conflict between self-determination and authorizing reason has no relevance. But we come to a similar conclusion about the conflict between self-determination and reason when the case is one of being driven by the master passion. If it is the pursuit of true and lasting happiness that obliges us to suspend, examine, judge and submit to reason, then reason stands in the service of the master passion. Our acts are then, in the first instance, not authorized by reason but compelled by the master passion. We are then compelled by the overriding desire to pursue what reason tells us to be true happiness. It is that compelling

---

14. All these statements are from Polin's article "John Locke's Conception of Freedom," p. 3.

desire that makes us submit to reason's authority. The question whether
there is a conflict between pure self-determination and determination by
reason then disappears as the most fundamental question, and is replaced
by the question whether it is possible to be truly self-determined if one is
subject to the master passion.

Thus, when throughout the preceding section I argued that, for Locke,
there are instances of pure self-determination in acts such as those of
suspension of action on desire, that was in fact a premature conclusion
based on an incomplete statement. For although they are determined by
neither reason nor *natural* passion, these acts are determined by the *master*
passion. Apart from the desire for true and lasting happiness there would
be no suspension of action on natural desire.

We have met Locke's statements from paragraph 50, that "no Body"
"accounts" the "constant desire of Happiness, and the constraint it puts
upon us to act for it," to be "an abridgment of Liberty, or at least an
abridgment of Liberty to be complain'd of"; for the more a person
complies with "the necessity of being happy" the nearer is "his approach
to infinite perfection and happiness." We saw that Locke does not take this
"constraint" as a curtailment of our freedom, but as "the foundation of
Liberty" (§51). To ascertain whether there is incoherence or contradiction
in Locke's position when he holds both that human beings must be self-
determined and that they are "necessarily" subject to the master passion,
we must grasp the important main ramifications of the assertion that it is
our own "constitution" that places us under the "necessity to pursue true
happiness." Hence near the conclusion of my discussion of human freedom we are forced to consider once again the concept of human nature.
Let me recapitulate and further connect some of its important aspects.

Locke believes there are four essential aspects to human nature. Three
of these are original essential aspects and two of these three, namely,
freedom and rationality, belong to new-born human beings only potentially. The third, the constant uneasiness which is the desire or passion for
happiness, belongs to all human beings during all stages of their existence.
To typify all three of these aspects as "original" is to say that human beings
originally possess the potential to become free and the potential to become
rational, and that they are also originally subject to the constant uneasiness
which is the desire for happiness.

That it is *natural* or unacquired passion that human beings experience
from the beginning of life onwards is a point Locke makes emphatically in
the first Book of the *Essay* when he writes it is "Nature" that "has put into
Man a desire of Happiness, and an aversion to Misery" and when he calls
this desire and this aversion "innate practical Principles" that "continue

constantly to operate and influence all our Actions, without ceasing" and
that "may be observ'd in all Persons and all Ages, steady and universal"
(1.3.3). Stressed as well is the point that this chief natural passion is not to
be trusted to lead to true and lasting happiness, that instead, if left unchecked, it tends to lead into misery. Because this passion is pervasive and
untrustworthy, it makes human life precarious: ours is a "feeble passionate
nature" (§67). We cannot undo our nature. That is, we cannot cease
desiring pleasure and feeling aversion to misery; we have no choice but to
pursue happiness. But if human beings were necessarily determined only
by their natural passions, this would make them part of the realm of
nature in which necessity rules to the exclusion of all liberty. Since such
incorporation would, for Locke, tend to lead people into misery and
bondage, he does not trust natural human passion.

Hence Locke insists that there is more to human passion than that of the
mere natural kind. There is the master passion—the fourth of the essential
aspects of human nature. That passion we have seen not to be original but
acquired. Unlike the desire for happiness, not all who should possess the
passion for mastery actually come to acquire it. Nevertheless, it is only
through giving free reign to the master passion that creatures become
truly human. For it is only when reason serves the master passion that
both the potentialities for freedom and reason come to be fully actualized.[15] And it is only when reason serves the master passion that the
desire for happiness can attain true fulfillment through persons' mastery
of their understandings which allows for the extension of mastery over
nature, that is, for having their fate in their own hands.

To be human is to be passionate. But it is only the master passion that
allows a person true humanity. Giving in to whatever desire presents itself
is an original natural impulse that tends to preclude the actualization of
human freedom and rationality, and thus tends to preclude the possibility

15. I have distinguished freedom and rationality from the master passion as "original
characteristics" from an "acquired characteristic." I have said as well that freedom and
rationality belong to human beings only potentially. But, of course, so does the master
passion. Nevertheless, there is an important difference. When children grow up, they cannot
but come to experience their freedom and they are bound to do some reasoning. To an
extent, therefore, their potentialities of freedom and reason actualize themselves naturally.
The master passion, on the other hand, can only be acquired through deliberate and repeated
exertion of both freedom and reason. Acquiring the passion for mastery is acquiring a habit.
For Locke, habit is not "nature" but is "second nature." Hence also the acquired master
passion is not an expression of "nature" but of "second nature." A corollary of this position is
that since beings are not truly human unless they acquire the master passion—as with
freedom and reason, the master passion is an *essential* characteristic—human beings are not
"natural" but are "self-made." I return to this point in my discussion of Locke's educational
writings.

of becoming truly human. It is Locke's firm conviction that human beings must become actually what they are potentially. Hence they must acquire the master passion. In this sense their own "constitution" makes them "necessarily" subject to the master passion.

Passion remains. But through suspension of action on desire followed by examination and judgment of the objects of desire, experiences of natural passion are to be replaced by expression of the master passion. It is our own constitution that places us under the necessity of acquiring the master passion. It is, indeed, natural to be subject to unexamined desire; but it is also natural to become rational and free, and it is only through the master passion that we can "raise our Nature to its Highest Degree of Perfection."[16] Thus only the master passion is to be trusted.

This is to say that it is only reason that is to be trusted. For it is only when reason (rather than prejudiced understanding) serves passion, that the desire in question is an expression of the master passion. As we have seen, Locke takes reason to be infallible. Absolutely trustworthy reason demands distrust of all it has not authorized. And since it authorizes only its own products, it necessarily demands distrust of all expressions of natural passion. This reason demands the stance of the revolutionary: its distrust is of the radical kind that requires rejection of whatever is distrusted. Thus Locke is consistent when he holds that expressions of the master passion must come to replace those of natural passion.

Of the four essential aspects of human nature, three are original. One of these is natural passion. It is necessary to human action in the sense that without it there would be no initial desire and hence no stimulation to action; there would then be no need for suspension of action on desire, no subsequent examination and judgment, and so no opportunity to achieve mastery. Nevertheless, natural passion must always be rejected as the proper guide to action. The fourth aspect, the non-original master passion, must take its place. Locke consistently stresses this role for the master passion. But is this emphasis in turn consistent with the insistence on self-determination? That question still remains to be answered.

For Locke, no one is constrained or determined to pursue pleasure in a particular way, or to pursue lasting and true, rather than ephemeral and apparent, happiness. No one is determined to suspend pursuit of immediate pleasure and to examine its object; and once it is known in what true

16. The words quoted are part of Descartes's original title for the *Discourse on Method* (see his letter to Mersenne of March 1636, in Kenny's *Descartes: Philosophical Letters*, pp. 27–29). The fact that they fit my account reveals the close affinity between Locke and Descartes. For both, mastery is to be achieved through submission to reason. The reason in question, for both, is of a reductionistic nature which dictates a revolutionary stance.

happiness consists, no one is determined to pursue it. People are committed to pleasure; they are not committed to true and lasting happiness—to mastery. They cannot escape pursuit of pleasure, but only they can determine their own pursuit of true and lasting happiness. They need not act in accordance with their nature, that is, they need not work at the full realization of their freedom and rationality. They can shrug off the "necessity" under which their "constitution" places them. We may ask, again, whether disregard of this necessity is not a more authentically autonomous act than compliance with it?

Before people achieve the mastery that is to entail true and lasting happiness, they are already masters of their fate in that they can choose for or against their acts being authorized by reason, for or against the mastery that results from heeding the "necessity" of their "constitution." They can choose good or evil. To use Polin's words, "It is not excessive to say that, for Locke . . . freedom represents a freedom for evil, the principle of . . . fundamental evil."[17] Because human beings are originally free and because they are creatures of foresight, they cannot escape giving concrete shape to their being. They cannot avoid choosing for or against the mastery that follows submission to reason.

Because no one can escape taking position with respect to mastery and because the position ought to be that of wanting to acquire and strengthen it, the master passion is fundamental *ethically* speaking; the "ought" in question is the fundamental feature of Locke's ethics. But *ontically* speaking, freedom is the more fundamental feature. Because the basic choice for everyone is that of what sort of creature one is to become—moral or non-moral—therefore Locke's ethics is founded on his ontology.

Why should one choose to act in such a way that one possibility rather than another—mastery rather than incorporation into nature—comes to be realized? The answer, for Locke, is not difficult. Human beings are creatures capable of exercising control, creatures who can become masters. It is foolish for such creatures to act in a way that bans freedom, removes control from their hands, and so deprives them of all mastery. To put this differently: human beings are creatures questing for pleasure. It is foolish for such creatures to act in ways that diminish pleasure and, in the long run, have as a possible consequence eternal misery. The reason why a person desires control in the first place is for the sake of attaining happiness. Originally capable of such control, it would be foolish to use it in a way that makes subsequent control (through acts of suspension, examination and judgment) more and more difficult and in the end nearly impossi-

17. "John Locke's Conception of Freedom," p. 3.

ble. Yet people make that foolish, irrational choice.[18] They do so whenever they choose not to act in accordance with their nature, that is, when they choose not to act in a way that actualizes rationality and so extends both freedom and control.[19] The first act of choice, that of what sort of creature one is to become, is an autonomous act. But it is, Locke believes, an act that can either tend to destroy autonomy or that can give it a fuller extension.

It tends to destroy autonomy when the act is one not involving submission to reason. For action on unexamined or insufficiently examined desire does not just have as a result something like less than full mastery. The nemesis of such acts is more severe. As we have seen, the unexamined or inadequately examined desires to which one freely abandons oneself become ever more difficult to resist in future instances and it therefore becomes ever more difficult to achieve any form of self-determination that consists in the actions of suspending desire and examining the desire's object. Even the self-determination that consists in a willful abandonment to desire with hardly a thought of the likely consequences, is an ability that then tends to become lost. The desire becomes nearly irresistible; giving in to it becomes virtually automatic. The habit thus formed becomes nearly unbreakable, and the person loses practically all control. The initial autonomous act in which one embraces unexamined desire was an act that fully depended on oneself; it was an expression of pure self-determination. Its outcome is incorporation in the mechanism of nature, a mechanism that tends to leave no control to those being incorporated in it. Apart from the original autonomous act it is, for Locke, only rational action that allows for control. It is only rational action that allows a person to achieve ever greater freedom and happiness. One's fate is in one's hands when, after suspension of a desire, one can choose either adequate examination of its object or abandonment to unexamined or insufficiently

18. Some commentators (e.g., John Dunn) would reject this conclusion because they interpret it too "existentially." Contrary to what Dunn believes to be the case, to choose what sort of creature one is to become does not make truth "depend upon human desire." Precisely because there is, for Locke, a law independent of human desire—and a world which is as it is, including the determination of good and evil, regardless of human will—precisely because there is the law of reason, therefore each person must choose to live in accordance with or in defiance of reason. As we shall see in a moment, the ability of, indeed necessity for, human beings to choose one way or the other, does not, in terms of his own doctrine, make "the life which Locke himself lived . . . a ludicrous exercise in self-denial." (The quotations are from Dunn, *Locke*, p. 87. See also p. 75.)

19. Because Locke holds that everyone is capable of making that irrational choice, his position is one in which original freedom plays a more fundamental role than original rationality. Here, again, there is close affinity with Descartes. See my "Descartes: La primauté du libre vouloir sur la raison," *Dialogue* 25, no. 2 (1986), pp. 211–21.

examined desire. If the first course of action is adopted, one remains master of one's fate. If the second, one is on the way to the loss of all mastery. Such loss of mastery coincides with ever decreasing happiness.[20]

Because the choice is an autonomous act, there is no explanation for why one goes this way rather than that. Locke deems the first course of action to be wise, the second foolish. Neither its wisdom nor its foolishness determines the act. Fundamentally, there is no explanation of why one becomes ever more fully human in the power of mastery, or ever less human in the force of "brute beasts."[21]

To the question: Why should one choose to act in accordance with one's nature? Locke, in the end, provides no answer. The self-determination of the act is total. That the choice ought to go one way rather than the other is Locke's moral judgment on the issue. The same holds for the statement that human potentiality ought to be actualized. The "compulsion" of human nature remains a moral compulsion; it morally justifies certain acts, but it cannot determine agents to carry them out. Locke is too un-Aristotelean to allow potentiality to prod or draw a person decisively one way rather than another. That is, human potentiality does not function as either an efficient or a final cause in the account of its own realization. Thus it is not an immanent potentiality that determines a person to pursue good rather than evil. Neither is that role filled by a transcendent deity. As we read in *A Letter concerning Toleration*, "God himself will not save men against their wills" (p.23).

No one is determined by fortuitous pleasure or by deliberate reason except through acts of self-determination. The question for this section was whether these acts are instances of pure self-determination or whether they are prompted by the master passion and, if the latter is the case, whether there is incoherence or contradiction in Locke's position at this point. Part of the answer is that it is not the master passion that prompts a person to mastery. But of course this was implied all along in the statement that the master passion is *acquired*. If a person achieves mastery that is taken to be an autonomous act. The reverse holds as well: no thorough incorporation into the mechanism of nature is possible apart from initial autonomy.

20. This conclusion fits the well-known statement from the *Second Treatise*, §57: "Could they be happier without it, the Law, as an useless thing would of it self vanish" and "the end of Law is not to abolish or restrain but to preserve and enlarge Freedom." "The law" is the law of nature, which coincides with the dictates of reason. Once it serves the master passion, human freedom is "preserved" and "enlarged," and happiness remains within the person's grasp.

21. For the legitimacy of my use of "beasts," see the *Second Treatise*, e.g., paragraphs 12, 16, and 63.

But does this entail that there is no incoherence or contradiction in Locke's position when he holds that one is truly self-determined? As an empiricist, he teaches that one experiences one's unconditioned freedom. Experience reveals this freedom to be fundamental: one chooses for or against acquiring the master passion, for or against the life of reason. It may thus seem as if incoherence is forestalled through the hierarchical ordering of self-determination and reason.[22] But is it?[23] May one coherently ascribe self-determination and passion for the pursuit of mastery to one and the same subject at all?

If we recapitulate what I said about the crucial aspects Locke ascribes to human nature we will see that he is in deep trouble at this foundational level of his position. (i) I can achieve mastery through autonomous submission to reason. Such submission will not just keep me from being incorporated into the mechanism of nature; it will allow me ever greater mastery over nature, which makes me more and more master over the events of my daily life,[24] and thus gives increasingly overt expression to my autonomy. Not to go this way of increasing autonomy would be foolish: it would prevent actualization of both my freedom and reason, and it would frustrate my innate propensity to pleasure by leading me into ever greater (possibly eternal) misery. (ii) But if I want to, I can be foolish. I can express my unconditioned self-determination—which is also a di-

---

22. That Locke's position on human freedom is fundamentally one of pure voluntarism may seem to conflict with his statement on divine freedom: "God Almighty himself is under the necessity of being happy; and the more any intelligent Being is so, the nearer is its approach to infinite perfection and happiness" (§50). However, the "necessity" under which God finds himself would, for Locke, not be different from that of human beings. And there are no pre-existing "eternal truths" to which God would have to conform his action in order to be happy. (Cf. 4.11.14.)

23. In a perceptive article on Dugald Stewart, Edward H. Madden presents Stewart's position on human freedom as one similar to what I argue to be Locke's. Madden concludes that Stewart's account "turns agent causality into pure voluntarism. An agent simply decides arbitrarily to follow reason or the passional life. The decision is authentically his . . . but voluntarism is not the base sought by the Scots for their agent causality and is incompatible with their view that reason should prevail and regulate the lower motives. Stewart might have responded that it is not impossible for agents to have a nature that inclines them to accept reason as a guide but does not require it. . . . The problem is that Stewart never saw the difficulty." It is clear from the tenor of Locke's argument that he did see "the difficulty," that of self-determination and compulsion by the master passion served by reason. His "solution" is that suggested by Madden: "foresight" would "incline" to rational action but does not "require," let alone make it inescapable. Hence pure voluntarism remains intact. Madden suggests this as a solution without exploring whether it involves further problems. (See Edward H. Madden, "Stewart's Enrichment of the Commonsense Tradition," *History of Philosophy Quarterly* 3, no. 1 (1986): 45–63. The quotations are from pp. 58–59.)

24. I return to the implied notion of progress in the next part of this chapter.

mension of my nature—by going the path of unexamined desire. I can prevent the rule of reason and commit myself to prejudiced understanding. Through a purely voluntaristic act which expresses unconditioned self-determination I thwart the expressions of other dimensions of my essence, those of reason, freedom, and the desire for realization of happiness. Conversely, actualization of my nature, of its dimensions of reason, freedom, and propensity to pleasure, requires that limits be placed upon unconditional self-determination.

Contrary to what some commentators would have us believe, the problem of Locke's theory of freedom is not that of the libertarian who finds himself forced into determinism. Instead, it is that of the libertarian who cannot reconcile the absolute *freedom* of pure voluntarism with the autonomy of mastery to be achieved through *submission* to reason and rejection of prejudiced understanding. Pure self-determination is incompatible with the pursuit of mastery. Yet Locke holds such self-determination to be a basic expression of human nature. But he also considers reason, freedom, and the desire for happiness to be such expressions. The expressions of the latter as basic aspects of human nature, are incompatible with that of the first. That is, Locke has ascribed fundamental features to human nature that cannot co-exist in it. In this respect his position is incoherent.[25]

4. The Master Passion and Progress

To say, as Yolton does, that "The moral agent is precisely the person who feels uneasy when not pursuing the moral good, who takes delight in right actions"[26] is to tell Locke's story well, as long as we keep firmly in mind that Locke means the uneasiness in question to be self-induced. And we must of course also remember that this self-induced uneasiness is not the only uneasiness to which a person is subject. As self-induced, it is distinct from the natural uneasiness that a person originally experiences as the manifestation of natural passion. In the moral life in which natural desire is constantly replaced by expressions of the master passion, natural uneasiness nevertheless remains a constant feature. People constantly feel

25. This problem of incoherence is hardly peculiar to Locke. See my *Descartes and the Enlightenment*, chap. 5, part 1.

26. The quotation is from Yolton's "Action and Agency," in *Locke and the Compass of Human Understanding*, p. 147. In the same volume, that position is ascribed to Locke by Aarsleff in his "The State of Nature and the Nature of Man in Locke" (see pp. 99–136). This position is a major theme in Polin's *La politique morale de John Locke*.

uneasy about whether the good that is theirs today will be theirs tomorrow; they constantly desire to consolidate and extend their control and so increase their autonomy. As long as they are to any degree at the mercy of things their reason cannot grasp and they cannot control, they feel uneasy. As creatures of foresight they know that human bodies may malfunction, that the society in which they now live in relative peace may come to be in upheaval, that (through drought or flood or other natural causes) their physical context may deprive them of the ease they have already attained. Natural uneasiness remains characteristic of human life even when the master passion rules. The desire for happiness remains insatiable, even if the particular desires that are being fulfilled all form parts of true happiness. Though masters, human beings are not gods. They remain finite creatures who have to exert themselves for limited satisfaction from day to day. Locke does not take this state of being as a tragedy. To the contrary: it is one ground for his belief in progress.

Since to be human is to be in a state of insatiable desire, no human being can be entirely caught up in the present moment. Even for those who have misused the freedom of self-determination and have chosen the unexamined or insufficiently examined pleasure of the moment—even for those for whom this action has become habitual so that it hardly remains one of choice—it is true that immediacy cannot hold total sway, that the occasion for escape from subjectivism and relativism continues to present itself, that the opportunity for mastery remains. We have seen earlier that life itself prompts to the breakthrough of reason.[27] We now see an additional factor: through the presence of uneasiness, the opportunity for mastery is built into human nature. This entails that the chance for gaining and extending control, the opportunity for progress, is built into human nature. For any human being—even those who are to a large extent incorporated into the mechanism of nature—can cease making the wrong choices and commence submitting to reason (cf. §69). Once under the sway of the master passion, their natural uneasiness will incite them to booking success upon success on the road of progress.

The task of human beings is to determine the kind of uneasiness they are to be under, the kind of desires they will have. To Locke's belief that to act humanly is to act rationally, add his conviction that to act rationally is to conform one's beliefs and actions to the nature of the universe. As creatures who constantly desire, no single state of happiness will be fully satisfactory if only because circumstances beyond their control may deprive them of it tomorrow. Since Locke shares the assumption of his age

27. See Chap. 4, section 2.

that "knowledge is power," therefore uneasiness incites to continual increase of knowledge of both physical and human nature. All knowledge comes to be developed only because people desire happiness; there is no knowledge for knowledge's sake, and the attitude of contemplation is to be exchanged for that of constant activity (cf. 4.12.12). Also the incentive for the development of knowledge is built into human nature. And, Locke believes, human beings have the capability to develop whatever knowledge their condition requires: "We shall not have much Reason to complain of the narrowness of our Minds, if we will but employ them about what may be of use to us; for of that they are very capable" (1.1.5). Rational creatures therefore have as task to know nature ever more adequately and to conform their actions to this knowledge ever more completely through purposely inducing in themselves the right kind of desires. If a person takes this task seriously, then the chronicle of increased control that results from this kind of self-determination relates an unending history of progress in the areas of both morals and nature, in both mastery of self and mastery of one's physical surroundings.[28]

If mankind wills it, it can be forever on the way of improvement of its lot. People will then have to renounce the way of "learned Ignorance," of the superstitions and prejudices embodied in the "general Maxims, precarious Principles, and Hypotheses laid down at Pleasure" (4.12.12). They will have to become masters of their own minds if they are to acquire the master passion. Only when compelled by reason can mankind attain the position of continued mastery of its destiny, of guiding this destiny to one of true and lasting happiness.

John Dunn has written of Locke as one who considers human passions to be "the corrupt passions released by the Fall."[29] As a description of the natural passions the characterization of "corrupt" is apt because, as we have seen, if left unchecked natural passions tend to deprive human beings of their autonomy and to make them part of the mechanism of nature; natural passions tend to lead to a loss of humanity and to reduce human beings to the level of "brute beasts." In acquiring the master passion a person undoes, or prevents, the consequences of the Fall. As we acquire the master passion, we are working out our salvation for time and eternity. This Locke takes not to be a matter of "working out your own

28. The spirit of the Enlightenment comes through clearly in this paragraph. Compare, for example, what Berlin and Crane Brinton write about the Enlightenment, the former in *The Age of Enlightenment*, p. 16; the latter in "Enlightenment," *Encyclopedia of Philosophy* 2:519. The points made in this paragraph all come to the fore in the *Essay*'s chapter "Of the Improvement of our Knowledge." See in particular 4.12.11–12.

29. Dunn, *The Political Thought of John Locke*, p. 194.

salvation with fear and trembling"; given that it is infallible reason that guides the process, it can be carried out with valor and confidence. Neither does he consider it a matter of it being "God [who] is at work in you, both to will and to work"; for we all determine ourselves to this process through acts of pure self-determination.[30]

Without the passion for mastery, human beings cannot become what their "constitution" "necessitates" them to be, that is, rational and free beings—masters. "Of Power" is part of Locke's answer to the question of how a person can achieve self-realization. A theme that runs through this answer is his rationalism: to each who will but listen, reason tells the same story about "happiness in general" and how to obtain it through each of life's particular experiences. In essence, the story is the same for all, because it is "reason unbiass'd" to which one listens. Whoever heeds reason cannot fail to progress on the path of self-realization, because "reason unbiass'd" is by its nature infallible. The doctrine of the infallibility of reason is presupposed throughout Locke's account of self realization and progress. The conclusion of my third chapter revealed the dogmatism inherent in this doctrine. This dogmatism now presents itself in the very core of Locke's account of how a person can achieve self-realization.

When we combine conclusions from the preceding and present sections of this chapter, it will be clear that dogmatism extends beyond that just mentioned. Locke states that we can all control our passions, suspend and examine action on our desires, and determine ourselves to act only on the dictates of reason. "Nor let any one say, he cannot govern his Passions, nor hinder them from breaking out, and carrying him into action; for what he can do before a Prince, or a great Man, he can do alone, or in the presence of God, if he will" (§53). But the last phrase of this statement contains a condition. It points to the doctrine that the passion for mastery is an acquired passion. This passion cannot itself determine that it be acquired. Acquiring the master passion is meant to be a matter of self-determination, purely a case of "if he will"; it excludes determination by known good as well as by the knowledge that ill befalls those who act irrationally. There are, therefore, no demonstrable grounds on which to base the doctrine that human beings will progress to ever greater self-realization simply because they possess the ability for such progress. Given Locke's doctrine of fundamental, unconditioned freedom, the po-

---

30. The quotations are from St. Paul's *Letter to the Philippians* (2:12–13). That, for Locke, God does not determine human self-determination is also clear from what he writes in the *Third Letter concerning Toleration, Works*, 1823, 5:397–98.

tentiality for mastery cannot necessitate its actualization. To the extent that Locke sounds a note of optimism about human progress, it is a groundless optimism. It is an article of faith for which reason can offer no guarantee nor revelation provide any foundation.

The doctrine of progress is a dogmatic assertion. Hence Locke's optimism—dare one say it?—is that of "enthusiasm." On it, Locke's verdict is severe. "Enthusiasm . . . founded neither on Reason, nor Divine Revelation" rises "from the Conceits of a warmed or over-weening Brain." He adds that "where it once gets footing" it "works" "more powerfully on the Perswasions and Actions of Men, than either of those two, or both together" (4.19.7). The history of the doctrine of progress since the writing of the *Essay concerning Human Understanding* provides abundant proof for the correctness of Locke's observation.

C
∾

The Education of a Potential Master

Human beings are essentially rational and free. If they determine themselves to be led by their reason in all the circumstances of their lives, they can become the kind of masters who, for time and eternity, have their fate in their own hands. There is a pressing question for one who, like Locke, holds these beliefs. If rationality and freedom are essential to being human, then why is there so little achievement of mastery? Why are so many in bondage to passions which their reason has not authorized, to superstition, to irrational doctrines, to evil institutions? From the immediately preceding chapter we know that the answer is, fundamentally, in terms of the original unconditioned freedom that pertains to human beings: we must choose to reason and to submit ourselves to our reason's dictates, and we can refuse to do either. Those who refuse are people who deliberately choose to act on desires their reason has not authorized, sometimes on desires they know their reason cannot authorize. Among these people are the domineering parents and prejudiced teachers of the *Essay* and the oppressing authorities of the *Toleration* and the *Second Treatise*. Their aim in life includes keeping others in thrall through inculcation of such beliefs and practices as secure their position of power. These people are "debased," "brutish," not really (or at least not fully) human. But Locke believes that most people are not like this. And many if not most of these are *subjected* to these prejudiced educators and oppressive authorities. Locke's answer, therefore, most frequently takes the form which focuses on this *subjection*. As we have seen, this form of the answer involves "principling," that is, the kind of education which, rather than making the young critical of current beliefs and practices, conditions them to an unquestioning acceptance of "the well endowed Opinions in Fashion" (4.3.20). Thus, with respect to most, Locke's explanation of the lack of achievement of mastery is in terms of wrong upbringing or education.

If the wrong kind of education stands in the way of mastery, can the right kind *guarantee* it? We already know that many recent commentators answer this question affirmatively. To be a master is to be a moral being, a person, for persons constantly strive to conform their actions to the dictates of their reason. Passmore argues it to be Locke's position that education can make one good, and Yolton—though with some qualifications—that the product of education is "moral man," the person. For both, habituation plays a crucial role in this process. But how habituation can produce a rational (revolutionary) autonomous being is a matter with which neither Passmore nor Yolton deals satisfactorily. And Nathan Tarcov's extensive treatment of Locke's educational writings explicitly avoids this central issue.

Especially in view of the Lockean doctrines of epistemic and moral autonomy described in the preceding sections, it is clear that more discussion is in order. As I now turn to Locke's works on education, it is not my intention to deal with all its various aspects. I disregard a large number of issues which, though not unimportant, are secondary to the main thrust. The main thrust derives from the way in which Locke relates his doctrine of the (potential) autonomy of the one to be taught with that of the authority of the teacher. Ironically, it is the main thrust that many recent treatments (such as Tarcov's) have by and large neglected in favor of secondary matters. Or, alternatively, it is this main thrust that influential writers (such as Passmore) have drastically misinterpreted.

I deal with the main thrust, with its nature and its relation especially to the *Essay concerning Human Understanding* but also to Locke's writings on politics and religion, as I explore questions such as the following. According to Locke, what is the nature of education? Who, or what, is the teacher? Is the (re-)education of adults essentially like the education of children? If it is wrong to live by precepts one has uncritically accepted (even if these are fully rational precepts) then what is the role of the teacher? Similarly, if the master passion (without which one cannot live a rational life) is an acquired passion which all must acquire for themselves then, again, what is the role of the teacher? If acquiring the master passion is acquiring a new habit and if (as many commentators hold) for Locke education consists essentially in instilling habits, then can education instill the master passion so that mastery is a direct consequence of proper education?

The last three of these questions appear to indicate tension: the first two would seem to make the teacher irrelevant while the third would seem to make education necessary for the achievement of mastery. Whether this is a tension in Locke's theory is one further question I attempt to answer in the following two chapters.

～7

Human Nature
and Education

This first of two chapters on Locke's educational theory has three divisions, each of which provides a part of the vantage point from which, in the next chapter, we can come to grips with the central thrust of this theory. The opening one connects these two chapters with the first two sections of this book. The following two present doctrines crucial to understanding Locke's educational writings: the first of these is the doctrine of the tabula rasa; the second, one I call "the doctrine of original neutrality."

1. "Of Power" and Locke on Education

If by nature human beings are potentially masters because by nature they possess foresight as well as the powers to suspend, deliberate and contemplate; if by nature they are responsible beings who can "by a due consideration" of the "true worth" of things, make themselves "uneasie in the want of it, or in the fear of losing it" (2.21.53) and thus determine their will to action conducive to well-being—then why are so many indiscriminate, shortsighted, precipitous, or irresponsible? I have stressed that ultimately there is no answer beyond pointing to the act of pure self-determination: neither education nor social pressure determines a person's way of life, at least not fundamentally. But education, social pressure and status, each play a role—a fact to which Locke draws attention in statements throughout "Of Power."

There is one passage in which he pulls together and reformulates these statements. Locke wrote it as an addition to "Of Power" paragraph 53, the paragraph ending with the sentence that so pointedly expresses individual autonomy ("Nor let any one say, he cannot govern his Passions, nor hinder them from breaking out, and carrying him into action; for what he can do before a Prince, or a great Man, he can do alone, or in the presence of God, if he will"). Locke decided not to include this new passage in the third edition of the *Essay*, presumably because he recognized that the points it emphasizes were already made in various places of the published version of "Of Power" and, in addition, in *Some Thoughts concerning Education*. But since the passage colorfully states answers to the question why people "abandon themselves" to injurious courses of action, and because it has much to say about the role of upbringing in general and education in particular, it forms an apt link between the discussion of reason and freedom on the one hand and education on the other. The passage may be found in Lord King's *The Life and Letters of John Locke*;[1] it is of sufficient interest to quote almost all of it.

> Perhaps it will be said, if this be so, that men can suspend their desires, stop their actions, and take time to consider and deliberate upon what they are going to do. If men can weigh the good and evil of an action they have in view; if they have a power to forbear till they have surveyed the conse-quences, and examined how it may comport with their happiness or misery, and what a train of one or the other it may draw after it; how comes it to pass that we see men abandon themselves to the most brutish, vile, irrational, exorbitant actions, during the whole current of a wild or dissolute life, without any check, or the least appearance of any reflection, who, if they did but in the least consider what will certainly overtake such a course here, and what may possibly attend it hereafter, would certainly sometimes make a stand, slacken their pace, abate of that height of wickedness their actions rise to? Amongst the several causes there may be of this, I shall set down some of the most common.
>
> 1st. It sometimes happens that from their cradles some were never ac-customed to reflect, but by a constant indulging of their passions have been all along given up to the conduct and swing of their inconsiderate desires, and so have, by a contrary habit, lost the use and exercise of reflection, as if it were foreign to their constitution, and can no more bear with it as a violence done to their natures. . . . Both the poor and rich, I fear, offend in this way; the one in not opening their children's mind at all, the other in letting them loose only to sensual pleasures; and hence the one never have their thoughts raised above the necessities of a needy drudging life, on which they are

---

1. Peter (Lord) King, *The Life and Letters of John Locke*. My quotation is from the London, 1884, edition, pp. 359–60.

wholly intent, and the other have no thought besides their present pleasures, which wholly possess them.

2nd. There seems to me to be in the world a great number of men who want not parts, but who, from another sort of ill education, and the prevalency of bad company and ill-imbibed principles of mistaken philosophy, cast away the thought and beliefs of another world as a fiction of politicians and divines conspiring together to keep the world in awe, and to impose on weak minds. . . . This I imagine is certain, that when in this age of the world the belief of another life leaves a man of parts who has been bred up under the sound and opinion of heaven and hell, virtue seldom stays with him; and then all his happiness being resolved into the satisfaction of his temporal desires, it is no wonder that his will should be determined, and his life guided, by measures that, by men of other principles, seem to want consideration.

3rd. To these we may add a third sort, who, for want of breeding, not arriving at a learned irreligion, or an argumentative disbelief of a future state, find a shorter cut to it from their own ill manners, than the others do from study and speculation; for having plunged themselves in all sorts of wickedness and villany, their present lives give them but a very ill prospect of a future state, they resolve it their best way to have no more thoughts about it, but to live in a full enjoyment of all they can get and relish here and not to lessen that enjoyment by the consideration of a future life, whereof they can expect no benefit.

Since these three cases concern people who "abandon themselves to the most brutish, vile, irrational, exorbitant actions, without . . . the least appearance of any reflection," it may be thought that Locke is here describing extreme cases or isolated instances. Even if this were so, this passage would lend itself for instruction: extremes, whether of the well-considered rational or of the unreflective irrational life, tend to make the relevant principles implicit in them easier to discern. But it is plausible to hold that Locke does not take himself to be describing isolated cases. The passage itself indicates as much. For according to Locke many if not most of "the poor" "offend" through "not opening their children's mind at all." And as for "the rich" the *Second Treatise* especially reveals that many of them are among "the most brutish." To them belong Kings Charles and James and their numerous ardent followers—all of whom Locke considers to be tyrants and supporters of tyrants who, through their irrational actions, reveal that they "live by another Rule, than that of reason" and hence "may be destroyed as . . . wild Savage beasts."[2]

---

2. See the *Second Treatise*, paragraphs 8, 11, 16, 172. Ashcraft's *Revolutionary Politics and Locke's Two Treatises of Government* has made it very clear that Locke himself was quite prepared to be personally involved in the "destruction" of these "brutish" characters.

A few comments on each of these three cases will establish that this passage from King's *Life and Letters* reinforces some of my earlier conclusions. At the same time they will indicate major issues that remain to be considered.

"1st." Human beings need to acquire the habit to suspend and reflect. That is, as they grow up their innate potential power of "reflection" must be actualized rather than (through giving in to pressures of the moment) become lost and hence "foreign to their constitution." They must be taught to resist immediate needs and desires so that the power of reflection is constantly and, after a while, habitually activated rather than suppressed or over-ruled by the passions that would lead the pressures of the moment to triumph. Depriving them, while still very young, of immediate satisfaction of desires, they can come to understand through subsequent experience that immediate satisfaction would have been wrong.

Important questions at once arise. Is not this a process of conditioning and, if so, can this conditioning be reconciled with acts of self-determination? Furthermore, if this is a process of conditioning then who conditioned the conditioner or, who taught the teacher? Is Passmore's position then defensible after all when he writes that Locke "opened up, in principle, the possibility of perfecting man by the application of readily intelligible, humanly controllable, mechanisms"?[3] These fundamental questions (to be dealt with in the next chapter) jump out at us. And there are additional important doctrines implicit in these statements.

"The poor," says Locke, "offend" "in not opening their children's mind at all" through allowing their attention to be fully absorbed by the procurement of daily necessities. Since this is an offense, the implication is that also for the offspring of the poor, education is mandatory. "Of Power," the *Conduct of the Understanding*, and *Some Thoughts concerning Education* were, of course, directly addressed to the middle and upper classes if only for the reason that, by and large, the lower class was illiterate. But it would be illegitimate to draw from this the conclusion that these works were not meant to have their impact on the lower class—a conclusion drawn in many discussions of Locke's writings on education. The doctrines of personal responsibility, of individual moral and epistemic autonomy, of the universal sameness of human nature and of the universality of reason—all of which we have seen in earlier chapters—rule out the rightness of that conclusion. Potentially, the poor are as human as the rich. Their total absorption into the activity of meeting physical needs is therefore both illegitimate and avoidable.[4] After all (as the *Conduct* puts

3. John Passmore, *The Perfectibility of Man* (London, 1970), p. 163.
4. Locke himself advanced a proposal whose implementation was to guarantee that total absorption of the children of the poor in eking out the wherewithal for their subsistence

it) "the difference, so observable in men's understandings and parts, does not arise so much from their natural faculties as acquired habits" (§4). Like Descartes in the opening paragraph of the *Discourse on Method*, Locke is thoroughly egalitarian about peoples' natural faculties.

Not implied is that if there is no total absorption minds will naturally

---

would be avoidable. It is his proposal for "working schools" which he presented in 1697 in his *Report to the Board of Trade*. (This proposal is reprinted as Appendix A to R. H. Quick's edition of *Some Thoughts concerning Education* [Cambridge, 1927]; the quotations in this footnote are from this three-page proposal.) Ironically, this proposal (at least in our century) has been systematically misread—as if Locke championed the kind of workhouses which, in a later century, aroused the ire of Charles Dickens. (For a recent example of such misreading, see W. M. Spellman, *John Locke and the Problem of Depravity* [Oxford, 1988], pp. 207–8.) Because this document is systematically misread, the following should be noted about it. Locke proposes the working schools for basically two reasons. (i) They are to make it possible for parents to provide adequately for their own physical needs and those of their pre-school children, and they are to supply major physical needs (food and warmth) for the school-aged children. This would take care of the first condition for successful education: it would allow for the "sound body" without which the "sound mind" could hardly be achieved. (ii) They are to teach school-aged children a trade *and* they are to make them literate and provide them with a general education. The second part of this reason is usually denied, and so the proposal is read as if Locke meant these schools to be primarily places to secure child labor, institutions which would condition these children "for their principal role in life as hewers of wood and drawers of water" (to quote from M. G. Jones, *The Charity School Movement: A Study of Eighteenth Century Puritanism in Action* [Cambridge, 1938], p. 76). *Locke meant these children's labor to make possible their education.* There are many indications of the correctness of this conclusion in the language of the proposal. Locke refers to these children as "the scholars." He argues that "the nourishment and teaching of such a child during the whole time will cost the parish nothing." The phrase "the whole time" spans over a decade (from age 3 to age 14); it does not take a decade for children to learn "spinning or knitting" (the chief sort of labor in these schools). Clearly, then, more teaching is to be going on than that required for learning these trades. This conclusion is supported by Locke's reference to these scholars' "schoolmasters or dames" and by his suggestion that if the school becomes large then "the boys and girls" may be "*taught* and kept to *work* separately." Finally, the "schoolmasters or dames" are to see to it that these "scholars" attend "church every Sunday . . . whereby they may be brought into some sense of religion." The result: by age 14 these children will have a good chance to become *persons*—as individuals who are "strangers" to neither "religion" (from church) nor "morality" and "industry" (from school) they can both think for themselves and provide for themselves and thus experience a considerable degree of autonomy. The scheme of working schools was to provide sufficient products from the children's labor to allow the parish to take care of their basic physical needs as well as hire their "schoolmasters or dames." And the labor in question was to leave sufficient leisure time for the education of these children who "with their belly-full of bread daily at school . . . will be healthier and stronger than those who are bred otherwise," and therefore capable to benefit from such education. Locke's proposal is meant to realize one of his main tenets, namely, that all human beings are to be guided by their own reason. It is to overcome what, in the closing pages of the *Reasonableness*, he identifies as a formidable obstacle to human progress: "the greatest part of mankind" are uneducated not because of lack of talent but lack of opportunity. (See also, again, the *Essay* 4.20.2–4.) (My conclusion here differs from Tully's. On the ground of this same document, he argues that Locke's "aim open. In that case there is no more than an opportunity for "opening of minds"; for a mind free from such absorption may come to be claimed entirely by present pleasures—the offense of the rich. Hence although the powers to suspend, to examine, and to reflect belong to human beings by nature, they are powers that need to be developed, habits that need to be acquired. Contrary, anti-rational, anti-natural habits can easily be contracted. What is by birth "foreign to their constitution" can become second nature; what is a natural potential can come to be experienced as "violence done to their natures." But for Locke this second nature is not human nature; it is less than human nature, debased because "abandoned" to "irrational . . . actions," to a "dissolute life" in which neither freedom nor mastery nor progress come to expression.

"2nd." Here we meet "another sort of ill education" (which implies that what was said under "1st" was also "ill education"), that which deems consideration of "another world" and "another life" irrelevant to the present world and life. A being thus educated may appear like the offspring of the indulgent rich, unreflectingly absorbed in total abandonment to pleasures of the moment. This appearance arises because, without consideration of a future state, the principle that orders life is limited to the here and now. But in this case life is, nevertheless, being ordered quite consciously and deliberately in terms of a "principle"; it is behavior consistently based on "a learned irreligion, or an argumentative disbelief of a future state." This form of "ill education" produces beings who are, in effect, as far from truly human as are the offspring of the poor consumed by daily cares or of the rich unthinkingly engrossed in fortuitous pleasures. The training (or lack of training) of all three results in preoccupation with immediacies. As a consequence, in view of the possibility of "another world," none of them are masters of their fate. In fact, their upbringing does not even allow them mastery of the present. For whether absorbed by the necessities of nature or by natural pleasures, in neither case has reason authorized this behavior; hence, in either case, the behavior falls short of human action.

"3rd." Locke here moves to the "ill bred" or "ill mannered," whom he juxtaposes to those of a "learned irreligion." This juxtaposition does not imply that their alternative is not one consciously chosen. The "ill man-

---

is . . . to fabricate an individual who is habituated to docility and to useful labour." See Tully's "Governing Conduct," p. 68. Both the notions of fabricating an individual and of habituation of human beings into docility run counter to several of Lock's oft-stated convictions about human nature. There is at least some support for my position in John Dunn, " 'Bright enough for all our purposes': John Locke's Conception of a Civilized Society," *Notes and Records of the Royal Society* [London], 43 [1989]: 143.)

nered" at first consider the prospect of a future state, at least as a possibility, and then deliberately reject it—not as irrelevant but (given their determination to enjoy the present) because its continued consideration would lessen the pleasures of the moment through awareness of the unhappiness they may entail. If they were to contemplate it seriously even as only a possibility, they might no longer be able to enjoy the pleasures to which they have become accustomed; a change of ways might be required to dispel the resulting uneasiness. Since the will has no power to resist such uneasiness, therefore assured continuation of "their present lives" is possible only if they prevent that uneasiness from arising, and the only way to forestall it is to prevent serious "consideration of a future life."[5] Absence of this kind of "consideration"—through deliberately keeping the peculiarly human power of "foresight" out of play—characterizes their behavior also as less-than-human.

Let us now move from Locke's unpublished addition to "Of Power" to his published writings on education. *Some Thoughts concerning Education* appeared in 1693, the year before the *Essay* saw its second edition. The most important changes and most extensive additions to this second edition were to "Of Power." From Locke's correspondence with Molyneux we know that these revisions were completed by August 23, 1693. Thus while Locke was thinking about freedom and desire, self-determination and habit, he was at the same time preparing *Some Thoughts concerning Education* for the press. There is clear continuity in doctrine between the *Essay* and the *Education*. This continuity extends also to Locke's other major work on education, *Of the Conduct of the Understanding*. That work (published posthumously in 1706) was initially meant as a chapter to a subsequent edition of the *Essay*.[6] Whereas the *Education* presents striking continuity especially with the *Essay*'s "Of Power" and chapters particularly relevant to "Of Power" (as with those of Book 1 on habit and "principling" and of Book 4 on error), the continuity between the *Conduct* and the *Essay* stands out especially with respect to methodology.[7] Axtell's typification of the relation among these works is apposite:

---

5. The situation Locke here sketches is quite analogous to an exercise of what, in a discussion of Descartes, I have called "the liberty of perversion." It is a conscious turning away from the good or the true that, you know, once considered with sufficient contemplative intensity, will determine the will. For the reference to Descartes, see my "Descartes: La primauté du libre vouloir sur la raison," *Dialogue* 25, no. 2 (1986): 211–21.

6. See Locke to Molyneux, 10 April 1697, in *Correspondence* 6: 87.

7. As M. A. Stewart put it: "That Locke meant the methodology of the *Essay* to carry through to every subject of knowledge is not particularly problematic: the message is clear enough in his own 'discourse on method,' the educational tract *Of the Conduct of the Understanding*." See Stewart's "Peter A. Schouls, *The Imposition of Method*," in *Canadian*

whereas the *Essay* "enquires into the constitution and history of the human mind," the *Conduct* "attempts to suggest rules and cautions for guiding and controlling its operations in the search for knowledge"; and "the *Education* can be considered partly a practical appendix to the *Conduct*" in that it attempts "to apply very concretely to the individual child the rules and cautions of the *Conduct*."[8]

The particular child to which these "rules and cautions" were to be applied was Edward Clarke's oldest son. The first part of this book makes clear that we have good grounds to agree with Axtell that "Locke's knowledge of the understanding" as presented in the *Essay* "is a universal knowledge: it applies to all men in all places." Hence we can agree as well with his conclusions that "the theory of education implicit within his philosophy is universal in application," and that since "the *Education* is the explicit application of the philosophy of knowledge latent within the *Essay*, we should expect the *Education* to be universally applicable in its main principles also."[9] That is, Axtell is correct if he means to say that Locke *believed* these principles to be universally applicable. For whether they are, or ought to be, is a moot point which Axtell did not discuss.[10]

The different emphasis in the *Education* and the *Conduct* (arising from the former's preoccupation with the child while the latter's focus is primarily on the adult) is not as important as the fact that the subject matter of these two treatises overlaps. Both concern potential masters, although in the first mastery is at least initially entirely potential while in the second some achievement of mastery is generally presupposed. Both insist on the

---

Philosophical Reviews 1, no. 2/3 (1981): 122. That Locke's thought is in fact highly coherent is only recently beginning to be recognized. Appreciation of this coherence is implicit throughout Yolton's *Locke: An Introduction*. In their "Introduction" to the Clarendon edition of *Some Thoughts concerning Education* (Oxford, 1989), John and Jean Yolton are less clear on this issue. On the one hand, they insist that Locke "of course worked within specific conceptual boundaries" and that Locke's "philosophy of man, theory of knowledge, and ethical and political doctrines are interrelated"; on the other hand, they caution against "forming an interpretation of some passage in one book based on what is said in another" (p. 3). If what is said in another book expresses one of Locke's often repeated tenets, this cautionary approach will turn out to be detrimental to a correct reading. On coherence, see as well Eric Matthews's "Mind and Matter in the 18th Century," *Philosophical Quarterly* 36 (1986): 421. However, the myth of lack of coherence (so eloquently reenforced by Laslett's "Introduction" to Locke's *Two Treatises*—see its p. 102) still persists. Witness William J. Sheasgreen's "John Locke and the Charity School Movement," *History of Education* 15, no. 2 (1986): 63–79; as well as Michael Lessnoff's review of Ruth Grant, *John Locke's Liberalism* in *Canadian Philosophical Reviews* 8, no. 1 (1988): passim.

8. *Educational Writings*, p. 57. Axtell here adopts Thomas Fowler's comments from the latter's Introduction to the 1890 edition of the *Conduct*.

9. Ibid., p. 51.

10. Ibid., p. 65.

necessity of autonomy, to be achieved through rejection of prejudice and breaking of habit. Underneath the differences in emphasis and focus there is the underlying unity of metaphysics, ethics, epistemology and methodology.

The *Education* opens with the paragraph containing the well-known assertions that "Men's Happiness or Misery is most part of their own making," and "of all the Men we meet with, nine Parts of Ten are what they are, Good or Evil, useful or not, by their Education."[11] These two statements might be taken to contradict one another: the first says that you are what you make yourself, the second that you are a product of your environment, particularly of your education. The apparent conflict disappears once we recognize that Locke means the first statement to involve a moral demand and judgment, while he presents the second as a matter of fact that most people are what they are because of their education. Putting these two statements together, Locke is saying that factual circumstances do not abrogate duty—and this, of course, is a doctrine we met repeatedly in the *Essay*. Thus the first assertion from the *Education* implies that you are capable of achieving mastery, that it is your duty to become a master, and that misery is bound to follow if you refuse to work at achieving it. The second, that your environment, particularly your education, either makes you what you are directly or places you in advantageous positions from which you can make yourself what you are meant to be (and in the latter case there is, of course, no conflict between the two statements). Explicitly with respect to the offspring of the middle and upper classes—but always implicitly and often explicitly also with respect to those of the lower class—Locke holds that none can legitimately abdicate responsibility for what they have become by claiming that they are a product of their environment. If you don't like where or what you are, the blame is primarily yours because you have failed sufficiently to exert yourself.

11. Locke put it more emphatically in the letter to Clarke which corresponds to this opening paragraph: "of all the men we meet with, nine of ten, or perhaps ninety-nine of one hundred, are what they are, good or evil, useful or not, by their education" (19 July 1684; *Correspondence*, 2:626). My treatment of this passage differs sharply from that of Tarcov. Because he does not recognize that the epistemology of the *Essay* requires that, *whatever the experience*, there is always (the demand for) epistemic autonomy, therefore Tarcov mistakenly believes that this passage "is not the assertion of individual responsibility." Hence right from the outset of his reading of the *Education* Tarcov would have debarred himself from dealing adequately with the central issue of Locke's educational theory, that of the apparent tension between autonomy and habituation. (I say "would have debarred himself" because, as I noted in my first chapter, Tarcov explicitly excludes this issue from his discussion.) See Tarcov's *Locke's Education for Liberty*, p. 83.

The empirical statement from the *Education*'s opening paragraph also implies a judgment. It implies that when people have become "good" or "bad" as an *immediate* result of education then, in either case, they have been subjected to the wrong kind of education. For if it is their *education* rather than *themselves* that made them so, their education has robbed them of their autonomy. When Locke says that nine out of ten (or, as in the parallel passage of the correspondence with Clarke, ninety nine out of a hundred) are what their education made them, Locke asserts that the vast majority of people have been wrongly educated. This interpretation fits the *Essay* and supports what I said in the two preceding sections of this study: most people have been "principled," and that is at least in part because of two or three thousand years of "bad logic" (i.e., wrong method). While this wrong method prevailed there was little progress in the sciences. Similarly, as long as this wrong kind of education dominated there was little progress in personal autonomy and (as a reflection of that in the public realm) in moral and political relationships. Nevertheless, in both the sciences and social relationships, there was *some* progress. And that is to be explained from the fact that people are *by nature* rational and free. Hence in each there is the natural tendency not to be "principled" but instead to test and initially reject whatever a particular cultural epoch would impose. Each has, by nature, the chance to start anew and to travel the right way.

Education and cultural milieu can incline one to virtue or vice, to mastery or slavery, to happiness or misery. Which inclination will dominate is, in the final analysis, the responsibility of each individual. Putting the matter this way immediately connects Locke's views on education with doctrines we have noted earlier about freedom and desire, self-determination and habit, and (the possibility of) progress. These are some of the obvious connections. Less obvious at this point but equally present are the doctrines of the tabula rasa and of the methodology or "revolutionary logic" of the *Essay*, as well as a doctrine I call the doctrine of original neutrality.[12] In what follows in these two chapters, I pay careful attention to these connections. In most of the remainder of this chapter, I deal with the concepts of the tabula rasa and of original neutrality.

To deal effectively with the notions of the tabula rasa and of original

---

12. Axtell writes of the "synaptic principles that bridge the *Essay* and the *Education*" and lists the following three as "perhaps the most important": the role of habit, the association of ideas, the theory of language. Although I would not deny that the third is one of the "synaptic principles," I hold that the first two are far more important than the third. I deal with these two in the next chapter, in the context of the doctrines which I have just listed. See *Educational Writings*, pp. 54–56.

neutrality, I must make some more general comments on the nature and role of education. In addition, more needs to be said about one of the fundamental aspects of education, that of "principling."

The exercise of our powers "leads us towards perfection" (*Conduct*, §4). But each of us is personally responsible for this "exercise": for both its nature and for the end to which this exercise takes place. Environment, particularly education, can keep one from exercising altogether, or can lead to the wrong exercise or to exercise for the wrong end. It is for this reason that viewing Locke as holding that both knowledge of truth and the desire to act on it can be inculcated through education—the view writers such as Brinton and Passmore promulgate—is too superficial. It is true that Locke held what Brinton has called "the simple view" of the "enlightenment man" that "the agent of progress is the increasingly effective application of Reason to the control of the physical and cultural environment." Nevertheless, we cannot simply accept what Brinton concludes to be Locke's position at this point, that "education" is "one of the major ways in which reason was to do its work of reform."[13] If education consists in exposing error and leading to truth and virtue, then it is legitimate to consider it as the tool that may help reason to achieve control of the environment so that progress can be assured. But Locke holds that there is bad as well as good education, that education, if it can lead to virtue, can also lead to vice.

Locke's comments written as an addition to 2.21.53 familiarized us with his use of the phrase "ill education." And in the *Essay*'s 1.2.27 we read of people "corrupted by . . . Learning, and Education," while 1.3.26 speaks of education that leads people to accept "absurdity" for truth and that paralyzes "the reasoning Faculties of the Soul" so that they no longer "know how to move, for want of a foundation and footing." Thus Locke insists that not all education allows for progress and leads to perfection. Again, no form of education, whether good or bad, *necessarily* leads anywhere. Passmore writes that it was in education that the eighteenth century "perfectibilists placed their trust" and adds that "it had first to be shown that education, as distinct from divine grace, was capable, even, of leading men to virtue. The great turning point, in this respect, is Locke's *Some Thoughts concerning Education*."[14] But Passmore is wrong in part.

13. *The Encyclopedia of Philosophy* 2:521. Of course, if Brinton means to say that the education in question is one itself proposed by reason, then no qualification is necessary beyond that which states that even a fully rational education cannot *immediately* make virtuous those submitted to it.

14. Passmore, *The Perfectibility of Man*, p. 159. There are still many who without question echo views of Locke like Berlin's and Passmore's. For a recent instance see Amy Gutman's

Whereas many thought of grace as irresistible, Locke clearly does not think of education and its results as irresistible. And precisely for that reason he thought he could retain hope. For in spite of "ill education" people must be held responsible for what they are, and this implies the promise that the vice, slavery and misery into which "ill education" would lead can be resisted or, if not at first resisted, can be overcome. And for all who allow themselves to be led by it, the right kind of education holds the promise that they can attain the most advantageous position from which to make the choice for truth and virtue, mastery and happiness.

A fundamental aspect of education, says Locke, is that of "principling." This aspect occupies a crucial place in both good and bad education. In the *Conduct*'s §41 we read that "Many men firmly embrace falsehood for truth . . . because . . . blinded as they have been from the beginning" they lack "a vigour of mind able to contest the empire of habit, and look into its own principles." They are "blinded . . . from the beginning" because of parents and teachers "principling their children and scholars" and often if not usually such "principling" "amounts to no more but making them imbibe their teacher's notions and tenets by an implicit faith, and firmly to adhere to them whether true or false."[15] In the realm of education there ought to be no room for faith. However, because of the self-interest of parents and teachers who want to safeguard their position through estab-

---

Democratic Education (Princeton, 1987). She asserts that for Locke "Education may aim to *perfect* human nature by developing its potentialities, to *deflect* it into serving socially useful purposes, or to *defeat* it by repressing those inclinations that are socially destructive. We can choose among and give content to these aims only by developing a normative theory of what the educational purposes of our society should be." Like Berlin and Passmore, Gutman fails to recognize that Locke would consider the first to be impossible (for only we ourselves can develop our potentialities) and both the second and third to be "ill education." In their "Introduction" to *John Locke: Some Thoughts concerning Education*, John and Jean Yolton remain ambiguous on this point. Some of their passages appear to assert the learner's autonomy: "The child begins . . . possessed of the necessary faculties and tendencies to learn about the world and to form a responsible self" (p. 15); and "to avoid coming under the absolute control of others" is one of the "major objectives for education" (p. 16). Other passages seem on the opposite side of this issue: "If civil society has the task of *protecting* the person, education has the task of *producing* persons" (p. 18); and "*Some Thoughts* gives parents a very specific manual on how to guide and mould their children into moral, social persons" (p. 2).

15. See also the *Conduct*, §6 (p. 216): "Principles." "There is another fault that stops or misleads men in their knowledge, which I have also spoken something of, but yet is necessary to mention here again . . . and that is a custom of taking up with principles that are not self-evident, and very often not so much as true." The principles in question are taken from tradition, or accepted because one respects those who hold them, etc. Locke's reference here is probably to passages like the *Essay*'s 4.20.8–10 (where we read that "principling" leads to "contrariety of opinion").

lishing dominion over the next generation, it is especially through the process of education that all sorts of beliefs are inculcated and no questions are allowed.

Often, if not usually, this "empire of habit" remains uncontested because the mind does not exercise the freedom to "look into its own principles" and so remains ignorant of how to proceed to gain knowledge in the various areas of life. People are not allowed to gain insight into the procedure of attaining knowledge because—so Locke continues in §41 of the *Conduct*—for the sake of self-interest, "teachers and guides . . . suppress, as much as they can, this fundamental duty [of looking into the mind's own principles] which every man owes himself, and is the first steady step towards right and truth in the whole train of his actions and opinions." Not knowing how to go about acquiring knowledge, and therefore not having a touchstone to test what is and is not knowledge, people can be habituated to accept almost anything as true, can be "principled" even to go against what "common sense" would tell them. And so we read in the *Essay*, for example, that "men, having been principled with an opinion that they must not consult reason in the things of religion, however apparently contradictory to common sense and the very principles of all their knowledge, have let loose their fancies and natural superstition" (4.18.11). Bad education consists in habituating the pupil never to question anything. This is the essence of bad "principling": to habituate the child to accept beliefs strictly on the authority of the proposer. Locke calls this "principling" because it rivets to the student's mind beliefs on which the student comes to act unquestioningly; that is, it provides the student with "principles" for thought and action.

So far, I have highlighted Locke's negative use of "principling." But Locke also has a positive use for it, for what he believes to be good education also consists in "principling." When Molyneux wrote to Locke that he was educating his son in accordance with the "Method of Education" implicit in the *Essay*[16] Locke replied: "pray let this be your chief care to fill your son's head with clear and distinct ideas, and teach him on all occasions, both by practice and rule, how to get them, and the necessity of it. This . . . is the true principling of a young man. But to give him a reverence for our opinions, because we taught them, is not to make knowing men, but prattling parrots."[17] These words echo a passage from the *Conduct*'s §41, written in the context of Locke's condemning the "principling" that occurs in bad education:

16. See Molyneux's letters of 7 May 1695 and 24 August 1695, in *Correspondence* 5: 363 and 428, respectively.
17. 30 March–early April 1696, in *Correspondence* 5: 596.

But as to the ingenuous part of mankind, whose condition allows them leisure, and letters, and inquiry after truth, I can see no other right way of principling them, but to take heed, as much as may be, that in their tender years ideas that have no natural cohesion come not to be united in their heads; and that this rule be often inculcated to them to be their guide in the whole course of their lives and studies, viz. that they never suffer any ideas to be joined in their understandings in any other or stronger combination than what their own nature and correspondence give them, and that they often examine those that they find linked together in their minds, whether this association of ideas be from the visible agreement that is in the ideas themselves, or from the habitual and prevailing custom of the mind joining them thus together in thinking.

Thus right education involves a kind of "principling" that is to be explicated in terms of a discussion of reason and freedom, and of method and the nature of ideas. I turn to this in the next chapter. First, I still need to discuss two important doctrines about human nature against the background of which Locke introduces his ideas of "principling" in both good and bad education. The first of these is that of the tabula rasa, the second that of *original neutrality*.

2. The Tabula Rasa

Locke introduces the tabula rasa in the context of the "principling" of bad education (*Essay* 1.3.22—a passage I will quote in a moment). This doctrine has important consequences for how Locke views human offspring. He sees them all as originally devoid of both knowledge and prejudice. This he stresses throughout the first book of the *Essay*. Implied is a form of egalitarianism: although there are the advantages or disadvantages of various cultural conditions, all children are potentially equal in the sense that there are no natural obstructions that would hinder the development of their innate faculties. Many recent commentators have stressed these two consequences.[18] At this point in my work, both need stating. In addition, there is a third, namely, that human beings are vulnerable from the very beginning. This implication has by and large remained unemphasized.[19]

---

18. For example, Yolton in *Locke: An Introduction*, pp. 20 and 134.

19. In the second of the references just cited, Yolton connects the tabula rasa with the "passivity" which "means involuntariness." From this it is only a small step to "vulnerability." But Yolton does not take that step. In his "Locke on Habituation, Autonomy,

The very young are vulnerable because they cannot help but experience their immediate environment.

> Children, when they come first into it, are surrounded with a world of new things, which, by a constant solicitation of their senses, draw the mind constantly to them, forward to take notice of new, and apt to be delighted with the variety of changing Objects. Thus the first Years are usually imploy'd and diverted in looking abroad. (2.1.8)

Because they are looking abroad they do not reflect or look within: "hence we see the Reason, why 'tis pretty late, before most Children get Ideas of the Operations of their own Minds" (ibid). As a consequence young children possess no valid criteria by which to judge the nature of the experiences that leave their traces on the "white Paper." "Their Notions are few and narrow, borrowed only from those Objects, they have had most to do with, and which have made upon their Senses the frequentest and strongest Impressions. A Child knows his Nurse" (1.2.27). Locke believes that what children experience is usually not the sort of thing reason can approve of. He is keenly aware of the fact that practical states of affairs reflect the attitudes of some, and holds that these attitudes tend to corrupt those of others.

> Doctrines, that have been derived from no better original, than the Superstition of a Nurse . . . may, by length of time, and consent of Neighbours, grow up to the dignity of Principles in Religion or Morality. For such, who are careful (as they call it) to principle Children well . . . instil into the unwary, and, as yet, unprejudiced Understanding, (for white Paper receives any Characters) those Doctrines they would have them retain and profess. (1.3.22)

And since the character of what they find in their surroundings is usually not determined by reason, therefore they are vulnerable to being imposed upon by the prejudices of their contexts.

Vulnerability is one side of the coin. The other side is that of opportunity. As we saw, many have jumped to the wrong conclusion mistakenly believing Locke to hold that if the context into which children are born and mature can be structured by reason, then experience inscribes no prejudices on the developing mind because it then inscribes only ideas whose connections reason approves because the ideas' "own nature and correspondence" (*Conduct*, §41) gives them such connections. But we know from earlier chapters that, because of the doctrines of epistemic and moral autonomy, we cannot posit an immediate, let alone a necessary, connection between right education and proper cultural conditions on the one hand and truth, virtue, and happiness on the other hand. The right kind of education affords children only an *opportunity* for mastery, an opportunity that is greater than that available in any other way. This opportunity arises in part because (as we saw in the exchange between Locke and Molyneux) good education does not attempt to *impose* truth: "to give them a reverence for our opinions, because we taught them, is not to make knowing men, but prattling parrots." Instead, it attempts to lead to a questioning attitude. The methodology that determines the character of this questioning stance demands initial rejection of whatever experience has so far imposed and, if one has not been brought up in the right sort of context, permanent rejection of most if not all of the beliefs to which these experiences gave rise because they cannot withstand the scrutiny of reason. Thus good education tends to overcome the vulnerability of the child as tabula rasa: the child's "unwary understanding" remains subject to having experiences (attitudes, doctrines) "instilled into" it; but (as we see in the next chapter) good education inclines children to the activation of their freedom of suspension of the action to which these experiences would immediately lead them, as well as to the acquisition of valid criteria by which to judge these experiences. In these ways it gives children the opportunity to overcome their initial vulnerability: they can erase whatever experience initially wrote on the tabula rasa.

To what, then, does the doctrine of the tabula rasa amount in these contexts of "principling Children well" or of "ill principling" them? It helps to explain why all children have a natural equal opportunity to achieve mastery. For that which places obstacles on the path towards mastery is something cultural: the superstitious nurse, the prejudiced parent, the opinionated power of church or state. And it helps to explain why "ill education" can be so disastrous: there is no natural resistance to, or no natural rejection of, that which is not rational. In addition to highlighting vulnerability, the doctrine points to opportunity. Although there is no natural resistance to the subversive influence of one's surroundings, neither is there a natural affinity with it. And this implies that, although prejudices can come to be riveted to the mind, they cannot come to constitute the mind itself. With effort, the slate can always again be wiped clean. A new beginning is always possible. But none of this entails that right education necessarily leads to perfection. That position is implied neither by the doctrine of the tabula rasa nor by the one I turn to next, that of original neutrality.

3. Original Neutrality

Locke rejects all but one of the forms of the doctrine of original sin.[20] Although his writings show clearly what this rejection commits him to, Locke's position gains greater relief if it is seen against the background of these rejected forms. Their consideration will bring into focus a doctrine he propounds in their stead, that of original neutrality. (The name for this doctrine is mine, not Locke's.) And it will make clear that the assumption of an original neutrality is of importance for both the education of children and the (re-)education of adults.

The phrase "original sin" covers a doctrine that, by Locke's time, had evolved into various distinct forms. Locke was well acquainted with its major expressions. One of the influential forms of the doctrine was articulated by the Council of Trent which, in 1546, had issued a three-page decree on it.[21] The Tridentine position is in part a reaction to

20. Spellman (in *John Locke and the Problem of Depravity*) presents Locke as far more a part of the Protestant tradition on the point of original sin than I am allowing for in this section. He asserts that "whereas in the world of Locke's youth" acts of "moral obliquity" and of "wilful inhumanity" would have been attributed to "the inborn depravity of the perpetrator," such acts would "a century later" be taken as originating in "circumstances external to the child," in "parental deriliction of duty" rather than in "childhood degeneracy." But neither of these really fits Locke: there is no original degeneracy, and the full blame for "individual failings" (or, for that matter, full praise for individual success) cannot be put at the door of "external circumstances." Circumstances can be a hindrance or a boon, but individuals remain personally responsible for failure or success. When Spellman portrays Locke as wedded to "a Christian view of human nature and human potential" (205) he remains unconvincing. Whereas he gives grounds for the correctness of this claim when it concerns many of Locke's contemporaries, when it touches Locke himself Spellman must admit that his evidence comes from "assumptions which inform the spirit" of Locke's work, "assumptions" which Locke "never plainly articulated" (ibid.). Locke did not articulate these assumptions because (as I shall argue) he did not hold them. As far as effects of the Fall are concerned, Locke's "view of human nature" is more that of the Socinians than of more orthodox Christians.

21. Locke had a copy of the Council's *canones et decreta*, as well as several books about the Council and its procedures. See John Harrison and Peter Laslett, *The Library of John Locke*, 2d ed. (Oxford, 1971), entries 2981 (p. 252), 1228 (p. 141), 2185 (p. 202), and 3052 (p. 257). See also entry 2611 (p. 229) which indicates that Locke possessed Jean François Senault's *L'homme criminel, ou La corruption de la nature par la péché*.

"Protestant heresies," some of which derived from St. Augustine. The particular formulation of some of the Council's canons was, in fact, to some extent precipitated through conflict with one of its outspoken members, the Augustinian theologian Seripando. Spending a few moments with the position of both Augustine and the Council of Trent will acquaint us with the two major views on original sin current in Locke's intellectual surroundings. The Augustinian-Protestant view was very much alive in Holland and England; the official Roman Catholic view, that of the Council of Trent, was equally alive in France.

The theological discussion of original sin up to Locke's time was not so much in terms of its nature as in terms of its effects. The dominant Augustinian-Protestant view was that there is essentially total debilitation of the intellect and will, and therefore a radical need for divine grace. The dominant Roman Catholic position stated that there is no total debilitation but only a darkening of the will and intellect.

Central to the Protestant doctrine is Romans 5:12—"Therefore as sin came into the world through one man and death through sin, and so death spread to all men because all men sinned." Augustine reads this text as saying that in Adam all people have sinned, i.e., that Adam's sin is imputed to all human beings, and that all suffer the consequences of this sin. These consequences are that human beings are radically enslaved to sin, that is, are by themselves incapable of truth or goodness, and thus are absolutely and totally dependent on grace for salvation. Since the Fall, the human intellect is almost blind. And the will of human beings is incapable of directing them to any good, not because they have no free will but because this free will now functions only within the sinful life which they freely chose through their original disobedience. People sin voluntarily, but have lost the freedom to live a life of rectitude, to serve and please God.

By and large, the Augustinian doctrine became the Protestant position. But there were dissenters, people who remonstrated against (among other tenets) the doctrine of total depravity. The writings of one of these, Jacobus Arminius (1560–1609), were still well known and influential during Locke's days. Locke's correspondence with Philip van Limborch, pastor of the Remonstrant congregation of Amsterdam, indicates that if Locke had any sympathy at all for either side, it was for the minority remonstrant rather than for the majority counter-remonstrant view. The counter-remonstrant position had carried the day. It was codified during the Synod of Dordrecht (1618–1619), a gathering of delegates of the Reformed Church of the Netherlands that had an international character through the presence of 27 delegates from other countries. Among these were delegates from the United Kingdom, apppointed by James I. This majority position was formulated in what came to be known as the *Canons of Dort* or the *Articles Against the Remonstrants*. Especially the first few articles of the "Third and fourth Heads of Doctrine" deal with the effects of original sin. The first states that "Man was originally formed after the image of God. His understanding was adorned with a true . . . knowledge of his Creator; his heart and will were upright, all his affections pure. . . . But, revolting from God by . . . his own free will, he forfeited all these excellent gifts; and . . . became involved in blindness of mind, horrible darkness, vanity, and perverseness of judgment; became wicked, rebellious, and obdurate in heart and will, and impure in his affections." The second article adds that "all the posterity of Adam . . . have derived corruption from their original parent, not by imitation . . . but by the propagation of a vicious nature." And the fourth states the effect of this propagation of Adam's sin with respect to the understanding: "There remains, however, in man since the fall, the glimmerings of natural light. . . . But so far is this light of nature from being sufficient to bring him to a saving knowledge of God and to true conversion that he is incapable of using it aright even in things natural and civil."

Romans 5:12 also dominates the Council of Trent's five canons on original sin; both the second and fourth canon quote it in full. And whereas the first canon states that "the first man Adam immediately lost the justice and holiness in which he was constituted when he disobeyed the command of God," the third insists (against both Pelagians and Erasmus) that "this sin in Adam . . . is communicated to all men by propagation not by imitation." This "communication" made Adam's sin "injurious" "to his descendants" (as the second canon puts it), to "even infants, who have not yet been able to commit any personal sins" (adds canon four). But (as the fifth canon asserts) by "the grace of our Lord Jesus Christ conferred in baptism the guilt of original sin is remitted" rather than "only brushed over or not imputed."

At first sight it may appear as if there is considerable agreement between the positions of Trent and Dordrecht. But one important difference comes to the fore once we answer the question: what, according to Trent, are the consequences of the imputation of Adam's sin to his descendants? These consequences are "death" and the fact that "both body and soul . . . changed for the worse" (first canon). The phrase "changed for the worse" does not have the radical connotation of the Augustinian position: a person may change for the worse but still be capable of truth and goodness. That a less than radical connotation is in fact intended is clear from the long decree which follows these five canons, that on justification. One of the canons of this decree recapitulates the Council's position on original sin and adds that free will "though attenuated in its powers and inclined [to evil] was by no means extinguished." It also asserts that there remained more than a glimmering of the natural light, that this light retained considerable efficacy in things natural and civil. Thus the contrast between the two positions is that, with various nuances, Augustinian Protestants held to a virtually total debilitation of intellect and will and therefore to a radical need for grace, while Roman Catholics held to a position in which there was a bending of will and darkening of intellect, neither of which required the infusion of grace in a radical sense in all areas of life. Those in the Tridentine tradition would never say—as does the fourth article of the Canons of Dort—that "this [natural] light, such as it is, man in various ways renders wholly polluted."[22]

Locke rejects both the Protestant and Catholic position. With respect to (i) reason, (ii) affections or passions, and (iii) will he discards the effects of original sin both in the radical Protestant and the mitigated Roman Catholic sense. This is, simply, because (iv) he explicitly refuses validity to their very notion of original sin. (v) The consequences of this total rejection color much of Locke's thought, and determine what he has to say about the attainment of mastery through education of the child and self-education of the adult. I will deal with each of these five points in turn.

(i) In his *Third Letter for Toleration*[23] Locke ridicules the thirteenth of the Church of England's Thirty-nine Articles because it states that "works done before the grace of Christ . . . are not pleasing to God . . . for that they are not done as God has willed and commanded them to be done . . . they have the nature of sin" (p. 397). To this Locke opposes that "reasoning impartially" is not in "the nature of sin," not only if this is about things natural and civil but even when it concerns eternal salvation (ibid.). Knowledge of God cannot, in fact, be "embraced" with "conviction and with an obedient heart" except through "considering, studying, and impartially examining matters of religion" (p. 405). These comments imply rejection of both the radical Protestant and mitigated Catholic views. In this *Letter* Locke comes close to their explicit rejection:

> The doctrine of original sin is that which is professed and must be owned by the members of the church of England, as is evident from the XXXIX

---

22. I have taken my quotations from the Council of Trent's *Canons* from George Vandervelde's *Original Sin* (Amsterdam, 1975). Those on original sin are from pp. 33–39; that on justification and the will is on p. 35. For the first, Vandervelde refers to pp. 1511–1515, for the second to p. 1521, of *Enchiridion Biblicum: Documenta Ecclesiastica Sacrum Scripturam Spectantia*. Auctoritate Pontificae Commissionis de Re Biblica Edita. 4th ed. (Rome, 1961).

23. I enter the page references directly in the text. They are to *Works*, 1823, vol. 6.

Articles . . . and yet I ask you, whether this be 'so obvious and exposed to all that diligently and sincerely seek the truth,' that one who is in the communion of the church of England, sincerely seeking the truth, may not raise to himself such difficulties concerning the doctrine of original sin as may puzzle him, though he be a man of study; and whether he may not push his inquiries so far, as to be staggered in his opinion? . . . And it is not impossible, that one, who has subscribed the XXXIX Articles, may yet make it a question, 'Whether it may be truly said that God imputes the first sin of Adam to his posterity?' (p. 411)

Since "reasoning impartially" is one way in which human beings express their nature, and since Locke takes them to be quite capable of it, of "sincerely"—and successfully—"seeking the truth," he holds that there is in this respect no fundamental corruption of human nature. Instead of original sin there is what might be called "original neutrality."

I use the phrase "original neutrality" rather than, for instance, "original innocence." The latter could imply a doctrine to the effect that human beings are originally, that is, without an exercise of their freedom and reason, inclined to what is good, to what, if God were to judge their actions on this inclination, would declare them innocent. Conclusions from Part B of this study preclude this from being a Lockean doctrine. Individuals freely choose or reject a life of reason. Depending on how they choose, God will declare them either innocent or guilty. No human beings start out from either innocence or guilt but from a position which, once left, will place them in the camp of the innocent or the guilty hence one best characterized as neutral. Some of Locke's statements directly support this characterization of his position as one that does not oppose original innocence to original sin, no innate inclination to good as opposed to one to evil. He wrote, "Men have a natural tendency to what delights and from what pains them. This universal observation has established past doubt. But that the soul has such a tendency to what is morally good and from evil has not fallen under my observation."[24]

Thus before partiality sets in, or before one knowingly acts on the truth, there is neutrality. In contrast to bad education, good education more readily allows for rational action, or makes it easier to reject prejudice that was already contracted. That is because good education aims for children to retain their original neutrality or for adults to come to use their power to

---

24. This is one of Locke's marginal notes in his copy of Thomas Burnet's tract on the *Essay concerning Human Understanding*. For these marginalia, see Noah Porter's "Marginalia Lockeana," in the *New Englander and Yale Review* 11 (July 1887). For a republication of Porter's article, see Peter A. Schouls, ed., *Remarks . . . concerning Humane Understanding*, volume 1 in *The Philosophy of John Locke* (New York, 1984), pp. 34–49. The quotation is from p. 38.

regain this neutrality. It aims at keeping or reaching the position from which they can reason and follow the dictates of their reason. Since "reasoning impartially" expresses a human being's true nature, then to the extent that people are kept from, or overcome, partiality, they can become truly human. Thus to the extent that good education leads to retention or regaining of neutrality, it can play its role in people's achieving what they are meant to be. It is "ill education" rather than original sin which "weakens" and makes "almost extinct" the "light that is in your minds," the "principle which dictates what is right, and inclines to good." It is partiality, prejudice, "prevailing custom, and contrary habits" through which "this principle was very much weakened."[25]

Is Locke skating on thin ice here? Has he now introduced ambiguities or even contradictions in his position such that, depending on what one emphasizes, it allows for an interpretation like Passmore's (that good education makes one moral, i.e., human) and mine (that good education is neither a necessary nor a sufficient condition for achieving one's true humanity)? The next chapter will show that Locke's text does not allow such contrary interpretations—it will support my earlier rejection of Passmore's interpretation in Chapter 2, section 3.

Here all we need to settle is Locke's view on original sin, and its consequences for his position on the nature of human beings. If one's reason is corrupt,[26] its corruption is to be explained in terms of one's irresponsible and preventable dealings with one's immediate context, not in terms of a distant past. And if (as Romans 1:28 has it) someone has "a reprobate mind," then "reprobate" does not indicate some deep-seated innate depravity. And so Locke's paraphrase of the word "reprobate" becomes "unsearching" and "unjudicious."[27] That reason is not corrupt by nature is clear, says Locke, from many observable facts. One of these is that if people free from prejudice for the first time hear and consider the "truths . . . owing to revelation" they accept them as "by no means to be contradicted" because they find them "to be agreeable to reason."[28] Had reason been affected by the Fall in a way taught by the Thirty-nine Articles and the Canons of Dort, it could hardly be expected to recognize revealed

25. These phrases are from Locke's paraphrase of and notes on Galatians 5:16, 17.

26. From Part A, Chaps. 3 and 4, we know that, for Locke, "corrupt reason" is really an illegitimate phrase. Reason is infallible and cannot be corrupted. It is therefore the person who is corrupt. People may become corrupt to such an extent that prejudice prevents their reason from being heeded or from speaking altogether. In that case, we ought no longer to speak of "persons," for what were (potentially) persons have then degraded themselves to the level of "brute beasts." See again the *Second Treatise*, §11, etc.

27. See note to Romans 1:28.

28. *Reasonableness*, p. 140.

truth when confronted by it, let alone be the judge (see the *Essay*'s Book 4, chapters 18 and 19) of whether or not there is in fact any truth present at all.[29]

That reason is unaffected by the Fall does not, in itself, dismiss the doctrine of original sin. For reason may be able to tell one the right way while passion or will prevent one from going that way. However, Locke's position is that each individual can autonomously choose or refuse to tread the path laid out by impartial reason. And that presupposes original neutrality rather than original sin also as far as passion and will are concerned.

(ii) Commentators sometimes give the impression that Locke espoused some form of the doctrine of original sin at least as far as the passions are concerned.[30] This impression ought to be dispelled—even though Locke himself sometimes gives some grounds for it as when, in the *Second Treatise*, he speaks of "the corruption and vitiousness of degenerate Men" (§128). If statements such as these refer to the passions at all, they are meant to be about the passions of the few so that (as Aarsleff has put it) "The very phrase 'degenerate Men' shows that Locke did not take degeneracy to be the normal and universal state of man."[31] Rather than congenitally evil, "The men of the *Two Treatises* were potentially good—that is, they were capable of recognizing their obligations and, in general, could be counted on to act upon them."[32]

Nevertheless, it is true that not only commentators' phrases but also Locke's expressions may make it appear as if, with respect to the passions, he accepted some doctrine of original sin. Out of context, statements from the *Education* especially could give rise to this appearance. Consider what he writes about children in §16: they take delight "in doing Mischief, whereby I mean spoiling of any thing to no purpose; but more especially the Pleasure they take to put any thing in Pain." But Locke immediately adds that with respect to delight taken in causing pain, he "cannot persuade" himself that it is "any other than a foreign and introduced Disposition, an Habit borrowed from Custom and Conversation." The phrase "spoiling of any thing to no purpose" is, perhaps, not a bad generic

29. In chap. 8, section 1, of *The Imposition of Method*, I have provided a somewhat different account of this matter; in both accounts I reached the same conclusion about Locke's view on the adequacy of reason.

30. See John Dunn, *The Political Thought of John Locke* (Cambridge, 1969), p. 194.

31. Aarsleff, "The State of Nature and the Nature of Man in Locke," p. 102.

32. These are Schochet's words, from his "The Family and the Origins of the State in Locke's Political Philosophy," in *John Locke, Problems and Perspectives*, ed. Yolton, pp. 81–98, pp. 95–96. He supports his judgment with reference to the *Second Treatise* §11, l. 31; §14, ll. 17–19; §124, ll. 8–9; and §136, ll. 5–6.

definition of "sin" so that "Delight in doing Mischief" becomes a synonym for "sin." Through the notion of "delight" sin is then placed in the passions; but through the phrase "foreign and introduced," sin in general and any particular expression of it is to be explained in terms of "Custom and Conversation." And so the notion of original sin is rejected. If this conclusion places too much weight on these phrases, it is in any case clear that delight in causing pain is not an inborn "Disposition."

Locke borrowed this particular passage from the *Education* from a letter he had written to Clarke. There also appear phrases in this letter that, taken out of context, might make one ascribe to Locke a form of the doctrine of original sin he in fact rejects. For in it he speaks of "the mastery of our natural inclination," of "that dangerous inclination which he ought by all means to subdue and suppress," of checking and subduing "the vicious inclinations" children "are apt to have" and of "vicious habits that are ordinary and natural."[33] But none of these expressions place Locke in either the Augustinian-Protestant or the Roman Catholic camp. For in that same letter he writes that all of these vices can be prevented, checked or removed through the right kind of upbringing or education. That, of course, also came to clear expression in the published version of these letters for, as we read in §139 of the *Education*, "few of Adam's Children are so happy, as not to be born with some Byass in their natural Temper, which it is the Business of Education either to take off, or counterbalance." This "Byass" is not Locke's name for original sin but simply refers to the fact that some children are naturally more easily prone to become irritated or petulant—vices they acquire more easily in wrong environments, and for which right education either allows no scope for development or removes if they have already been acquired in the wrong environment. Neither special grace nor Holy Spirit nor rite of baptism ever makes its appearance in this discussion. These vices are "ordinary" and "natural" only in the sense that, given the wrong context, human beings are apt to contract them and so acquire "vicious inclinations." On the other hand, given the right upbringing, human nature is such that people are apt to acquire inclinations or habits that make it easier for them to pursue the paths of truth and virtue.

(iii) I can afford to be very brief about the will. The Council of Trent speaks of "free will inclined to evil," and the Synod of Dort juxtaposes the pre-lapsarian "upright will" to the "wicked, rebellious, obdurate will" which is said to exist after the Fall. Strictly speaking, Locke cannot accept

---

33. See Axtell, *Educational Writings*, pp. 366, 368, and 371; and 19/29 April 1687; *Correspondence* 3:172–84.

either position to the extent that they imply an independent, undetermined, "free" will. The will is never free but always determined by desire or passion. And as we have just seen, Locke has no room for a doctrine of original sin in the context of his discussion of the passions. With respect to the will the question, for Locke, is whether it is determined in the way it ought to be determined. It ought to be determined by desires reason has authorized. It ought not to be determined by desires not approved by reason. Locke says people can see to it that their will is determined by desires approved by their reason. They possess this ability apart from the grace that may become theirs through baptism or the Holy Spirit. It is because he believes people to possess this ability by nature that, in the *First Letter concerning Toleration*, Locke can write about the American Indians as "innocent pagans, strict observers of the rules of equity and the law of nature."[34]

(iv) It will hardly be a surprise when I say that Locke *explicitly* rejects the dominant forms of the doctrine of original sin. The opening pages of *The Reasonableness of Christianity* leave no doubt about it. Its first two sentences[35] state, "It is obvious to any one, who reads the New Testament, that the doctrine of redemption, and consequently of the Gospel, is founded upon the supposition of Adam's fall. To understand, therefore, what we are restored to by Jesus Christ, we must consider what the Scriptures show we lost by Adam." And what we lost, says Locke, is "bliss and immortality" (p. 5). "Nobody can deny . . . that death comes on all men by Adam's sin" (p. 6). "And thus men are, by the second Adam, restored to life again" (p. 9). "Only," he adds, "they differ about the word death." Some hold that when God said " 'in that day that thou eatest of the forbidden fruit, thou shalt die' " he meant, "thou and thy posterity shall be, ever after, incapable of doing any thing, but what shall be sinful and provoking to me." This, the Augustinian-Protestant view, Locke rejects: "If by death, threatened to Adam, were meant the corruption of human nature in his posterity, it is strange, that the new Testament should not any where take notice of it, and tell us that corruption seized on all, because of Adam's transgression, as well as it tells us so of death. But, as I remember, every one's sin is charged upon himself only" (p. 7). Implicit in this statement is the rejection of the Catholic position as well: human beings are capable on their own to achieve their salvation, to gain a blissful life eternal:

---

34. The first *Letter concerning Toleration, Works*, 1823, 6:36.
35. The page references are to the edition of 1823; I shall enter them directly in the text.

And thus men are, by the second Adam, restored to life again; that so by Adam's sin they may *none of them lose any thing, which by their own righteousness they might have a title to*: for righteousness, or an exact obedience to the law, seems, by the Scripture, to have a claim of right to eternal life . . . *If any of the posterity of Adam were just, they shall not lose the reward of it, eternal life and bliss, by being his mortal issue*: Christ will bring them all to life again; and then they shall be put every one upon his own trial, and receive judgment, as he is found to be righteous, or not. (P. 9, my italics)

So the only form of original sin Locke acknowledges is that which sees physical death as the effect of Adam's fall. But Christ's death has made physical dying the passage to "eternal life and bliss" for those who, acting freely on the dictates of their own natural reason, live righteously. The only use Locke has for "grace" is that God will bestow the gift of heaven on all those who consistently attempt to live a life of reason but sometimes fail in doing so: the goodwill portrayed in this partial success is ground enough for God to bestow eternal bliss, and the partial success is each individual's own achievement. In this form of the doctrine there is no room for congenital corruption of will or intellect—a statement that fits exactly what we have just seen about reason, passion, and free will.

Locke's rejection of the dominant forms of the doctrine is dictated by his individualism. The opening paragraph of the *Reasonableness* supports this contention in terms of contract theory. That Adam's posterity would be incapable of good because of Adam's fall and thus "doomed to eternal, infinite punishment" is unjust because "millions had never heard of [Adam], and no one had authorized [Adam] to transact for him, or be his representative."

But what, then, of Romans 5:12 ("Wherefore, as by one man sin entered into the world, and death by sin; and so death passed upon all men for that all have sinned") the cornerstone of all positions on original sin? Locke's paraphrase of this verse is as follows:

Wherefore, to give you a state of the whole matter from the beginning, you must know, that as by the act of one man, Adam, the father of us all, sin entered into the world, and death, which was the punishment annexed to the offence of eating the forbidden fruit, entered by that sin, for that all Adam's posterity thereby became mortal.

In a footnote he adds " 'Having sinned,' I have rendered became mortal" because that is the relationship which St. Paul puts between sin and mortality in I Corinthians 15:22. And the reason why St. Paul spoke less clearly in Romans than in Corinthians Locke then ascribes to St. Paul's "great liking of the beauty and force of antithesis" as a literary device. So much for the cornerstone of the doctrine of original sin.[36]

(v) The consequences of his rejection of these forms of the doctrine are evident in many of Locke's major tenets. These consequences made their weight felt long before the explicit dismissal of the doctrine in the *Reasonableness of Christianity*. In the *Essay*'s "Of Power," for example, they are a backdrop to the thesis operating throughout the chapter and are clearly visible in paragraph 51: that human beings are capable on their own to seek and to attain true happiness. Because they are not naturally corrupt they can autonomously act in accordance with right reason or moral obligation. We have already noted its presence in the *Second Treatise* and in the *Letters on Toleration*.

What are the consequences for Locke's position on education? There is original neutrality, that is, a human being has no innate inclination to either good or evil. And the opening paragraph of the *Education* contains the assertion that "of all the Men we meet with, Nine Parts of Ten are what they are, Good or Evil, useful or not, by their Education." Putting these two statements together, does that yield the conclusions that commentators such as Passmore draw? Are children infinitely malleable? Can people be educated into virtue? Does the educator bestow moral character on children through conditioning them to have the right habits?[37] In other words, does Locke's rejection of original sin go hand-in-hand with an advocacy of progress based on an apology for social control? Is the assumption of original neutrality the key which unlocks the door for the social engineer? Where, then, would this leave the natural freedom and rationality, the autonomy, of individuals? We have now reached the vantage point from which we can deal decisively with questions such as these.

36. One might justly object that to the extent that there is a connection between Locke's individualism and his form of the doctrine of original sin, Locke stopped short of asking a final crucial question. If Adam's sin cannot make me naturally unrighteous, why should Adam's punishment for Adam's sin—death—"naturally" become a part of my life as the only possible passage from its temporal to its eternal phase? (Incidentally, it is on the ground of Locke's statement that "Christ . . . at the cost of his own painful death, purchased life" for those who live uprightly, that Spellman bases much of his claim about Locke's view on human depravity. But a statement such as this concerns only the passage from temporal life to eternal bliss: whereas Christ has opened this passage, it is up to each individual to enter and traverse it. See William M. Spellman's "Locke and the Latitudinarian Perspective on Original Sin," *Revue Internationale de Philosophie* 42, no. 165 [1988]: 215–28.)

37. See again Passmore, *The Perfectibility of Man*, pp. 159–61. See, as well, pp. 68 and 74 of Sheasgreen's "John Locke and the Charity School Movement," and the passages quoted from John and Jean Yolton in note 14 above. (The passages from their pp. 2 and 18 are no aberration for them; similar sentiments come through on pp. 3, 8, 12, 17, 21, and 28.)

～ 8

Education, Reason, and Freedom

1. "Principling," Reason, and Freedom

A human being's original neutrality does not guarantee eventual mastery, for only those who act upon the dictates of their reason can walk the path of mastery and enjoy a master's freedom. To obtain these dictates requires an exercise of freedom. Hence the mastery and freedom that reason is to make possible themselves presuppose the freedom necessary for the achievement of knowledge. We have seen that this original freedom can be misused. One instance of misuse occurs when we determine ourselves to disregard our reason, to act on desires our reason has not authorized. Then this freedom entraps us in prejudice, precludes mastery, and tends to incorporate us in the mechanism of nature—a process whose outcome is that we become ever less able to exercise even this original freedom. Thus if knowledge is a necessary condition for the freedom characteristic of mastery, original freedom is a necessary condition for attaining knowledge. In Locke's theory of education this necessary condition holds for both adults and children.[1]

---

1. As a parallel example, this condition holds as well in the area of politics. To enjoy political mastery, that is, to be free as autonomous citizens, the behavior of both rulers and citizens must conform to rational rules. Such rules properly relate the right concepts or mixed modes. But it is those who are (to become) citizens who compose these mixed modes and who relate them to make the rules to which they then submit themselves. There is no inescapable compulsion on anyone to compose the right mixed modes and to relate them to make rational maxims. Neither is there inescapable compulsion on anyone to submit to

For education to be possible and for knowledge to become achievable through education, those to be educated must possess original freedom that the educator must leave inviolate. To the extent that the educator encroaches on this freedom, education becomes the kind of training or conditioning whose product is not knowledge but belief, prejudice or superstition. The consequence of action on such inculcated beliefs is the same as that which ensues if individuals deliberately disregard their reason: the freedom of mastery recedes and they become enmeshed in the bondage of prejudice.[2]

The right kind of education helps to make knowledge accessible; and knowledge is the means to further freedom. But even when education allows for the acquisition of knowledge, it does not follow, for Locke, that such education necessarily leads to that freedom. Though a necessary condition for mastery, knowledge is not a sufficient condition. The truth does not necessarily make one free for (as we saw in Part B) reason or knowledge alone is not a motivating power. Even right education cannot therefore without further ado be introduced as the means that guarantees progress, for even if it were a sufficient condition for the attainment of knowledge, it is not a condition sufficient to secure action on that knowledge. Thus, whether good or bad, education can never completely determine human action because, for Locke, there always remains the genuine possibility of free choice between alternatives. But none of this prevents Locke from assigning an important role to "praise, blame, persuasion, education." That role, however, will turn out to be limited—a limitation that precludes the inevitable effectiveness of social control.[3]

---

these maxims. Freedom is presupposed in action on the laws that ought to govern a political association as well as in the very making of these laws. This freedom can be used to make the right laws or the wrong ones or none at all. Only through the first of these, and through the right kind of uncoerced action following it, can one realize political mastery, that is, individual political freedom.

2. Rousseau's affinity with Locke is clear at this point. The concept of freedom is at the heart of Rousseau's thought. This freedom, as James Miller has written, may be distinguished into " 'positive freedom' (to realize mastery of oneself) and a 'negative freedom' (to do without the interference of others)." For Locke, the latter becomes a condition for the former, in that all interference except that of legitimate "principling" creates the prejudices which prevent (or at least make more difficult) the mastery of oneself and one's cultural context. See James Miller, *Rousseau, Dreamer of Democracy* (New Haven, Conn., 1984), p. 166.

3. If, in the rest of this chapter, I can demonstrate that what I have so far asserted to be Locke's position is so in fact, then I will have shown a view such as Isaiah Berlin's to be mistaken. Berlin (as we will recall from my fifth chapter) ascribes to Locke the doctrine "that free will is tantamount to capacity for being (causally) affected by praise, blame, persuasion, education, etc." This is a doctrine which Berlin rejects because he takes it to deny the

What, then, is the educator's task? Recall Locke's statements that the freedom of a human being is the "freedom of the understanding" and that "It is conceit, fancy, extravagance, any thing rather than understanding, if it must be under the constraint of receiving and holding opinions by the authority of any thing but their own, not fancied, but perceived evidence" (*Conduct*, §12). Recall as well that if we hold opinions on the authority of another (even if, as we saw in the preceding chapter, the other is the enlightened tutor John Locke or the sensitive parent William Molyneux) then "we impose upon ourselves in that part which ought with the greatest care to be kept free from all imposition" (ibid.). "Borrowed reason" will not do. [4]

But if even rational parents or good educators are not to impose their ideas on their children and pupils, if their actions are to be determined by their children's or pupils' freedom, then what—according to Locke—are they to do? As I deal with this question, I assume what I have postulated from the beginning of this study: that it is appropriate and illuminating to read Locke's works on education with doctrines from the *Essay* and admonitions from his correspondence firmly in mind as directives for interpretation. I am acutely aware of the Yoltons' (and others') cautionary remarks that "Too much can be made of interconnections between works" and that "One simply has to read carefully, keeping in mind the total body of Locke's writings while examining any one book."[5] In my attempt to follow the injunction contained in the second of these statements, I am far from sanguine about the "simplicity" of such an enterprise. But it is clearly correct to hold that the interconnections, if there are any, will have to reveal themselves from Locke's own words. In the remainder of this section, I therefore proceed by drawing attention to well-known passages from the *Education*. Important interconnections between the *Education* and the parts of Locke's writings I have already discussed will then begin *to present themselves* if we are willing to give at least some of these passages a reading different from the traditional one. With such a reading these passages will allow the beginnings of an answer to the question put in the opening sentence of this paragraph in terms of

---

existence of freedom: "Whether the causes which are held completely to determine human action are physical or psychical or of some other kind . . . if they are truly causes—if their outcomes are thought to be as unalterable as, say, the effects of physical or physiological causes—this of itself seems to me to make the notion of a free choice between alternatives inapplicable" (*Four Essays on Liberty*, p. 65). Locke would have agreed with Berlin's rejection of this doctrine.

4. See above, Chap. 2, section 2; and Chap. 6, section 2, note 13.

5. "Introduction" to *John Locke, Some Thoughts concerning Education*, p. 5.

the child's freedom and the parents' or teacher's "principling." In addition to "freedom" and "principling" the term "reason" will again play a role; but most of what I have to add about reason in the context of education I leave for the next section.

Near the end of the *Education* (in §200) Locke sums up his "present Thoughts concerning Learning and Accomplishments."

> Teach him to get a Mastery over his Inclinations, and submit his Appetite to Reason. This being obtained, and by constant practice settled into Habit, the hardest part of the Task is over. To bring a young Man to this, I know nothing which so much contributes, as the love of Praise and Commendation, which should therefore be instilled into him by all Arts imaginable. Make his Mind as sensible of Credit and shame as may be: And when you have done that, you have put a Principle into him, which will influence his Actions, when you are not by, to which the fear of a little smart of a Rod is not comparable, and which will be the proper Stock, whereon afterwards to graft the true Principles of Morality and Religion.

This passage states the four major aspects of what Locke takes to be right education. Education (*a*) demands mastery over desire or inclination, (*b*) requires that desire be judged by reason, (*c*) is to instill, through the use of praise and blame, the "principle" or "habit" that allows for the "mastery" that submission to reason makes possible, and (d) thus leads those educated to the position most favorable for increasing the freedom best described as "autonomous action": no longer subject to "the fear . . . of a Rod" they can adopt as principles for their actions "the true Principles of Morality and Religion." Let me deal with each of these aspects in turn.

(*a*) *Mastery over desire*. The "great Principle and Foundation of all Vertue and Worth," says Locke, is "That a Man is able to deny himself his own Desires, cross his own Inclinations, and purely follow what Reason directs as best, tho' the Appetite lean the other way" (§33). Shortly afterwards (in §38) Locke reiterates this doctrine in a formulation I have used throughout this study: "the Principle of all Vertue and Excellency lies in a Power of denying our selves the Satisfaction of our own Desires, where Reason does not authorize them." This "Principle" or "Foundation" is, in fact, a "Power." It is a "Power . . . to be got and improved by Custom, made easy and familiar by an early Practice"—a practice that is to start as early as possible in our lives: "Children should be used to submit their Desires, and go without their Longings, even from their very Cradles" (ibid.). For if a child "has not a Mastery over his Inclinations" and thus "knows not how to resist the Importunity of present Pleasure or Pain, for the sake of what Reason tells him is fit to be done," then this child does not possess "the true Principle of Vertue and Industry; and is in Danger never to be good for any thing" (§45).

This "Principle," so these paragraphs state, is the "Power" "of all Vertue and Worth," "of all Vertue and Excellency," "of Vertue and Industry." "Worth," "Excellency" and "Industry" are concepts that direct us not to restrict "moral" to the sphere of mastery over self in the narrow sense of "mastery of the Understanding." The principle makes both knowledge and action on knowledge possible. Such knowledge may be narrowly about mastery over self or broadly about mastery over one's cultural and physical contexts.[6]

This "Power," in the narrow sense, is that of suspension of action on desire in order to examine the beliefs that action on this or that desire will produce genuine or lasting happiness. In the broader sense, education is to result in the attitude that makes one refuse simply to accept and act upon what one's senses convey (whether that is about the state of one's body or of the external world), or what people say, or what one finds written (whether this be called "ethics," "politics," "revelation," or "physical science"). That is, education is to lead one to acquire the "Power" of the thoroughly critical stance that makes one question all "common received Opinions" (§81). The educator's major task has been achieved once the pupil is capable of action only "for the sake of what Reason tells him is fit to be done" (§45).

If I am told by reason, I must be told by my own reason, for I cannot know it is reason speaking unless my own reason reveals that. Here we can see the connection between this "great Principle" and the "principling" discussed in the preceding chapter. In the last four paragraphs of its first section, we noted that there is a positive use of "principling." It consists in "teaching" the child "how to get" "clear and distinct ideas" and, once it knows how to obtain and relate them, giving the child's mind

6. Mastery over what extends beyond the self presupposes mastery over the self. Without control over one's understanding and inclinations, the right thoughts cannot be thought or, if they could be thought, they cannot command that action be in compliance with them. Even though, in the physical sciences, we are debarred from the kind of truth or certainty that "morals" allows us (Locke alludes to the *Essay*'s position on this in paragraph 190 of the *Education*), it is nevertheless the case that we can obtain the "knowledge" or beliefs sufficient for comfortable lives. This "knowledge" too presupposes the mastery over self which is the *Education*'s primary interest. Hence the *Education* is concerned with mastery over the self and with mastery over one's cultural and physical contexts. On the latter, see paragraphs 193–95. In paragraph 94 Locke writes that the "great Work of a Governour is to fashion the Carriage, and form the Mind; to settle in his Pupil good Habits, and the Principles of Vertue and Wisdom," so that the pupil can then "by his own Genius and Industry afterwards" direct his attention to that "which will be of most and frequentest use to him in the World."

the freedom to "look into its own principles." We saw that Locke proclaims this "looking into one's own principles" to be a "fundamental duty" "which every man owes himself." We can now see quite clearly what is at stake: through implementation of the "great Principle" (that is, through freedom from desire) there is room for the reflection which reveals the "principles" of reason and hence the criteria by which to judge all beliefs, desires and actions.

Because they are initially incapable of denying their own desires and crossing their own inclinations, that is, incapable of suspension of action on desires and examination of the beliefs attached to them, young children are initially incapable of acting only "for the sake of what [their own, not their parents' or teacher's] Reason tells" them. Thus the tutor's major task may also be characterized as follows: "to teach the Mind to get the Mastery over it self; and to be able, upon Choice, to take it self off from the hot Pursuit of one Thing, and set it self upon another with Facility and Delight"—the outcome of which is to be that "the Mind" achieves "an habitual Dominion over it self, lay[s] by Ideas, or Business, as Occasion requires, and betake[s] it self to new and less acceptable Employments without Reluctancy or Discomposure" (§75).

A question (one to be left until part *d* of this section) now naturally presents itself: how does one "teach" "Mastery," the ability to determine oneself "upon [one's own] Choice"? How does one teach autonomy? The mind's "habitual Dominion over it self," so this paragraph states explicitly, requires that it "lay by Ideas, or Business," that it suspend action on beliefs or desires. But (to use phrases from a later paragraph) how are "Children . . . brought to deny their Appetites" or how are "their Minds . . . made vigorous" so that they obtain "the Custom of having their Inclinations in Subjection"? (§107). How can there even be talk of the pupil's autonomy if such autonomy results from the teacher's work, whose "chief Business" is "to form the Mind of his Scholars, and give that a right disposition"? Before I answer this question, I need to state and explore some of the ramifications of the doctrine that relates reason and desire.

(*b*) *Reason judging desire.* From a number of the passages presented in (*a*) we might be tempted to draw the conclusion that the task of the educator begins with the attempt to rid children of all desires or passions. That would be the wrong conclusion to draw; the role of desire remains crucial for action, as much so in the *Education* as it was in the *Essay*. One of the first passages I quoted in (*a*) indicates as much: children must learn to deny themselves the satisfaction of desires "where Reason does not authorize them." As Locke puts this two paragraphs earlier: "The having Desires . . . is not the Fault; but the not having them subject to the Rules and

Restraints of Reason" and "The Difference lies not in the having or not having Appetites, but in the Power to govern, and deny our selves in them" (§36).

The problem, as we just saw, is that children experience desires before they can submit these desires to their reason. It is during this period that the task of the educator is crucial. "He that is not used to submit his Will to the reason of others, when he is Young, will scarce harken or submit to his own Reason, when he is of an Age to make use of it" (ibid.). For the actually rational human being, a necessary condition for virtuous action is that he "submit" his desires "to his own Reason." A near-necessary condition for acquiring the habit of subjecting one's desires to one's reason is to become "used to submit his Will to the Reason of others, when he is Young."[7] Compliance with this near-necessary condition does not make children virtuous, but it does instill the habit or principle which is a necessary condition for virtuous action. This is the principle introduced in (a): the power of suspending action on any of one's desires in order to examine the belief that action on these desires will give genuine happiness. Early education must result in internalization of this principle.

At this point it becomes possible to read the well-known passage from paragraph 42 with greater justice to Locke's intentions than the usual (e.g., Passmore's) reading allows: "he that is a good, a vertuous and able Man, must be made so within. And therefore, what he is to receive from Education, what is to sway and influence his Life, must be something put into him betimes; Habits woven into the very Principles of his Nature." It remains true that "a vertuous and able Man, must be made so within" or (to quote from a later paragraph) that it is "Vertue, which is the hard and valuable part to be aimed at in Education" (§70). Virtue is to be the chief fruit of education. But it is not the immediate outcome. Virtuous action presupposes the knowledge and freedom of the actor, but neither knowledge (of one's duty) nor freedom (exercised in gaining this knowledge and

---

7. This is a "near-necessary" condition because it usually holds. Locke allows for exceptions. Young children so "spirited" that they are quite unwilling to submit themselves to others may in later life turn out to be capable of rejecting all their earlier opinions and of commencing a life consonant with the dictates of their own reason. In fact, says Locke, these "spirited" children have a better chance at mastery than those whose "spirit" has been broken, that is, those whose freedom their parents and teachers have consistently violated (see §46). The existence of these very "spirited" ones is, presumably, what makes Locke cautious in the opening paragraph of the *Education*: "*Nine* Parts of Ten are what they are, Good or Evil, useful or not, by their Education." So "there are some Men's Constitutions of Body and Mind so vigorous, and well framed by Nature, that they need not much Assistance from others, but by the Strength of their natural Genius, they are from their Cradles carried towards what is Excellent. . . . But Examples of this Kind are but few."

in submitting to it) can be imposed or instilled. Hence virtue can only "be *aimed at* in Education." If (to continue with phrases from that same paragraph) "the Labour, and Art of Education should furnish the Mind with [virtue], and fasten [it] there," that is only because, through consistent postponement or denial of satisfaction of desires, education has formed in children the habit which allows to bring into play their powers of foresight, suspension, examination, and submission to their own reason. And that can lead conditioned virtuous behavior (behavior for the sake of parental applause) to become autonomous virtuous action (voluntary action on desires authorized by one's own reason). The "highest Perfection" one can achieve is not that of living by "borrowed reason" and "imitated virtue." The "true Principle and Measure of Vertue" remains located in "the Knowledge of a Man's Duty" and "the following the Dictates of that Light God has given him" (§61). Hence "the highest Perfection, that a Man can attain to in this Life" is the "right improvement, and exercise of our Reason" (§122). Following "the Sober Advices he has received from his Governors" must give way to heeding "the Counsel of his own Reason" (§94).

We are now ready to look at details of (*c*) how education, whose "chief Business" is "to form the Mind . . . and give that a right disposition," can be seen as (*d*) leading to autonomy.

(*c*) *Instilling a "Principle" or habit*. We have seen that the "Principle" to be instilled is: no desire should be immediately gratified, so that all objects of desire may come to be rationally examined to determine whether pursuing them would lead to true happiness. Rational examination requires suspension of action on that which is desired. At the age when children are still incapable of rational examination, they can be conditioned to suspend action on desire through the process of denying them immediate gratification of desires. Such conditioning is possible in part because young children are dependent on others for gratification of their desires, and these others can impose delay or denial of gratification.

Very young children are incapable of discerning that it is wrong to desire one object and right to desire another. At that age it is important to deny (immediate) satisfaction of both these kinds of desires. If it were to cry for the first and to pacify it were given the second this would, for the child, amount to indiscriminate fulfillment of desire. Such fulfillment will not lead children "to be able to bear a Denial of that Satisfaction"; instead of making the "Principle" of suspension their own, it will make a home in them for "the Spring from whence all the Evil flows," that is the habit of immediate indiscriminate satisfaction of fortuitous desire (§55).

The principle to be instilled is thus not a maxim with a specific content concerning a limited set of desires. At first (at a very young age) the principle is simply that of unbalking compliance with postponement or denial of desire-fulfillment, a principle that is to become internalized through parental disapprobation if the child protests and parental applause if it willingly complies (see §§58–61). The children's interest in applause or "Esteem" will increasingly make them want to comply. Hence—given that parents are both the source of eventual satisfaction of some desires and of disapproval or applause—this Principle will come to be riveted to their minds, that is, the process is one of "forming of their Minds" (§70). Once they realize that applause or esteem follows upon unbalking compliance with denial, hindsight comes to activate foresight and they begin to realize that esteem will be gained when, after they have made clear that they desire something, they at the same time indicate that they will not attempt immediate satisfaction of the desire. At that stage the reward ought not to be merely esteem, but the gift of some room for independent action: "The constant loss of what they craved . . . should teach them . . . a Power to forbear" (§107) and "If . . . they accustom *themselves* early to silence their Desires . . . they may be allowed greater liberty; when Reason comes to speak in them, and not Passion" (§108).

At this early stage the "Reason" that "comes to speak in them" is that of parents or teacher; their rationality is presupposed throughout Locke's discussion in the *Education*. Indiscriminate and immediate satisfaction of desires will "draw" on children "the *just* Displeasure of their best Friends" (§60). And a father must do nothing before his child which he would not have him imitate, for to be avoided at all costs is the "Arbitrary Imperiousness of a Father, who, without any Ground for it, would deny his Son the Liberty and Pleasures he takes himself" (§71; see also §81).[8]

The parents' non-arbitrary action is not to be confused with mere habitual behavior. Habitual behavior can be irrational and imperious. The behavior of the tyrant (whether that be of the "divinely ordained" king in the political state or of the "divinely ordained" father in the patriarchal family) tends to be quite predictable and habitual. Here of course comes the catch for Locke, the problem he will have to surmount if education— and this "principling" that is at the heart of it—is to allow the child to live by reason instead of by habit. When children establish a pattern of action that avoids censure and gains them esteem this is, to begin with, habitual

---

8. Note again the parallel with the *Second Treatise*. The aim of that treatise may be said to be the removal of "arbitrariness" from public life. (See, e.g., Laslett's "Introduction" to the *Second Treatise*, p. 125.) In it, he who "would deny" others "the Liberty and Pleasures he takes himself" would act "imperiously," irrationally, tyrannically: one of the "brutes" who is not to be imitated but to be removed.

behavior. As such, it falls short of free action. Children's behavior justly applauded is behavior whose principle is imitation of rational examples whose rationality is still hidden from these children. The child's behavior is then determined by external causes it does not fully understand. Even if the behavior thus imposed is rational action for the one who is the example, it is not rational action for the one on whom it is imposed as an example, for it is not the child's own reason that has authorized this action. The question thus remains: how does the imposition of this principle allow for a life of free action, a life in which one is guided by one's own reason?

(*d*) *Education for autonomy.* Reason, for Locke, is the agent of progress; and he holds that there is a good opportunity for rational action to become established in the life of individuals through giving them the kind of education that stresses inculcation of right habits. But this does not imply that Locke means his advocacy of progress to become an apology for social control. Instead, his advocacy of progress is bound up with that of an individual's autonomy.[9] Although it requires initial "control" over the child, education is to result in autonomy; hence it must as soon as possible make "control" both unnecessary and illegitimate.[10]

How do children become autonomous beings? We have seen that indiscriminate satisfaction of desire precludes the achievement of autonomy and, instead, leads into servitude.[11] We saw as well that forced submission to others' reason gives a chance for it: once children become accustomed to not acting on desires immediately, there will (as they grow older) be room for their reason to judge the objects of their desires, and so they will

9. It is for this reason that John Dunn is correct when he writes that Locke's position "offers no encouragement whatsoever for the more extreme Enlightenment hopes of reforming human nature *en masse* through . . . control of the environment in which individuals develop" (*Locke*, p. 74). It is this same reason which makes Passmore's opposite conclusion (see Chap. 2, section 3, above) the wrong one to draw. To reiterate earlier points: Regardless of education (good or bad) the origin of progress lies in an individual's decisions to reason and to heed his or her reason's pronouncements; education can make room or create obstacles for such decisions, but cannot determine them; for their rational acts people deserve more credit and for their irrational acts they deserve greater blame than do their parents or teachers.

10. In this sense, too, Locke stood for what came to be known as "Enlightenment." He would have been able wholeheartedly to support Kant's dictum that "Enlightenment" is the human being's emergence from nonage, where "nonage"—more literally, "not having a voice of one's own"—is the inability to use one's own understanding without another's guidance.

11. Parents who allow indiscriminate fulfillment of desire are charged with "encouraging Intemperance in their Children." The passage in which this phrase appears (§37) again indicates that Locke intended his directives to apply to the poor as well as the rich.

have opportunities for responsible action. Their forced submission to others' reason, enforced through accentuation of their desire for esteem, then comes to be replaced by their free submission to their own reason. Education has then led them to autonomy. In the remainder of this section and the next, I can complete the account of the process through which Locke envisages this change to occur.

Paragraphs 95 and 98 of the *Education* are suitable vantage points from which to complete this account. In the first of these we read that parental disapproval or applause, though "one main Instrument, whereby their Education is to be managed," "should be relaxed, as fast as their Age, Discretion, and Good-Behaviour could allow it."[12] As soon as possible during the youth of his son, the father should

> ask his advice, and Consult with him, about those things wherein he has any knowledge, or understanding. By this, the Father will gain. . . . That it will put serious Considerations into his Son's Thoughts, better than any Rules or Advices he can give him. . . . And if you admit him into serious Discourses sometimes with you, you will insensibly raise his Mind.

Although the father is said to "put serious Considerations into his Son's Thoughts," the father is only the indirect cause of these considerations. To "put into" here consists in creating room for the son's *opportunity* to use his liberty and reason for thinking certain thoughts, not in imparting these thoughts themselves. In addition the father is said to "raise his [Son's] Mind." But no one's "mind" can be "raised" except through the direct agency of the "mind" to be "raised." Hence, again, the father's role is that of creating the *opportunity* for the child's free agency that results in the "raising" of the child's "mind." That my introduction of the child's liberty and agency explicates Locke's intentions is clear from his juxtaposition of the father's procedure in this instance with that of the earlier imposition of parental approbation or disapprobation. (By "earlier" I here refer to the period in which children are to "perfectly comply with the Will of their Parents" because "Their Want of Judgment makes them stand in need of Restraint and Discipline" and determines that "Liberty and Indulgence can do no Good"—as paragraph 40 puts it.) It is clear as well from Locke's

---

12. When Yolton writes that, for Locke, a person acts rationally only because of disgrace or esteem, he is really writing about neither "persons" nor "actions," for both of these terms apply only to those who are autonomous. The autonomous are persons and perform acts (rather than evince behavior conditioned by esteem or disgrace) because of their *free* submission to their *own* reason. See Yolton's *Locke: An Introduction*, p. 24.

juxtaposition of this procedure with that of imposition of rules: he believes it to be "better than any Rules" the parent "can give him."

Paragraph 98 amplifies the move made in 95. Not just the parent but also the tutor must give room for the student's self-development once the stage has been reached in which the student has become accustomed to not acting on beliefs immediately. The tutor must stop "magisterially dictating" and start "using him to reason about what is propos'd." "Particularly in Morality, Prudence, and Breeding, Cases should be Put to him, and his Judgment asked." The student's initiative or freedom are, again, implied when Locke juxtaposes this approach to the inculcation of "Maxims," and to submission to the tutor's "Logical Disputes" or "set Declamations." Putting "cases" to the student and so "using him to reason," "opens the Understanding better than Maxims;" and "Disputes" or "Declamations" at this stage only "spoil the Judgment, and put a Man out of the Way of right and fair Reasoning."

These two paragraphs have, implicitly, introduced the theme of *compulsion versus liberty* or (what amounts to the same thing in this context) of submission to others' reason versus reasoning on one's own. This brings us to the verge of the next part of the chapter where we will see how, for Locke, the nature of reasoning makes it possible that—although initially requiring compulsion—education can result in autonomy. But first I need to establish more clearly that liberty—one of the terms of this theme—is more than implicitly present in the *Education*.

A basic motif in Locke's writings on education is that "Children have as much a Mind to show that they are free, . . . that they are absolute and independent, as any of the proudest of you grown Men" (§73). This freedom, though not to be given its reign from its earliest manifestations, is to be carefully nurtured; the "rough Discipline of the Rod" is to make way for the situation in which children are "satisfied that they act as freely" in their learning as in their "sports and Play" (§74). This freedom is a "natural Freedom" (§76), a "Liberty" which "Children love" and which dictates to parents and educators that children "should be brought to do the things are fit for them, without feeling any restraint laid upon them" (§103). Children "should be allowed the liberties and freedom suitable to their Ages, and not be held under unnecessary Restraints. . . . They must not be hindered from being Children . . . but from doing ill: All other Liberty is to be allowed them" (§69). And of course this holds especially for the liberty expressed in the child's willingness to reason: "if he show a forwardness to be reasoning about things that come in his way, take care as much as you can, that no body check this Inclination in him" (§122).

Passages such as these make it legitimate to speak of *compulsion versus liberty* as a basic theme in Locke's *Education*. Locke himself characterizes this theme as so fundamental that it expresses "the true Secret of Education":

> He that has found a way, how to keep up a Child's Spirit, easy, active and free; and yet, at the same time, to restrain him from many things he has a Mind to, and to draw him to things that are uneasy to him; he, I say, that knows how to reconcile these seeming Contradictions, has, in my Opinion, got the true Secret of Education. (§46)

If parents act rationally in denying their children's desires and praise them when they don't balk at this denial or berate them when they do, then children are restrained by their parents' reason which will then "incline them to the right" (§56). To "incline them to the right" is not to result in a situation in which maturing children pay ever greater heed to parental approval or disapprobation. Commendation is to be given "when they do well," disapprobation to be expressed "upon doing ill" in order that "it will in a little Time make them sensible of the Difference" (§57). This "Difference" is not between commendation and disapprobation but between "doing well" and "doing ill." It is in terms of knowledge of the latter difference, not in terms of approval or disapproval of those in power over them, that the end of education finds its realization. Statements from paragraph 61, including some I have discussed before, express this as clearly as one could wish. We there read that the "true Principle and Measure of Vertue" is not really actualized when the maturing child acts for the sake of "Reputation," for even when "Reputation" is acquired under the aegis of rational parents, it can amount to no more than "the Testimony and Applause that *other People's Reason* . . . gives to virtuous and well-ordered Actions." "Love of Credit" and "Apprehension of Disgrace" can only function as "the proper Guide and Encouragement of Children, *till they grow able to judge for themselves, and to find what is right by their own Reason.*" The "true Principle and Measure of Vertue" becomes actualized once "the Knowledge of a Man's Duty" results in the free determination of "following the Dictates of that Light God has given him."

Indeed, the importance of applause or disapprobation is not to be minimized, for in most cases conditioning is crucial. But it is the parents' or teacher's "*just* Displeasure" or *warranted* "Applause" which "alone ought to hold the Reins, and keep the Child in order" (§60). When a parent forces children to postpone or to forego altogether satisfaction of a desire, this act is to condition children to place themselves in a position where they have the time in which all fortuitous desires can be called before the bar of their reason. The end of forced postponement, or of disapprobation if such postponement is resisted, is that children come to recognize the necessity of such postponement or the justness of such displeasure. This necessity exists for the actualization of their freedom and rationality, and the displeasure comes into play when—as their reason is being denied its role as authoritative examiner—capriciousness usurpes the place of liberty. (See §§104–5 as contrasted with §73 as a statement of capriciousness contrasted with true liberty.) It is the parents' reason that insists on postponement and that sanctions applause or censure.

Since it is the parents' *reason* that forces the child to the freedom of rational action, it is, in effect, reason that is the child's teacher. But children cannot know this until they themselves begin to reason. When children know that it is reason that is the teacher, the need for the applause or disapprobation of others is past, for it is then their own reason that approves or disapproves of their actions. With their own reason as their teacher, autonomy is theirs and the end of education has been attained.[13]

2. Education and Methodology, or Reason as the Teacher

Because most education is in the hands of the prejudiced, it involves the wrong sort of "principling," namely, the kind which prevents such a "principled" mind from "looking into its own principles." As long as there is no awareness of the mind's own principles, one does not possess the criteria for knowledge, and without such criteria one is precluded

13. Thus Gutman's interpretation is wrong in a crucial aspect when she characterizes Locke's as the prime example of educational theories under the rubric "The State of Families" and when she then writes that "the state of families . . . places educational authority exclusively in the hands of parents, thereby permitting parents to predispose their children, through education, to choose a way of life consistent with their familial heritage. . . . John Locke maintained that parents are the best protectors of their children's future interests" (*Democratic Education*, p. 28). For Locke, the parents' "predisposition" of their children is a predisposition to reasoning. Parents can be good teachers only if their reason is their teacher. Unless a "life consistent with their familial heritage" is a life in which reason's dictates are enacted, that life has to be rejected. And if it is one directed by reason then, given the universal uniformity of reason and of its dictates, it will not differ essentially from any other. Furthermore, given that the locus of reason is in each individual and that individuals must personally come to recognize and accept reason's dictates, Locke's position (as we shall see even more clearly in the following section) is closer to what Gutman calls "The State of Individuals" (pp. 33–35) than to "The State of Families."

from acting rationally, that is, one cannot be a person. We encountered these Lockean doctrines in the first part of the preceding chapter. (See the four paragraphs at its end.) From them we progressed, in the first part of the present chapter, to Locke's advice for rational parents and educators. I discussed the "principling" to which they subject children in terms of creating room for the child's reasoning.

We now need to shift our focus and pay attention to *how* a child becomes aware of the "principles" involved in reasoning. The room created for the child's reason to function at the same time established room for the child to introspect or reflect, that is, for becoming aware of reason's mode of procedure or reason's principles as it does its work.

Once children become aware of their reason's mode of procedure, they can adopt reason's principles as guides for life. If they elect to be directed by their reason's principles, then they opt for autonomous action: self-consciously directed by their own reason, they are *persons*. In persons, education (the process of learning submission to others' reason) has reached its goal of "producing" autonomous beings (people submitting to their own reason). The outcome of the change of focus is, therefore, the shift from habitual or causally determined behavior to autonomous or free action. For us to understand how this effect can come about, we must focus on that aspect of "producing" that consists in becoming self-conscious of one's reason's mode of procedure. (This still leaves the matter of *electing to act in accordance with reason's principles*—an issue on which there will be a last word in the final section of this chapter.)

This shift may be characterized as that from the young child to the older child or adult. It may be seen as the move from "nurture" to "nature." To say that this change of focus involves the transition from *Some Thoughts concerning Education* to *Of the Conduct of the Understanding* would not do justice to the content of the first of these. It is, however, the case that, in the *Conduct*, Locke is more explicit about the nature of the principles of reasoning than he is in the *Education*. Hence (except for one quotation from Locke's *Some Thoughts concerning Reading and Study for a Gentleman*) I shall first turn to the *Conduct* and then revert to the *Education*.

If in addition to Locke's notions of right and wrong "principling" I introduce that of "bottoming," then good education may be said to be that which avoids the wrong kind of "principling" and imposes the right kind, in order to allow room for "bottoming" and for reflection on this process of "bottoming." When Locke tells us what "in short, is right reasoning" he writes that it consists in "find[ing] out upon what foundation any proposition advanced bottoms; and to observe the connexion of the intermediate ideas, by which it is joined to that foundation upon which it is erected, or that principle from which it is derived."[14]

Although I have so far not used the word "bottoming," it is not new to Locke's vocabulary; he used it, for example, in the *Essay*'s 1.3.24. The activity for which it stands is one I discussed earlier, for example, in Chapter 1, sections 1 and 3. It is the complex activity of attempting to reduce one's beliefs to their clear and distinct, self-evident foundation (if they have such a foundation) and then to reconstruct these beliefs by tracing the necessary connections between and among the ideas in them, including that self-evident idea or principle on which they are "founded" or on which they "bottom." Or it is the construction of entirely new propositions on the "foundation" or "bottom" of self-evident ideas or principles, making certain that all connections between and among their ideas are necessary connections. If this process of reconstruction or construction has been carried out successfully, it warrants replacing the term "belief" with the term "knowledge." The process, of course, is that of reasoning; it is the application of the *Essay*'s revolutionary logic. As we now turn to the *Conduct* and then to the *Education*, we will see that this process functions as centrally in these works as it did in the *Essay*. And it will become clear how, through becoming aware of reason's procedure, one's own reason may become one's teacher and those so taught achieve autonomy in education.

Through reflection one becomes aware of the principles of reason. But (as we saw in the first section of Chapter 7) "both the poor and the rich" "offend" through the kind of "principling" whose outcome is that their children "were never accustomed to reflect" and so have "lost the use and exercise of reflection, as if it were foreign to their constitution, and can no more bear with it as a violence done to their natures." Children can only become accustomed to "reflect" if they become accustomed to "bottoming" (for it is *that* process on which they must reflect to begin with) and they become accustomed to "bottoming" through their parents' and teacher's use of examples.

As we now turn to the use of examples, it is to be stated once more that the examples of interest are, initially, those in the realm of *general* knowledge. Locke himself stresses this when, in the *Conduct*'s sixth paragraph, he writes that this treatise is about "strict reasoning" or "to trace the dependence of any truth, in a long chain of consequences, to its remotest principles, and to observe its connexion."

---

14. *Some Thoughts concerning Reading and Study for a Gentleman*, in *Works*, 1823, 3:294.

It is to general knowledge that the notion of "bottoming" is crucial, for the "remotest principles" of this knowledge are the clear and distinct, self-evident ideas which serve as foundation or "bottom." In the *Conduct's* fifth paragraph Locke states that he will not concern himself with "the *getting* clear and determined ideas." "Getting" such ideas is necessary for the very possibility of general knowledge; it is its precondition, for it is the process of decomposition or abstraction that gives us our simple universals, the most fundamental clear and distinct ideas on which our discursive reasoning bottoms. Locke adds that he will not deal with this process here because it is an issue he has "sufficiently enlarged upon in another place," namely, in various parts of the *Essay*.[15] We shall see that although he will not "enlarge" on it, he will regularly refer or allude to this process; and that is no surprise, for this activity is a crucial part of the mode of reason's operation of which we become conscious through reflection on the process of bottoming. Locke alludes to it, for instance, when (in §9) he juxtaposes that which "outward corporeal objects" give the mind, to the "abstract ideas" that do "not offer themselves to the senses" (and he then typically adds that he will say no more on this topic because what is "said in the third book of my Essay will excuse me"). We now need not be detained by this process, although some of it will present itself naturally as we deal with examples.[16]

When, in the fourth paragraph of the *Conduct*, Locke states his optimistic belief in the possibility of progress—"We are born with faculties and powers capable almost of anything"—he insists that one condition for realization of progress is practice through examples: "it is only the exercise of those powers which gives us ability and skill in any thing, and leads us towards perfection." Practice through examples has two results: (i) through reflection on this practice the mind becomes aware of its own principles, and (ii) the practice creates the habit of implementing these principles. The resulting habit therefore does not come about through learning rules by rote; instead, it becomes established through practicing these rules through following the examples which embody them. For "Nobody is made any thing by hearing of rules, or laying them up in his memory; practice must settle the habit of doing, without reflecting on the

15. One might say that Locke has "enlarged" on this topic in various *other* parts of the *Essay* for, as we know, the *Conduct* was written as a chapter for the *Essay*.

16. I have dealt with this part of Locke's doctrine before, in section 3 of the first chapter of this book and, at greater length, in *The Imposition of Method*, chap. 7. The interpretation I developed in the latter place has since found confirmation in Peter Alexander's *Ideas, Qualities, and Corpuscles* (Cambridge, 1985) when he writes (on p. 106) that "for Locke, simple ideas are usually, perhaps always, the products of the analysis of our experiences."

rule" (ibid.). (Note how this dovetails with what was said in the preceding section through my introduction of the *Education*'s paragraphs 95 and 98).

At first, practice takes place "without reflecting on the rule" because the rule is implicit in the examples, hence not immediately accessible. Once we understand the examples we can reflect on them. Such reflection allows for cognition of the rules implicit in them as well as for increasing ability to apply these rules elsewhere. Reason is then becoming conscious of its own mode of procedure. Thus those who understand and reflect on the examples are becoming self-conscious and, in their developing self-consciousness, they can begin to determine themselves to act rationally. The vulnerability of the very young (who, still incapable of reflection, are without the criteria of truth and hence incapable of rational action)[17] is being overcome. Through conscious application of these rules in other instances they determine that their action in these other instances is rational; that is, they determine themselves to be persons. Through seeking out opportunities for application of these rules, rational action is to become habitual, and personhood becomes firmly established. These statements need to be related to Locke's text in order to show that they in fact express his position.[18]

A good place to start is a passage from the *Conduct*'s sixth paragraph, whose opening lines are familiar to us because I used them in my first chapter (section 4):

> Would you have a man reason well, you must use him to it betimes, exercise his mind in observing the connexion of ideas, and following them in train. Nothing does this better than mathematics, which, therefore, I think should be taught all those who have the time and opportunity; not so much to make them mathematicians, as to make them reasonable creatures; for though we all call ourselves so, because we are born to it, if we please; yet we may truly say, nature gives us but the seeds of it: we are born to be, if we please, rational creatures; but it is use and exercise only that makes us so, and we are, indeed, so no farther than industry and application have carried us.[19]

17. See above, Chap. 7, section 2, the second paragraph.

18. As in Chap. 1, section 4, it is again clear that Locke's position has strong affinities with that of Descartes in the *Rules for the Direction of the Mind* and the *Discourse on Method*. For both, there is no imposition of rules that do not find their origin in the mind for which they are to become habits. Positively, for both, through introspection the mind becomes aware of its proper mode of procedure, and the rules it can then formulate are a functional definition of reason. And as we shall see in what immediately follows, Locke shares Descartes's insistence that mathematical examples are the best for this practice of whose principles one is to become aware through introspection.

19. The phrase "we are born to be, if we please, rational creatures" (emphasized through its repetition) evokes the *Second Treatise*'s argument, particularly that of the chapter "Of

It is "use and exercise" that makes one rational. The right training ground for such exercise is, to begin with, that of examples from mathematics. This is because of Locke's position that in mathematics there is hardly room for prejudice; hence its concepts can relatively easily be seen to be clear and distinct ("there is most knowledge . . . in mathematics, where men have determined ideas," he says in paragraph 31). That makes these examples the most suitable to serve as instances in which reflective awareness may observe the principles of reasoning. What are then observed are not just the principles of mathematical reasoning, for reason's mode of procedure does not differ from one subject to another in the realm of general knowledge. This aspect of Locke's doctrine we saw before (see the final six paragraphs of my first chapter). To relate it firmly to the *Conduct* all we need is to read part of its seventh paragraph:

> I have mentioned mathematics as a way to settle in the mind a habit of reasoning closely and in train; not that I think it necessary that all men should be deep mathematicians, but that, having got the way of reasoning, which that study necessarily brings the mind to, they might be able to transfer it to other parts of knowledge, as they shall have occasion. For, in all sorts of reasoning, every single argument should be managed as a mathematical demonstration; the connexion and dependence of ideas should be followed, till the mind is brought to the source on which it bottoms, and observes the coherence all along.

Locke adds that the outcome of such training is "freedom" for the understanding because, once habituated to reasoning, one will no longer "be led into error by presumption, laziness, or precipitancy." All three of these rule out "bottoming" and so all three are paths into the bondage of superstition and prejudice. Cognizance of the principles of reason is the key to discerning these paths (although as we know it is not the guarantee that we will in fact shun them).

Although "God has made the intellectual world harmonious and beautiful" that does not detract from the fact that "it will never come into our heads all at once; we must bring it home piecemeal, and there set it up by our own industry," lest we "have nothing but darkness and chaos within, whatever order and light there be in things outside us" (§38). Turning to a

---

Paternal Power": "Children, I confess are not born in this full state of Equality, though they are born to it"(para. 55). In the *Conduct*, maturing children, "if they please" to concentrate on mathematical examples, bring the "seeds" of personhood to fruition. This rationality or personhood is the condition for freedom from "paternal power" in the *Second Treatise*: "Age and reason as they grow up . . . leave a Man at his own free Disposal" (ibid.).

being slightly less than God: "Euclid" is "allowed to be knowing, and to have demonstrated" what he said; "and yet . . . Till we ourselves . . . perceive it by our own understandings, we are as much in the dark and as void of knowledge as before, let us believe any learned author as much as we will" (§24). And it is "the study of mathematics" which "would show . . . the necessity there is in reasoning, to separate all the distinct ideas." "This [separation of all ideas] is that which, in other subjects, besides quantity . . . is absolutely requisite to . . . reasoning." Whatever the subject-matter, one cannot "reason as it were in the lump," for "that mind is not in a posture to find the truth, that does not distinctly take all the parts asunder" (§7; see also §39). All our beliefs, theories, and "conceptions," are "nothing but ideas, which are all made up of simple ones" (§29) and we cannot judge or understand any of these beliefs or theories unless we first grasp these "simple ones"—their "bottoming" or foundational ideas and principles. These, in turn, we cannot understand unless they are clear and distinct or self-evident (see §§21, 31, 42). For the "only way to get true knowledge is to form in our minds clear settled notions." These a person needs "to state the question right, and see whereon it turns; and thus he will stand upon his own legs, and know by his own understanding" (§15).

Now one can be *told* to "bring it home piecemeal," "to separate all the distinct ideas," to "distinctly take all the parts asunder"; but the one cannot *do* it for the other. Once room for thought and for reflection on thought has been created, all that can be done is to invite exercise. Once exercise in mathematics is engaged in, this discipline "*necessarily* brings the mind to . . . the way of reasoning." There the reflecting mind cannot but "*observe*" the process of "bottoming;" "the study of mathematics would *show* them . . . reasoning." This part of the "production" of an autonomous being is therefore *self-production*.

There is, for Locke, far more to reasoning than what I have highlighted. There is the combination of ideas that gives us complex ideas, and the combination of these complex ideas to give us our knowledge-statements and our theories. We need not spend time with these doctrines now. Reasoning—knowledge—*begins* with the reductive process of "distinctly taking all the parts asunder." "This is that which, in other subjects, besides quantity, is what is absolutely requisite to just reasoning"(§7). Hence it is the process we must learn first of all, and of which we must become reflexively aware. We must learn to execute this process ourselves and we must do our own reflection.

As reflection acquaints us with the principles of reason it at the same time gives us our foremost principle of rational action. For the process of reasoning demands decomposition of all "knowledge" that comes "as it were in the lump." This decomposition is tantamount to initial rejection of whatever we experience as complex. But it is Locke's doctrine that all our immediate experience is characterized by complexity. Hence the dictate for rational action is: never begin with accepting as true or good whatever our experience initially presents to us. It requires that we decompose all "common received Opinions." Thus it stipulates that we adopt the revolutionary stance we have recognized as part of Locke's position in my first chapter. To be rational is to be critical—where "critical" has the revolutionary meaning Locke shared with Descartes and the philosophes. (See Chapter 1, section 1.)

This is the doctrine of the *Conduct of the Understanding*. It is also that of *Some Thoughts concerning Education*—the last point to be established in this section.

Parents and teachers must reason with children as soon as they have the use of language (see §81). That does not mean they are then immediately ready to reason about the topic of chief interest to the *Education*, that of morals. For

> The Foundations on which several Duties are built, and the Fountains of Right and Wrong, from which they spring, are not perhaps easily to be let into the Minds of grown Men, not used to abstract their Thoughts from common received Opinions. Much less are Children capable of Reasonings from remote Principles. (Ibid.)

As long as they cannot "abstract" and thus not grasp the "Foundations" or "remote" ideas—"as long as they shall be under another's Tuition or Conduct," as paragraph 82 puts it—they are bound to imitate the examples of their elders. The time of "Tuition" coincides with the time during which they are unable to obtain abstract ideas through "decomposition" of the complexity of the contents of their sentient states. That is, it coincides with the time in which they are not very proficient in reasoning.[20] Since education is designed to obviate "another's Tuition" and so to "produce" a moral being capable of "following the dictates of that Light God has given him" (§61), therefore the child must be led to making abstractions. The teacher must "accustom him to Distinguish well, that is, to have distinct Notions, where-ever the Mind can find any real differ-

20. Since they *can* follow examples discerningly, their reason *is* stirring. For not all examples they encounter are the right ones to imitate: no one's context is fully free from "passion." Hence we read, "Children . . . distinguish early betwixt Passion and Reason: and they cannot but have a Reverence for what comes from the latter" (§77).

ence" (§195). For his "Mind" must start from "the simplest and most uncompounded parts it can divide the Matter into" and he must avoid all use of "terms, where he has not distinct and different clear Ideas" (ibid.). How to learn to abstract? "*Arithmetick* is the easiest, and consequently the first sort of abstract Reasoning, which the Mind commonly bears, or accustoms it self to" (§180). Once he can reach and comprehend "the Foundations" in mathematics, this procedure may be transferred to morals in order to wean the child from imitation and lead it to rational action. As in mathematics, the "leading" is to be in terms of confrontation with examples. To return to paragraph 98:

> Particularly in Morality . . . Cases should be Put to him, and his Judgment asked. This opens the Understanding better than Maxims, how well soever explain'd, and settles the Rules better in the Memory for Practice. . . . He will better comprehend the Foundations, and Measures of Decency, and Justice; and have livelier, and more lasting Impressions, of what he ought to do, by giving his Opinion on Cases propos'd, and Reasoning with his Tutor on fit Instances, than by giving a silent . . . Audience to his Tutor's Lectures.

In both the *Conduct* and the *Education*, the process of reduction that allows for "bottoming" or "comprehending the Foundations" is at the same time the process of cleaning the slate from all that experience has inscribed on it and that the individual's own reason has not yet authorized. That is, it is the process of becoming autonomous. My own reason tells me to carry out this process. Since it is my own reason that carries me to this autonomy, this process of being taught is itself an exercise in autonomy.

3. Mastery and Progress

In this final section, I want to draw together more explicitly the main tenets of Locke's educational writings and crucial doctrines from the *Essay concerning Human Understanding*. This exercise will afford me the opportunity to present some of my conclusions in bolder relief. The two conclusions I want to emphasize will be seen to be intimately connected. The first is that Locke's prescriptions for education present the *Essay*'s doctrine in practice.[21] The second is that, in terms of his own position, the

21. Peter Gay is one of the few commentators who is convinced of the existence of this relationship, and writes about it in unambiguous terms. "*Some Thoughts . . .* was an evident offspring of Locke's major work, the *Essay*. . . . To its many approving readers in the

optimism with respect to progress—an optimism that permeates the works that have been my main focus—is unfounded. I shall develop these related conclusions together.

Children can become free but cannot be compelled to become free even if their cultural milieu never presents them with beliefs and attitudes that reason cannot justify. And adults can free themselves from prejudice even if, from childhood on, they have constantly been subjected to "ill education." Both child and adult can achieve mastery, but neither can be forced to do so. Only their own freedom and reason allow them to achieve it; and what Locke believes to be the case about reason and autonomy precludes the necessity or inevitability of this achievement. There is a kind of mastery implicit in Locke's notion of autonomy and this mastery entails that Locke's optimism about progress is an article of faith. We all originally possess the mastery that determines that we are "self-made." But what we make ourselves to be need not be human—it may be subhuman.

Let us consider the salient details of these interrelated doctrines and conclusions. A good place to begin is by returning to the *Essay*'s "Of Power." In its fifth paragraph we read:

> This at least I think evident, That we find in ourselves a Power to begin or forbear, continue or end several actions of our minds . . . barely by a thought or preference of the mind ordering, or as it were commanding the doing or not doing such or such a particular action. This power which the mind has, thus to order the consideration of any Idea, or the forbearing to consider it . . . in any particular instance is that which we call the Will.

Thus, in addition to awareness of ideas that are forced upon the mind in the course of perception of external objects as well as in the course of a relatively uncontrolled train of association, the mind can order itself to consider certain ideas. The ordering here is a thoughtful ordering, that is, it involves "thought or preference of the mind." Circumstances may force ideas on a person. One of these "circumstances" is the educator who, through manipulation of the environment, attempts to determine which ideas the pupil will obtain through perception. But circumstances, including those created by the educator, cannot force a person to reason about these ideas. For reasoning requires the thoughtful "ordering" that consists in the selecting, decomposing, comparing and relating of ideas; and no

---

eighteenth century, *Some Thoughts* was the new philosophy in action; Locke's philosophy of education deserved a hearing and demonstrated the importance of its subject, because it was Locke's philosophy *in* education" (*The Enlightenment, An Interpretation, 2: The Science of Freedom*, p. 501).

such effort is expended "in any particular instance" except through "that which we call will." This will "the mind" determines to "the consideration of any idea, or the forbearing to consider it."

Of course it is true as well that no such effort is expended unless there is uneasiness or desire. It is precisely at this point that educators have their great opportunity to influence their charges who, if happiness is to become theirs, must act on some but not on other of these desires. The rational educator attempts to inculcate habits that lead to fulfilment of the right desires, the irrational educator inculcates quite different ones. Whichever is the case, as children mature and their reason and freedom begin to stir, desires habitually satisfied (whether good or bad) need to be examined. For children to become fully human they must become responsible for their habits. If we call the inculcation of habits the formation of character then, for children to become human, *they have to take responsibility for their character—a character they may well have to reconstitute.* We have seen that commentators are by and large agreed on the point that, for Locke, education consists in the formation of character, and that they often add or imply that therefore education makes a person virtuous or evil. I take it that the various parts of my exposition drawn together make it incontrovertible that this is an erroneous interpretation based on an incomplete account that stresses one aspect of Locke's position and (to a greater or lesser extent) neglects another. In terms of the opening paragraph of the *Education*, it emphasizes that "of all the Men we meet with, Nine Parts of Ten are what they are, Good or Evil, useful or not, by their Education," and it disregards the importance of the statement that "Men's Happiness or Misery is most part of their own making."[22]

Both habit and autonomy must be given their due. Overemphasis of habit conflicts with more than the opening paragraph of the *Education*; it conflicts with many of the specific injunctions of this work, as well as with broad outlines and many details of Locke's other works. That it militates against Locke's position in the *Essay* is clear enough from my exposition in Part B of this book. To that exposition let me now add these two considerations.

First. The closing paragraphs of "Of Power" strongly emphasize indi-

---

22. In the preceding chapter we took note of the fact that in his letter to Clarke, from which Locke adapted this paragraph, he wrote "nine parts of ten, or perhaps ninety-nine of one hundred." But this letter was written in 1684, during the period that Locke still held that you cannot know the good and not do it, and before the time that the role of desire and the emphasis on autonomy in its context made its appearance in the second edition of the *Essay*. Once that shift is made, "ninety-nine of one hundred" no longer fits Locke's position and, I would suggest, even "nine out of ten" may then be too strong as well.

vidual responsibility for what each person is and ought to be. The heading of paragraph 70 states that "Preference of Vice to Vertue" is "a manifest wrong Judgment," and in the opening sentences of that paragraph we read

> But whatever false notions, or shameful neglect of what is in their power, may put Men out of their way to Happiness, and distract them, as we see, into so different courses of life, this yet is certain, that Morality, established upon its true Foundations, cannot but determine the Choice in any one, that will but consider: and he that will not be so far a rational Creature, as to reflect seriously upon infinite Happiness and Misery, must needs condemn himself, as not making that use of his Understanding he should.

Preference of vice to virtue is a wrong judgment because it is an irrational judgment. Through 2.21.5, we were reminded of Locke's doctrine that there is no consideration of ideas apart from willing such consideration and there is no such willing unless the mind determines the will to do so. Now suppose that through education the mind were to become bound up with prejudice in ways that no longer allowed it to determine itself to consider certain kinds of ideas. That would entail that certain prejudices could never be expelled and hence that certain modes of behavior could never be examined. This would in turn imply that education can permanently fix a being's character and that (for better or worse) there is room for the social engineer. There are good grounds why no part of this supposition can be accepted as Locke's doctrine.

To mention just one of these: it excludes consideration of the permeating role of desire for happiness, for fleeing pain and pursuing pleasure— the only inclination that human beings possess innately, and of which neither parents and educators nor their own actions can ever rid them. In order to achieve happiness at all, reason must play its role. It is true that (as Locke continues in 2.21.70) "False notions" "may put Men out of their way to Happiness." But if "infinite Happiness and Misery," if "the eternal State is considered but in its bare possibility, which no Body can make any doubt of," then reason will identify as prejudice those tenets that would prevent one from action that does not constitute an insurance policy against "infinite Misery." Regardless of one's circumstances, all human beings remain personally responsible for their eternal weal or woe. If they fail to act on it, that is a "shameful neglect of what is in their power." Neither rational nor irrational action, neither reasoning that leads to rejection of "false notions" nor the "shameful neglect" of such reasoning, is either precluded or dictated by one's upbringing. For Locke, it remains one's own choice whether one will act in accordance with reason or with unexamined desire. Regardless of the significant role education no doubt plays, one's destiny remains in one's own hands. For good or for ill we are, each one of us individually, masters of our fate. The uneasiness from which we cannot escape in the various experiences that constitute human life are, each of them, opportunities for setting out, or progressing, on the path of mastery. Hence human life itself precludes the triumph of the social engineer.

Second. If we consider what "Of Power" teaches about the acquiring of habit, the conclusion just reached will be reinforced: autonomy and habit both must be given their due, but autonomy plays the more fundamental role simply because habit is to be contracted autonomously. On this point "Of Power" (§§68 and 69) is quite explicit; and so its doctrine fits that of the educational works when they teach that one is responsible for one's own character. In these paragraphs Locke argues that some of the actions that lead to true happiness may be unpleasant; and it appears "so pre-posterous a thing to Men, to make themselves unhappy in order to Happiness, that they do not easily bring themselves to it." But they can "bring themselves to it," they "can change the agreeableness or dis-agreeableness in things," hence it would be "a mistake to think, that Men cannot change the displeasingness, or indifferency, that is in actions, if they will do but what is in their power." "A due consideration will do it in some cases; and practice, application, and custom in most." That is, reason can guide action into new habits. To be more precise, it is reason joined with the freedom of self-determination that creates new habits, for no new habits can be contracted apart from suspension of the action prescribed by the old habits, followed by "due consideration" and rational selection of new actions. The pursuit of these new actions is to occur repeatedly and this repetition, authorized by reason, creates the new habits. These new habits continue to be acted out both because there is pleasure in the very fact of habitual action and because these habits, authorized by of reason, ensue in true happiness. As Locke writes in paragraph 69:

> Habits have powerful charms, and put so strong attractions of easiness and pleasure into what we accustom our selves to, that we cannot forbear to do, or at least be easy in the omission of actions, which habitual practice has suited, and thereby recommends to us . . . Every one's Experience shews him . . . that Men can make things or actions more or less pleasing to themselves; and thereby remedy that, to which one may justly impute a great deal of their wandering. Fashion and the common Opinion having settled wrong Notions, and education and custom ill habits, the just values of things

are misplaced. . . . Pains should be taken to rectify these; and contrary habits change our pleasures, and give a relish to that, which is necessary, or conducive to our Happiness. This every one must confess he can do, and when Happiness is lost, and misery overtakes him, he will confess, he did amiss in neglecting it; and condemn himself for it.

This process of acquiring new habits through the acts of self-determination in the suspension of action on old habits and in placing oneself under the authority of one's reason, is a matter of both reconstitution of one's character and self-re-education. This reconstitution and re-education are necessary if original education saddled one with "ill habits." Of course, original education need not have done so. But even if education inculcated the right habits, those who have such habits do not know that they are the right habits unless they examine them and discern that the principles which inform them are rational principles. And even if one need not reconstitute one's character because, upon examination, one's habits prove to be the right ones, the examination and acceptance of this examination's outcome are the processes through which one accepts responsibility for one's character. In our discussion of the *Education* we saw that good habits acquired through upbringing but never made into objects of reflection cannot, once they are acted on, constitute a fully human life. For though such a life may appear good because it is reason-authorized, it is the parents' or teacher's reason and not one's own which authorizes it. In view of Locke's epistemic individualism, the life thus led is one of belief rather than of knowledge. It is like the life of the unenlightened flock which slavishly acts out the rational principles held up by the enlightened preacher. Since, for Locke, faith is to be judged by reason and one's ultimate task is to know rather than to believe, such a life hardly even qualifies as second best.[23]

23. The parallel in doctrine between the writings on education and on religion is clear. In the first *Letter concerning Toleration* Locke states that "such is the nature of the understanding, that it cannot be compelled to the belief of any thing by outward force" (p. 11). Hence "Although the magistrate's opinion in religion be sound, and the way that he appoints be truly evangelical, yet if I be not thoroughly persuaded in my own mind, there will be no safety for me in following it" (p. 28). Regardless of the sincerity of the parents' or teacher's desire to impart knowledge, the children must carry out the process of "bottoming" and of (re-)construction for themselves if they are to gain truth. And "How great, soever, in fine, may be the . . . concern for the salvation of men's souls, men cannot be forced to be saved whether they will or no; and therefore, when all is done, they must be left to their own consciousnesses" (ibid.). Locke never abandoned this stance. As we read in the *Third Letter for Toleration*, "force may be pertinent . . . to make men hear, but not to make them consider" if by "consider" we mean "consider so as to embrace" where "embracing" is the result of confrontation with the truth that one's own "considering" reveals, rather than for the sake of

Proper upbringing stimulates reason into activity. Once activated, it ought to exercise itself to the point where it becomes conscious of its mode of operation. Short of attaining such self-consciousness "men are guilty of a great many faults in the exercise and improvement of this faculty of the mind," faults "which hinder them in their progress, and keep them in ignorance and error all their lives" (*Conduct*, §2). As we have seen, once such self-consciousness is attained and the mind has trained itself to act in accordance with its own rules, then the educator's task is accomplished, for then the pupil's mind has acquired "that freedom, that disposition, and those habits, that may enable him to attain any part of knowledge he shall apply himself to, or stand in need of in the future course of his life" (*Conduct*, §12). Right methodic procedure guarantees that needs encountered in the course of life can be met.

We know that Locke considers these needs to be endless in number. For any state of uneasiness is a state of need, and it is part of being human constantly to fall short of complete satisfaction, constantly therefore to experience need. It is human to be subject to insatiable desire. But it is also human constantly to be able to some degree to meet each legitimate need, to fill each proper desire. It is human to be able to satisfy needs in such a way that, in this process, we work at "our happiness in general."

For Locke, right methodic procedure, that is, reason applied unencumbered with prejudice, guarantees increasing mastery. Rational procedure is the path of progress. What Locke did not see was the problem inherent in the ascription of autonomy to each individual, an autonomy retained irrespective of cultural context or education good or bad. It is an autonomy that demands a decision on the part of each individual to be or not to be compelled by rational desires, an autonomy which characterizes each as "self-made." The ascription of this kind of autonomy not only precludes the inevitability of successful social engineering; it also excludes the guarantee of increasing mastery through individual autonomous action. On both counts, it makes the expectation of indefinite progress into an article of faith.

In the course of this study we encountered another article of faith that Locke took to be a matter of fact. It is the issue to which I devoted my third chapter, that of the infallibility of reason. Even if Locke's doctrine of the original mastery implicit in autonomy were not to make belief in

---

"outward conformity" (p. 397). Parents, teachers, preachers, magistrates—none of them ought to pretend to powers which God (if he could) would not employ: as the first *Letter* has it, "God himself will not save men against their wills" (p. 23). (All quotations from the letters on toleration are from *Works*, 1823, vol. 6.)

progress an item of faith, his acceptance of the infallibility of reason would pose problems for it. With reason as the agent of progress, reason's presumed infallibility helps to account for the optimistic tone that pervades Locke's works: "We are born with faculties . . . capable almost of any thing, such at least as would carry us further than can easily be imagined . . . towards perfection" (to quote the *Conduct*'s fourth paragraph once more). Each of these articles of faith would by itself cast doubt on the reasonableness of Locke's optimism; together, they make it quite unwarranted. In Locke's own terms, this optimism betrays the presence of the "Enthusiast." For as we noted, "Enthusiasm fails of Evidence," whether that of "Reason" or of "Divine Revelation" (*Essay*, 4.19.7, 11).

Thus I conclude with a re-affirmation of two of my findings. The first of these Locke would no doubt reject as unfairly applied to his position and, he would say, it in any case deserves no serious consideration because the statement of it contains a contradiction. With respect to the second, he would concur with only part of it. The first is that, in some respects, Locke was an "enthusiastic" philosopher, that is to say that Locke the revolutionary was also Locke the dogmatist. The second is that, in spite of incoherence within crucial doctrines, Locke's work as a whole is far more coherent than most commentators have been able to see or willing to grant.

Bibliography

Primary Sources

The Correspondence of John Locke, ed. E. S. deBeer. 8 vols. Oxford. 1976–88.
John Locke: An Essay concerning Human Understanding, ed. P. H. Nidditch. Oxford, 1975.
John Locke: A Paraphrase and Notes on the Epistles of St. Paul, ed. Arthur W. Wainwright. 2 vols. Oxford, 1987.
John Locke: Questions concerning the Law of Nature, ed. and trans. Robert Horwitz, Jenny Strauss Clay, and Diskin Clay. Ithaca, N.Y., 1990.
John Locke: Some Thoughts concerning Education, ed. John W. Yolton and Jean S. Yolton. Oxford, 1989.
John Locke: Two Treatises of Government. Rev. ed., ed. Peter Laslett. Cambridge, 1963.
Works of John Locke. London, 1823. Rpt. Aalen. 1963.

Secondary Sources

Aaron, Richard I. *John Locke*. 3d ed. Oxford, 1971.
Aarsleff, Hans. "The State of Nature and the Nature of Man in Locke." In *John Locke, Problems and Perspectives*, ed. John W. Yolton. Cambridge, 1969.
Abrams, Philip. *John Locke: Two Tracts on Government*. Cambridge, 1967.
Adam, Charles, and Paul Tannery, eds. *Oeuvres de Descartes*. 11 vols. Paris, 1965–75.
Alexander, Peter. *Ideas, Qualities, and Corpuscles*. Cambridge, 1985.
Ashcraft, Richard. *Revolutionary Politics and Locke's Two Treatises of Government*. Princeton, 1986.

Axtell, James L. *The Educational Writings of John Locke*. Cambridge, 1968.

Ayers, Michael. *Locke. Volume I: Epistemology*. London, 1991.

Ayers, Michael. *Locke. Volume II: Ontology*. London, 1991.

Beck, L. J. *The Method of Descartes*. Oxford, 1952.

Berlin, Isaiah. *The Age of Enlightenment: The Eighteenth Century Philosophers*. Oxford, 1956.

Berlin, Isaiah. *Four Essays on Liberty*. Oxford, 1969.

Blackmore, Sir Richard. *The Creation: A Philosophical Poem demonstrating the Existence and Providence of God*. London, 1712.

Brandt, Reinhard, ed. *John Locke: Symposium Wolfenbüttel 1979*. Berlin, 1979.

Brinton, Crane. "Enlightenment." *Encyclopedia of Philosophy*, ed. Paul Edwards. Vol. 2. New York, 1967.

Brown, S. C., ed. *Philosophers of the Enlightenment*. Hassocks, U.K. 1979.

Chappell, V. C. "Locke on the Freedom of the Will." *British Journal for the History of Philosophy* 1 (1992).

Chisholm, Roderick M. "Freedom and Action." In *Freedom and Determinism*, ed. Keith Lehrer. New York, 1966.

Clapp, J. G. "Locke, John." *Encyclopedia of Philosophy*, ed. Paul Edwards. Vol. 4. New York, 1967.

Colman, John. *John Locke's Moral Philosophy*. Edinburgh, 1983.

Condillac, Etienne Bonnot de. *An Essay on the Origin of Human Knowledge*, trans. Thomas Nugent. New York, 1974.

Condorcet, Antoine-Nicolas de. *Sketch for a Historical Picture of the Progress of the Human Mind*, trans. June Barraclough. London, 1955.

D'Alembert, Jean. *Encyclopédie, Discourse preliminaire*. Paris, 1751.

Dennett, Daniel C. *Brainstorms: Philosophical Essays on Mind and Psychology*. Hassocks, U.K., 1978, rpt. 1981.

Dennett, Daniel C. *Elbow Room*. Oxford, 1984.

Descartes, René. *The Philosophical Writings of Descartes*, trans. John Cottingham, Robert Stoothoff, Dugald Murdoch. Vols. 1 and 2. Cambridge, 1985.

Dunn, John. " 'Bright enough for all our purposes': John Locke's Conception of a Civilized Society." *Notes and Records of the Royal Society* 43 (1989): 133–53.

Dunn, John. *Locke*. Oxford, 1984.

Dunn, John. *The Political Thought of John Locke*. Cambridge, 1969.

Dunn, John. "The Politics of Locke in England and America in the Eighteenth Century." In *John Locke, Problems and Perspectives*, ed. John W. Yolton. Cambridge, 1969.

Dunn, John. "Revolution." In *Political Innovation and Conceptual Change*, ed. Terence Ball, James Farr, Russell Hanson. New York, 1989.

Gay, Peter. *The Enlightenment: An Interpretation, 2: The Science of Freedom*. London, 1970.

Grant, Ruth W. *John Locke's Liberalism*. Chicago, 1987.

Grimsley, Ronald. *Jean D'Alembert*. Oxford, 1963.

Gutman, Amy. *Democratic Education*. Princeton, 1987.

Harrison, John, and Peter Laslett. *The Library of John Locke*. Oxford, 1971.

Hoyt, Nelly S., and Thomas Cassirer. *Encyclopedia Selections*. Indianapolis, Ind., 1965.

Humphrey, Ted. *Immanuel Kant, Perpetual Peace and Other Essays*. Indianapolis, Ind., 1983.

Jenkins, John J. *Understanding Locke*. Edinburgh, 1985.

Johnson, Merwyn S. *Locke on Freedom*. Austin, Tex., 1977.

Jones, M. G. *The Charity School Movement: A Study of Eighteenth Century Puritanism in Action*. Cambridge, 1938.

Kenny, Anthony, ed. *Descartes: Philosophical Letters*. Oxford, 1970.

King, Peter (Lord). *The Life and Letters of John Locke*. London, 1884.

Koyré, A. "Introduction" to *Descartes, Philosophical Writings*, ed. G.E.M. Anscombe and Peter Geach. London, 1954.

Kraus, Pamela, "Locke's Negative Hedonism." *The Locke Newsletter*, no. 15 (1984), pp. 43–63.

Laslett, Peter. "Introduction" to *John Locke, Two Treatises of Government*. Cambridge 1960, amended 1963.

Leibniz, G. W. *New Essays*, ed. and trans. Peter Remnant and Jonathan Bennet. Cambridge, 1982.

Lessnoff, Michael. "Ruth Grant's *John Locke's Liberalism*." *Canadian Philosophical Reviews* 8, no. 1 (1988).

McCracken, Charles. *Malebranche and British Philosophy*. Oxford, 1983.

Mackie, J. L. *Problems from Locke*. Oxford, 1976.

Madden, Edward H. "Stewart's Enrichment of the Commonsense Tradition." *History of Philosophy Quarterly* 3, no. 1 (1986): 45–63.

Manuel, Frank E. *The New World of Henri Saint-Simon*. Cambridge, Mass., 1956.

Matthews, Eric. "Mind and Matter in the 18th Century." *Philosophical Quarterly* 36 (1986): 420–29.

Miller, James. *Rousseau, Dreamer of Democracy*. New Haven, Conn., 1984.

Milton, J. R. "Before the Drafts: Locke's Intellectual Development 1658–1671." A paper read to the British Society for the History of Philosophy Conference on John Locke, Oxford, November 15, 1986.

Molyneux, William. *Dioptrica Nova. A Treatise of Dioptrica*. London, 1692.

Neill, Alex. "Locke on Habituation, Autonomy, and Education." *Journal of the History of Philosophy* 27, no. 2 (1989): 225–45.

Paine, Thomas. *The Age of Reason*. 1794. Prometheus Books, 1984.

Parry, Geraint. *John Locke*. London, 1978.

Passmore, John. "The Malleability of Man in Eighteenth-Century Thought." In *Aspects of the Eighteenth Century*, ed. Earl R. Wasserman. Baltimore, 1965.

Passmore, John. *The Perfectibility of Man*. London, 1970.

Polin, Raymond. "John Locke's Conception of Freedom." In *John Locke, Problems and Perspectives*, ed. John W. Yolton. Cambridge, 1969.

Polin, Raymond. *La politique morale de John Locke*. Paris, 1960; rpt. New York, 1984.

Porter, Noah. "Marginalia Locke-a-na." *New Englander and Yale Review* (1887), 33–49.

Prior, Matthew. *Dialogues of the Dead and Other Works in Prose and Verse*, ed. A. R. Waller. Cambridge, 1907.

Quick, R. H., ed. *Locke, Some Thoughts concerning Education*. Cambridge, 1927.

Rabb, D. J. *John Locke on Reflection: A Phenomenology Lost*. Lanham, Md., 1985.

Rabb, D. J. "Reflection, Reflexion and Introspection." *The Locke Newsletter* no. 8 (1977): 35–52.

Rogers, John. "The Empiricism of Locke and Newton." In *Philosophers of the Enlightenment*, ed. S. C. Brown. Hassocks, U.K., 1979.

Ryan, Alan. *Property and Political Theory*. Oxford, 1984.

Schankula, H.A.S. "Locke, Descartes, and the Science of Nature." In *John Locke: Symposium Wolfenbüttel 1979*, ed. Reinhard Brandt. Berlin, 1981.

Schochet, Gordon J. "The Family and the Origins of the State in Locke's Political Philosophy." In *John Locke: Problems and Perspectives*, ed. John W. Yolton. Cambridge, 1969.

Schouls, Peter A. "Critical Notice of Richard Ashcraft, *Revolutionary Politics and Locke's Two Treatises of Government*." *Canadian Journal of Philosophy* 19, no. 1 (1989), pp. 101–16.

Schouls, Peter A. *Descartes and the Enlightenment*. Edinburgh, 1989.

Schouls, Peter A. "Descartes as Revolutionary." *Philosophia Reformata* 52, no. 1 (1987): 4–23.

Schouls, Peter A. "Descartes: La primauté du libre vouloir sur la raison." *Dialogue* 25, no. 2 (1986): 211–21.

Schouls, Peter A. *The Imposition of Method: A Study of Descartes and Locke*. Oxford, 1980.

Schouls, Peter A. "John Locke: Optimist or Pessimist?" A paper given at the John Locke Conference, Christ Church, Oxford, 5–7 September 1990.

Sheasgreen, William J. "John Locke and the Charity School Movement." *History of Education* 15, no. 2 (1986): 63–79.

Smith, Norman Kemp. *Studies in the Cartesian Philosophy*. 1902. New York, 1962.

Spellman, W. M. *John Locke and the Problem of Depravity*. Oxford, 1988.

Spellman, W. M. "Locke and the Latitudinarian Perspective on Original Sin." *Revue Internationale de Philosophie* 42, no. 165 (1988): 215–28.

Stewart, M. A. "Peter A. Schouls. *The Imposition of Method*." *Canadian Philosophical Reviews* 1, no. 2/3 (1981): 119–23.

Strauss, Leo. *Natural Right and History*. Chicago, 1953.

Tarcov, Nathan. *Locke's Education for Liberty*. Chicago, 1984.

Taylor, Charles. "Atomism." In *Powers, Possessions and Freedom, Essays in Honour of C. B. Macpherson*, ed. Alkis Kontos. Toronto, 1979.

Taylor, Richard. "Determinism." *Encyclopedia of Philosophy*, ed. Paul Edwards. 2: 359–73. New York, 1967.

Tully, James. *A Discourse on Property: John Locke and His Adversaries*. Cambridge, 1980.

Tully, James. "Governing Conduct." In *Conscience and Casuistry in Early Modern Europe*, ed. Edmund Leites. Cambridge, 1988.

Vandervelde, George. *Original Sin*. Amsterdam, 1975.

Watts, Isaac. *Logick: Or, The Right Use of Reason in the Enquiry after Truth*. London, 1726. New York, 1984, ed. Peter A Schouls.

Woolhouse, R. S. *The Empiricists*. Oxford, 1988.

Woolhouse, R. S. *Locke*. Brighton, 1983.

Woolhouse, R. S. *Locke's Philosophy of Science and Knowledge*. Oxford, 1971.

Woozley, A. D. "Introduction" to Locke's *An Essay concerning Human Understanding*. New York, 1974.

Yolton, John W. *John Locke and the Way of Ideas*. Oxford, 1956.

Yolton, John W. *Locke: An Introduction*. Oxford, 1985.

Yolton, John W. *Locke and the Compass of Human Understanding*. Cambridge, 1970.

Yolton, John W. *Perceptual Acquaintance from Descartes to Reid*. Minneapolis, 1984.

Yolton, John W., ed. *John Locke, Problems and Perspectives*. Cambridge, 1969.

Index

Library of Congress Cataloging-in-Publication Data

Schouls, Peter A.
    Reasoned freedom : John Locke and enlightenment / Peter A.
Schouls.
        p.   cm.
    Includes bibliographical references and index.
    ISBN 0-8014-2758-4.   —   ISBN 0-8014-8037-X (pbk.)
        1. Locke, John, 1632–1704.   2. Liberty—History—17th century.
3. Education—Philosophy—History—17th century.   I. Title.
B1297.B295   1992
192—dc20   92-52771